CW01636572

Legal Imperialism

Sovereignty and Extraterritoriality in Japan, the Ottoman Empire, and China

Legal Imperialism examines the important role of nineteenth-century Western extraterritorial courts in non-Western states. These courts were created as a separate legal system for Western expatriates living in Asian and Islamic countries, and were developed from the British imperial model, which was founded on ideals of legal positivism. Based on a crosscultural comparison of the emergence, function, and abolition of these court systems in Japan, the Ottoman Empire, and China, Turan Kayaoğlu elaborates a theory of extraterritoriality, comparing the nineteenth-century British example with post–World War II American legal imperialism. He also provides an explanation for the end of imperial extraterritoriality, arguing that the Western decision to abolish their separate legal systems stemmed from changes in non-Western territories, including Meiji legal reforms, republican Turkey's legal transformation under Atatürk, and the Guomindang's legal reorganization in China. Ultimately, his research provides an innovative basis for understanding the assertion of legal authority by Western powers on foreign soil and the influence of such assertion on ideas about sovereignty.

Turan Kayaoğlu is Assistant Professor of International Relations at the University of Washington, Tacoma. Kayaoğlu studied international relations at Bilkent University and the University of Denver before receiving his Ph.D. in political science from the University of Washington, Seattle. His articles have appeared in *International Studies Review* and *International Studies Quarterly.*

Legal Imperialism

Sovereignty and Extraterritoriality in Japan, the Ottoman Empire, and China

TURAN KAYAOĞLU
University of Washington, Tacoma

CAMBRIDGE
UNIVERSITY PRESS

CAMBRIDGE UNIVERSITY PRESS
Cambridge, New York, Melbourne, Madrid, Cape Town,
Singapore, São Paulo, Delhi, Mexico City

Cambridge University Press
32 Avenue of the Americas, New York NY 10013-2473, USA

Published in the United States of America by Cambridge University Press, New York

www.cambridge.org
Information on this title: www.cambridge.org/9781107617889

First published 2010
First paperback edition 2013

A catalogue record for this publication is available from the British Library

Library of Congress Cataloguing in Publication Data
Kayaoglu, Turan.
Legal imperialism : sovereignty and extraterritoriality in Japan, the
Ottoman Empire, and China / Turan Kayaoglu.
p. cm.
Includes bibliographical references and index.
ISBN 978-0-521-76591-6 (hardback)
1. Extraterritoriality. 2. Extraterritoriality – Japan – History.
3. Extraterritoriality – China – History. 4. Extraterritoriality – Turkey – History.
I. Title.
KZ3678.K39 2010
341.4–dc22 2009038043

ISBN 978-0-521-76591-6 Hardback
ISBN 978-1-107-61788-9 Paperback

Contents

Tables and Figures — *page* vi
Acknowledgments — vii

Introduction: Extraterritoriality in British Legal Imperialism — 1
1 Positive Law and Sovereignty — 17
2 Extraterritoriality and Legal Imperialism — 40
3 Japan's Rapid Rise to Sovereignty — 66
4 The Ottoman Empire's Elusive Dream of Sovereignty — 104
5 China's Struggle for Sovereignty — 149
Conclusion: American Legal Imperialism – Extraterritoriality Today — 191

Bibliography — 205
Index — 223

Tables and Figures

TABLES

1. Rise and Decline of British Extraterritoriality *page* 5
2. Rise and Decline of Extraterritoriality in Japan 67
3. Legal Codification in Japan 93
4. Courts and Legal Personnel in Japan 94
5. Competing Legal Systems in the Ottoman Empire 118
6. Legal Codification in Turkey 136
7. Rise and Decline of Extraterritoriality in China 151
8. Legal Codification in China 178

FIGURES

1. Japan's Economic Capacity Compared to Major Home States 75
2. Japan's Military Capacity Compared to Major Home States 75
3. Japan's IGO Membership Compared to Home States 90
4. Japanese IGO Membership 90
5. Courts in Japan 94
6. The Ottoman Empire/Turkey IGO Membership 109
7. China in the League of Nations Council Elections 159

Acknowledgments

I would like to thank several individuals for their encouragement and feedback on this project. I owe the initial idea for this project to Jack Donnelly. At the University of Washington, Seattle, I worked with a fascinating group of advisers. Reşat Kasaba's insights on the comparative and historical development of Turkey's political institutions helped me to understand the Turkish case. One cannot combine academic inquiry and humor better than Jon Mercer; in addition to providing critical feedback, he always managed to have me leave his office with a smile. Finally, Beth Kier constantly reminded me that everything I wrote could be written more concisely and every argument I made could be made more rigorously.

I have been fortunate to have great colleagues at the University of Washington. Jessica Beyer, Rob Farley, Lisa Glidden, Mary Alice Haddad, Yuko Kawato, Terence Lee, Glenn Mackin, Kate Marshall, and Kate Stenger Knutson read and provided feedback on various chapters. In particular, Kate Marshall, Mike Strausz, and Jason Scheideman read various versions of the chapters and provided invaluable comments and suggestions. Yuko Kawato and Hironori Sasada helped me by locating and translating Japanese sources. The participants of the Turkish Studies seminars were the first to be exposed to and critically evaluate some of the ideas presented here. Among the members of the Turkish Studies seminars, Zeynep Akbulut-Kuru, Elif Andaç, Senem Aslan, Arda Ibikoğlu, Ali Iğmen, Ahmet T. Kuru,

Tuna Kuyucu, Işık Özel, and Brian Mello read and provided written comments on various drafts of the chapters.

Michael Forman, Katie Baird, Mary Hanneman, and Yonn Dierwechter – my colleagues at my new institution, the University of Washington, Tacoma – provided excellent feedback on both the content and presentation of my argument. Also in Tacoma, David Corbett read the entire manuscript with a lawyer's sense of precision and perspective. Alan Wood and Adam Cathcart corrected many of my mistakes on the history of Republican China. I substantially benefited from the comments of several other colleagues including Tony Anghie, James Caporaso, George Gavrilis, Margaret Levi, Austen Parrish, Kal Raustiala, Henrik Spruyt, and Alexander Wendt.

Finally, I want to thank several family members. My brother, Tuncay Kayaoğlu, never allowed me to feel lonely despite the two continents that divided us. My parents, Hanım Kayaoğlu and Sadullah Kayaoğlu, who despite – or maybe because of – their lack of any formal education have encouraged me to continue my education wherever it takes me. Their prayers have been and continue to be the best source of inspiration and strength throughout my lengthy formal education. And with her unconditional love and constant optimism, my wife, Sarah Al-Marri, kept me both focused and balanced. I dedicate this book to these family members.

Introduction

Extraterritoriality in British Legal Imperialism

Great powers have commonly used law as an imperial tool. During the late nineteenth and early twentieth centuries, Western powers imposed a system known as extraterritoriality in Japan, the Ottoman Empire, and China. Western extraterritorial courts – not local courts – had jurisdiction over Westerners in Japan (1856–1899), the Ottoman Empire/Turkey (1825–1923), and China (1842–1943). During the mid-1880s, for example, forty-four Western extraterritorial courts operated in Japan's treaty ports. In 1895, thiry-two British courts operated in the Ottoman Empire. Three decades later (circa 1926), twenty-six British, eighteen American, and eighteen French courts dotted China's ports and cities. Even though Japan, the Ottoman Empire/Turkey, and China were not formal colonies of the West, Western states used extraterritorial courts to extend their authority, making these countries, in Mao's term, semicolonies. In so doing, these states limited, and eventually eliminated in collaboration with groups in the local elite, the authority of indigenous legal systems. They replaced them with Western legal categories and practices. This book examines the emergence, function, and abolition of this system of extraterritoriality and offers a new perspective on the development of sovereignty in the nineteenth century. This historical perspective integrates Western colonial expansion and jurisprudence with non-Western political development and legal institutionalization.

Extraterritorial courts had jurisdiction over cases involving Western foreigners. Some cases became notorious examples of Western imperial injustices from the perspective of local people. For example, on October 24, 1886, a storm caught the British freighter *Normanton* off the coast of Oshima Island, Japan, whereupon the freighter hit a rock and sank. All of the Japanese passengers drowned, but the British officers and crew took the two lifeboats and survived. In the subsequent legal action, the British extraterritorial court, Her Britannic Majesty's Court at Hyogo, Japan acquitted the crew of any misconduct even though similar cases involving European passengers frequently resulted in convictions for murder or manslaughter.[1]

Two decades later, while passing through a village in China's Yunan Province, Henry Demenil, a U.S. citizen, killed a Tibetan Buddhist lama. District Attorney Arthur Bassett of the U.S. District Court for China brought the case to the court in Shanghai in December 1907 (*US v. Demenil*). Drawing on Demenil's diary, which described the incident as unintentional, the judge acquitted Demenil and concluded that the killing was due to the defendant's "nervous condition" and physical debilitation, brought on by "the rarefied mountain air of the locality, the loneliness of the place, and wilderness of surroundings."[2]

Extraterritorial courts were the organs of Western legal expansion in non-Western countries. As opposed to territoriality, where a state claims exclusive jurisdiction over all the people within its territorial boundaries regardless of their nationality, extraterritoriality refers to a legal regime whereby a state claims exclusive jurisdiction over its citizens in another state. In world politics, a state uses territorial jurisdiction within its boundaries, and extraterritorial jurisdiction within the boundaries of another state. Extraterritorial institutions like Her Britannic Majesty's Court in Hyogo and the U.S. District Court for China in Shanghai embodied the semicolonial status of these non-Western states.

Using their court systems, even small Western countries could evade non-Western jurisdiction over their citizens. On July 21, 1905, a bomb targeting the Sultan of the Ottoman Empire killed twenty-six people but missed the Sultan. Among the people arrested for the explosion was Charles Edouard Joris, a Belgian citizen who confessed that he had prepared and placed the bomb. Arguing that only Belgian consular courts

1 Chang (1984: 81–98).

2 Scully (2001: 129–130).

could try Belgians in the Ottoman Empire, the Belgian government demanded that the Ottoman government surrender Joris. The Ottoman government initially refused, and tried and sentenced Joris to death. The Belgian government, however, rejected the Ottoman court's judgment as a violation of Belgian extraterritoriality. In a dramatic reversal, the Ottoman government subsequently yielded and released Joris.[3] In this case, the Belgian claim rested on extraterritorial rights embedded in the larger system of Western extraterritoriality in the Ottoman Empire. These rights enabled Belgium and fourteen other Western states to claim jurisdiction over their citizens in the Ottoman Empire.

Naturally, given such polarizing circumstances, increasing non-Western nationalism, and burgeoning press in these countries, extraterritoriality incited much resentment in non-Western states. Eventually, Japan, the Ottoman Empire, China, Iran, and Thailand gained jurisdiction over Western foreigners after a period of long and agonizing negotiations with Western states. Among these states, this book focuses on Japan, the Ottoman Empire, and China. Extraterritoriality negotiations offer rich observations to study how nineteenth-century positive law and Western colonial expansion constructed not only empires, but also the sovereign state system itself.

EXTRATERRITORIALITY IN THE NINETEENTH CENTURY

This book addresses three main questions: First, what does extraterritoriality reveal about the origins and nature of sovereignty? Second, why did Western states, in particular Great Britain, abolish extraterritoriality? Third, how do specific hegemonic powers and their legal regimes shape the way these powers extend their legal system into other countries?

Extraterritoriality and Nineteenth-Century Sovereignty

In addressing the first question, I propose that the story of the rise and decline of extraterritoriality is also a story about the origins and

[3] For the Joris case, see the reports the *London Times* published in 1906 and 1907. *American Journal of International Law* (1907: 485) published an editorial comment on the case. Murat Bardakçı (1999) provides details of the case.

nature of sovereignty. As I elaborate in the first two chapters, two nineteenth-century developments produced the modern conceptualization of sovereignty: the dominance of legal positivism and European colonial expansion. Mostly associated with the legal philosophy of English philosophers Jeremy Bentham and John Austin, legal positivism assumed a narrow definition of law: state (sovereign) legislated commands backed by state coercion. This approach to law had significant influence in shaping nineteenth-century legal episteme, or the collective understandings and discourses of law determining the scope, application, and underlying values of law. The nineteenth-century understanding of sovereignty and international law grew out of positivist legal episteme.

European colonial expansion was also important for the development of nineteenth-century sovereignty. In the process of this expansion, legal positivism became an imperial legal episteme in influencing initially British and later Western imperial ideas and policies. Western imperial, particularly British, encounters with Asian societies further developed and consolidated the norms and practices of sovereignty that first appeared in legal positivist understandings and discourses. Jurists and legal scholars as policymakers and advisers were integral to the development of agenda of imperial encounter. In these encounters, the practices of the British state and the ideas of British jurists clarified, crystallized, and consolidated the concept of sovereignty doctrine in part to exclude Asian entities from it. The rise and decline of British extraterritoriality illustrates how construction of positive law and nineteenth-century sovereignty severely limited the authority claims of non-Western states within their territorial domains.

The British extraterritorial empire was the most organized, extensive, and durable (Table 1). British courts operated in Japan (six around the mid-1880s), the Ottoman Empire (sixty-six in 1900), and China (twenty-six in 1926).[4] In the early years, the courts had simple procedures, and British citizens in these countries were denied many of the legal rights British citizens enjoyed at domestic British courts. It was usually one man, the consul, who belonged to the executive branch rather than the judiciary, who rendered the decision. Throughout

[4] I discuss the numbers of extraterritorial courts in China and Japan later. For the Ottoman Empire, see Kocabaşoğlu (2004: 158–159).

TABLE 1. *Rise and Decline of British Extraterritoriality*[a]

Country	Establishment	Abolition	Method of the Abolition[b]
Algeria	1825	1830	Occupation (France)
Tunisia	1825	1881	Occupation (France)
Zanzibar	1886	1890	Protectorate (Britain)
Tonga	1879	1890	Protectorate (Britain)
Madagascar	1865	1896	Occupation (France)
Samoa	1879	1899	Occupation (Germany/ United States)
Japan	1856	1899	Negotiations
Congo	1884	1908	Occupation (Belgium)
Korea	1883	1910	Occupation (Japan)
Morocco	1825	1912	Protectorate (France)
Tripoli	1825	1912	Protectorate (Italy)
Egypt	1825	1914	Protectorate (Britain)
Turkey	1825	1923	Negotiations
Iran	1825	1928	Negotiations
Thailand	1855	1937	Negotiations
China	1833	1943	Negotiations

[a] In places where Levant Company operated (Algeria, Tunisia, Morocco, Turkey, Iran, Egypt) I use the abolition of the company and the transfer of its legal authority to the British government as the emergence date. For China, I use the Charter Act of 1833 in which the British government took over the East India Company's judicial authorities in China as indicative of the emergence of extraterritoriality in China. All other pre-1925 dates are from Liu 1925.

[b] When a Western imperial power established de jure jurisdiction such as occupation and protectorate over a non-Western state where extraterritoriality existed, other extraterritorial states gave up their claims of extraterritorial jurisdiction. While the Ottoman Empire, China, and Japan were imperial powers themselves, they were traditional land-based empires with different types of rules and ideologies compared to European empires of the nineteenth century. (For comparisons of traditional and European empires, see Abernethy 2000.)

the nineteenth century the courts and their procedures evolved and became more elaborate, in part to bridge the gap between justice rendered in the British domestic and extraterritorial courts. Eventually, the courts had their own substantial codes as well as codes for civil and criminal procedures, enforcement, and appeals.[5] British jurists and bureaucrats at the Colonial Office prepared these rules. As the number of courts increased, the British government organized them in a legal hierarchy. For example, the British Supreme Court at Istanbul was the highest British court in the Ottoman Empire, and the British Supreme Court at Shanghai was the highest British court in China.[6] These supreme courts acted as the first level of appellate courts in their respective geographical regions, in the Levant and East Asia. For example, appeals in cases from the British courts in Japan and Korea were heard at Shanghai. The Privy Council in London was the final appellate court of the British extraterritorial courts.[7] With this extensive and organized presence, the British extraterritorial empire operated for most of the nineteenth and early twentieth centuries in those non-Western states lacking formal colonial governments.

Legal imperialism is the extension of a state's legal authority into another state and limitation of legal authority of the target state over issues that may affect people, commercial interest, and security of the imperial state. Extraterritoriality was quintessential legal imperialism; it extended Western legal authority into non-Western territories and limited non-Western legal authority over Western foreigners and their commercial interest. The production and maintenance of extraterritorial legal authority required both a legal framework to deny non-Western law and sovereignty and also the material capability to defend these extraterritorial court systems against the non-Western elites and populations who became increasingly uncooperative and even hostile to these courts.

5 For rules of the British Supreme Court for China, see Kennett (1918).

6 The Supreme Court at Constantinople was created in 1857. In 1858 the court had 22 personnel including a judge, two policemen, and two prison guards. Kocabaşoğlu (2004: 108).

7 For cases appealed from the British Supreme Court at Istanbul see Tarring (1887: 15–17). The U.S. Circuit Court in California acted as the appeals court for the U.S. Court for China, but no case from China reached the Supreme Court. For more about the U.S. District Court for China, see Ruskola (2005: 2008).

Any analysis of legal imperialism requires a balancing of the relative roles of material power and ideas. This combination is difficult to sustain in the academic studies of international relations where the constructivists' power of ideas and realists' ideas of power divide the discipline's research agenda. Both of these reductionist positions are unable to explain fully the rise and fall of transnational legal structures, such as nineteenth-century extraterritoriality, in world politics. An argument based solely on power and self-interest is unable to explain the broad patterns of extraterritoriality. First, extraterritoriality was not imposed on the weaker European or on any Latin American states. In Latin America, as in Asia, in the mid-nineteenth century, economically and militarily powerful Europeans and Americans demanded legal immunity and jurisdictional protections based on claims of local injustice and lawlessness.[8] British, French, and Spanish consular officials often lobbied for their citizens' legal immunity.[9] For example, in Uruguay, foreigners demanded the right to invoke consular jurisdiction to create a separate legal system, similar to extraterritoriality. Yet, despite legal and economic conditions that resembled those of the Asian states, Western states never imposed extraterritoriality in Latin America.[10]

Second, not all the Western states benefiting from extraterritoriality were great powers. The rational, self-interested application of material power alone cannot explain how minor Western powers like Belgium, Greece, and Switzerland acquired extraterritorial rights in the Ottoman Empire or China.[11] Even if one considers minor powers' alliances with a great power, this cannot explain the extraterritorial rights of these states. Why would a great power use its military leverage to undertake the costs to substantiate a minor power's extraterritorial rights in non-Western states? This is especially the case when the citizens of a great power and a minor power were in direct economic

[8] Benton (2002, 211).

[9] Benton (2002, 214).

[10] The only exception is that for a brief period, the government of Uruguay established a Comisión Mixta (made up of one Frenchman, one Englishman, and two Uruguayans) to consider claims by British and French subjects in 1857. See Benton (2002: 215–216). These complaints, however, sometimes triggered Western intervention for debt collection in these countries. Also see Benton (2002: 236–251), Keene (2007), Finnemore (2004), and Obregon (2006).

[11] Sousa (1933).

competition with one another in a non-Western state, as in the Greek-British commercial competition in the Ottoman Empire during which both states had extraterritorial rights in the Ottoman Empire. One may argue that it was in Britain's self-interest to present itself as, and carry the responsibilities of, the representative of the entire "civilized" world in imposing extraterritoriality. While this might be true, it demands an ideational framework, rather than material factors, to establish extraterritoriality with civilizational differences.

The relations between great powers on extraterritoriality also defy the predictions of power politics. Surprisingly, there is little evidence that the great powers used extraterritoriality for geopolitical competition. On the contrary, they often collaborated with each other to sustain extraterritoriality in non-Western states. Extraterritoriality never became a tool for strategic competition among European imperialists. British Foreign Office documents concerning Japanese extraterritoriality contain ample correspondence with the other great powers regarding the likely responses of these powers to Japanese demands for the revision of extraterritoriality. In major international conferences, such as at the Tokyo Conference (1882), the Washington Conference (1921), and the Lausanne Conference (1923), Western extraterritorial states always presented a united front on extraterritoriality.

Third, while minor Western powers had extraterritoriality, that right was denied to major non-Western powers. For example, the Ottoman Empire had interests (substantial Muslim minorities existed in the small Balkan states), religious authority (Ottoman Sultans with their claim to the Muslim Caliphate), and power, but this never translated into an Ottoman legal claim, or even an attempt, of extraterritoriality even in the small Balkan states. Japan is the only exception to the non-Western states not claiming extraterritoriality: It effectively imposed its jurisdiction over Japanese citizens in China and Korea only after the abolition of extraterritoriality in Japan. The abolition of extraterritoriality in Japan indicated that Japan had been admitted into the group of "civilized sovereign" states, and thus Japan was granted the rights of civilized sovereign states, including extraterritoriality.[12]

[12] For a similar argument, see Suzuki (2009). For a history of Japan's "legal colonization" in Korea, see Kim (2009).

The absence of extraterritoriality in Latin America and small European states, the minor European powers' of extraterritoriality in the Ottoman Empire and China, and the absence of non-Western claims for extraterritoriality all support the arguments of international relations scholars who offer an ideational and cultural perspective such as constructivists and English School scholars. They argue that power and material self-interest alone cannot explain the patterns of legal imperialism. The categories of extraterritoriality were the categories of civilization: Western versus non-Western. Western jurists, statesmen, and diplomats perceived extraterritoriality to be a Western right in non-Western states. Constructivists argue that sovereignty norms have changed over time – most notably in the transformation from the medieval to the modern international system of Westphalian sovereignty.[13] Constructivists as well as English School scholars differ on which ideas are most relevant in explaining the consolidation of Westphalian sovereignty.[14] Yet, they agree that the consolidation of Westphalian sovereignty, as well as other types of systemwide normative changes, is a two-step process: the emergence of norms in Europe and their subsequent diffusion to non-European entities through state socialization. Sovereignty norms emerge from the norm-generating European core, and then diffuse into the norm-receiving non-European periphery.

This two-step approach limits the emergence of sovereignty geographically (to Europe) and normatively (European ideas and practices of equality, recognition, and territoriality). In addition to being Eurocentric in its invocation of non-Western examples, only to illustrate their incompatibility with European ideas and practices,[15] this two-step approach allows scholars to ignore the systematic sovereignty-violating and oppressive practices such as Western colonization and extraterritoriality. This tendency often exists in constructivist studies' neglecting the implications of the role of power asymmetry in norm-construction. Most constructivists emphasize *shared* ideas, thereby suggesting that norm-construction is a benign process leading to normatively better

[13] Ruggie (1993), Biersteker and Weber (1996).

[14] Spruyt (1994), Reus-Smit (1999), Philpott (2001).

[15] Such as the Chinese "suzerainty system," or the Ottomans' alleged "house of war" versus "house of peace" Islamic worldview. For example, see Spruyt (1994: 16–17) and Philpott (2004: 15–20); also see Acharya (2004).

outcomes.[16] They thus fail to adequately theorize the role of structural power dynamics in norm-construction.[17] Norm-construction emerges simultaneously with categories of norm-exclusion. In the nineteenth century, Western jurists, statesmen, and diplomats reformulated the sovereignty doctrine during Europe's imperial encounter with non-European states. Non-Western states became the nonsovereign "other" and were excluded from the realm of sovereignty. On the one hand, this process systematically marginalized, excluded, and disempowered non-European entities and enabled and justified European intervention, coercion, and imperialism in these entities.[18] On the other, this European-led process triggered non-Western reforms and modernization by setting the terms by which previously excluded players could (and eventually did) join the system of sovereign states and benefit from it.

Connected to the last point, extraterritoriality also reveals how the sovereign state system extended into Asia. Absolute territorial jurisdiction is a unique feature of the modern international system. Various international relations scholars have suggested that territorial jurisdiction is constructed through the interactions of various state, nonstate, and international actors.[19] The authority claims of Western and non-Western rulers over Western foreigners in Asia waxed and waned before Western rulers recognized the non-Western states' exclusive territorial jurisdiction. The variation in the timing of the abolition of extraterritoriality shows that the diffusion of territorial sovereignty into non-Western countries occurred from the end of the nineteenth century to the middle of the twentieth century.

[16] For this teleological logic, see Wendt (1999).

[17] Kurki-Sinclair (2007).

[18] Lake (2003: 303).

[19] In the last two decades, a significant literature has emerged to explore the constructed nature of territorial sovereignty. Jackson (1990) examines how the territorial sovereignty of African states is constructed through external legitimization. Ashley (1984, 1989) and Thomson (1994) examine how rulers came to legitimize foreign rulers' rights to domestic violence in the international system. Ruggie (1983, 1993) and Spruyt (1994) explore how modern states with mutually exclusive territorial jurisdiction came to dominate the modern international system. Bartelson (1995), Walker (1993), and Weber (1995) focus on discursive practices in the construction of territorial sovereignty. Wendt (1999) emphasizes ideas about the "self" and "other"; Onuf (1998) and Philpott (2001) highlight, respectively, the roles of secular and religious ideas about political authority in the construction of territorial sovereignty in the international system.

Extraterritoriality and its abolition also reveal another quality of sovereignty: its ability to coordinate authority claims in the international system. A state's law-making and law-enforcing authority has an international dimension. Domestic legal arrangements affect transnational interactions and foreign nationals in a state. The coordination of states' legal claims facilitates transnational interactions and safeguards a state's citizens in another state. For example, transnational commercial transactions would be difficult if business groups did not know about legal and property rights in other countries. The business groups' willingness to interact will be without credible information about the enforcement of these rights. The need for legal coordination and the security of foreigners makes state rulers accountable to each other regarding their domestic legal arrangements.

The "revival" of Roman law in continental Europe and later the supremacy of positive law in Britain in the nineteenth century established the preconditions for sovereign territoriality. These preconditions enabled states to coordinate their legal structures through territorial jurisdiction and thus facilitated transnational interactions. Territorial jurisdiction allowed state rulers to claim jurisdiction over their subjects and citizens as well as the subjects and citizens of other rulers if these people were in their territory. Yet this right of territorial jurisdiction was contingent on all state rulers establishing institutions to make and enforce laws. More specifically, modern sovereignty as developed by positivist jurists requires state law institutionalization. State law institutionalization means the codification of laws, the establishment of a statewide court system, and the consolidation of the state's legal hierarchy.

Explaining the Abolition of Extraterritoriality

This book also engages a second set of questions about why extraterritoriality was abolished and the factors that explain the variation in the timing of the abolition process. Legal institutionalization explains the timing of the abolition of extraterritoriality. Facing the Asian states' resistance to extraterritoriality, Western states required the institutionalization of state law, in the form of positive law, as a condition for the recognition of Asian sovereignty. Institutionalized state law compatible with a positive legal order facilitates transnational trade by providing information about legal and property rights, credibly enforcing these rights, and making the state accountable for the legal system within its boundaries.

During the nineteenth century, Asian legal systems were fragmented because state rulers shared legal authority with societal groups and local communities. The absence of a state-centered legal system meant that local and foreign trading parties did not have the same degree of information about the rules, the past behavior of local people, and the ability to retaliate in the future. These asymmetries of information and enforcement empowered local people against distant parties, particularly foreigners. Situations that favored locals over foreigners were reversed by extraterritorial regimes mandating that conflicts between local and Western traders fall under the jurisdiction of Western courts. The asymmetries of information and enforcement that extraterritoriality created resulted in the empowerment of distant parties against local people.

The timing of a state's legal institutionalization explains the timing of the abolition of extraterritoriality. Meiji legal reforms in the 1880s, Republican Turkey's legal transformation under Atatürk in the 1920s, Reza Shah Pahlavi's legal reforms in Iran in the 1920s, Thai legal development in the 1930s, and the Guomindang's legal reorganization in China in the 1930s explain Western – particularly British – decisions to end extraterritoriality in these states.

Hegemony, Law, and Imperialism

The third set of questions this book examines addresses whether and how the forms of legal imperialism depend on the specific hegemonic state and its legal regime. I focus on showing how British hegemony and positivism shaped nineteenth-century legal imperialism and extraterritoriality. If specific legal regimes shape the forms of legal imperialism, the rise of American hegemony should produce some differences, and my concluding chapter provides some preliminary evidence to show how American hegemony and American legal realism together justify and shape American legal imperialism in the post–WWII international system.

Imperialism and international law have returned to the international relations research agenda.[20] However, they rarely meet. In one corner, the imperialism research agenda has focused on the validity, features, sources, and implications of the American empire. While legal themes are inherent in these debates, exemplified with references to terms like the *constitution* of the world order, *contractual* relations between American and peripheral countries, *legal* and political institutions, and *allocation of rights,* scholars often overlook the underlying legal episteme – the collective understandings and discourses of law, which determine the scope, application, and underlying values of law – and shape these terms. In the other corner, the international law research agenda has focused on the legalization of international relations. While scholars examining international legalization often acknowledge the role of power asymmetries, they largely overlook the extensive role of power in international institutionalization, legalization, and law.

The notion of legal imperialism focuses on the nexus of imperial power and legal practices. In place of establishing formal colonial empires to extend its rule, American imperialism relies heavily on the legal means of limiting and replacing the indigenous legal systems. Not only does the diffusion of nationalism and sovereignty make it difficult to maintain a formal empire,[21] but the cultural antipathy to formal empires, and the constitutional limitations to justifying formal imperial structures,[22] also make a traditional empire difficult to reconcile with the American legal system. Moreover, the legalistic nature of American culture and the power of its judicature reinforce the legal character of American imperialism. Thus, more than its British predecessor, American imperialism has a legalistic character, albeit a different one. Examples like the increasing use of U.S. federal courts to enforce American foreign policy goals abroad, and the removal of local courts' authority over American military personnel and contractors abroad, reveal the legal character of American hegemony.

[20] Nexon and Wright (2007).
[21] Philpott (2001).
[22] Lawson and Seidman (2004).

THE PLAN OF THE BOOK

This introductory chapter provided a broad picture of the nineteenth-century extraterritoriality and linked this picture to the debates about sovereignty and imperialism in international relations scholarship. The first two chapters present the theoretical foundations of my argument about the origins of sovereignty and the abolition of extraterritoriality. Chapter 1 elaborates an alternative to the view that the modern notion and practice of sovereignty originated with the Peace of Westphalia in 1648. It contends that the modern conceptualization of sovereignty is related to two nineteenth-century developments: the dominance of legal positivism and European colonial expansion. This chapter examines the replacement of natural law with positive law in Western jurisprudence during the nineteenth century. This chapter then argues that the supremacy of positivist legal jurisprudence delegitimated Asian law and claims to sovereignty, thus facilitating Western legal imperialism in Asia.

Chapter 2 discusses extraterritoriality as a form of legal imperialism. Drawing on the European imperial encounter with Asian states in the nineteenth century, the chapter first links positive law and sovereignty to the construction of Western – particularly British – imperial expansion in the form of extraterritoriality. Second, the chapter describes Asian resistance to extraterritoriality and illustrates how Western requirements to recognize Asian sovereignty were tied to the institutionalization of positive law in Asia. Third, it provides the theoretical foundations of my argument regarding the abolition of extraterritoriality by explaining the effects of state law institutionalization on the abolition of extraterritoriality. Finally, the chapter discusses how my legal institutionalization approach relates to arguments that link the abolition of extraterritoriality to the growing material and military capacity of non-Western states or their westernization.

Three empirical chapters then illustrate the role of positive law and the institutionalization of a state's legal monopoly in the construction of modern sovereignty in Asia. Chapter 3 explains the abolition of extraterritoriality in Japan. The Japanese case is striking because of the short life of extraterritoriality. Extraterritoriality appeared in Japan in 1856, later than in the Ottoman Empire (1825) or China (1843). Yet in 1899, Japan became the first non-Western state in which extraterritoriality was abolished. Much of the literature on the early abolition of extraterritoriality in Japan emphasizes the role of Japanese power and Japanese Westernization. I offer an explanation based on Japanese legal reforms. The Meiji's impressive transformation had a legal foundation. This legal change contributed to both the rise of Japanese power and the promotion of Japan's image as civilized. In conjunction with these two, but more importantly, Japanese legal institutionalization satisfied Western legal demands – the clarification of legal rights, their enforcement, and the establishment of government's legal accountability for these – and its responsibility for the abolition of extraterritoriality.

Chapter 4 examines the abolition of extraterritoriality in the Ottoman Empire/Turkey. In many ways, starting with the conquest of Constantinople (1453), the Ottoman Empire played an integral role in European politics, making it different from the later ancillary roles of China and Japan. The significant position of the empire in the European international system presents a dilemma for scholars who make a cultural argument linking the abolition of extraterritoriality to the expansion of international society. I bridge these contradictory observations by offering a legal institutional argument combined with insights from realism to explain the abolition of extraterritoriality. The Ottoman Empire's legal system in part embedded in Islamic religious law and ethics and the Ottoman Empire's geopolitical weakness contributed to European resistance to abolish extraterritoriality. Extraterritoriality negotiations from the Treaty of Paris (1856) to the Treaty of Lausanne (1923) show a legal-institutional logic. I argue that the abolition of extraterritoriality in the Turkish case was related to the comprehensive legal reforms that accompanied the transition from the Ottoman Empire to the Turkish Republic.

Chapter 5 analyzes the abolition of extraterritoriality in China. Despite vehement and sometimes violent Chinese opposition to extraterritoriality, Western states maintained extraterritoriality until 1943. Western states' tenacity was transformed into an unexpected concession during the Second World War. The United States and Britain initiated the abolition process when the issue was not a priority for the Chinese government. Wartime abolition (1943) led many to suggest that American and British strategic calculations explain the abolition of extraterritoriality in China. I challenge this focus on strategic calculations and instead stress the role of the legal institutionalization. Compared to Japan and the Ottoman Empire, large-scale Chinese legal reforms started much later, in the early twentieth century. China was also slow to consolidate a comprehensive and statewide legal structure as reported by the Commission on Extraterritoriality in 1926. Eventually, Guomindang's legal reforms in the 1930s and the normative shift away from extraterritoriality under American international preeminence explain the abolition of extraterritoriality in 1943.

The conclusion reevaluates the relationship of the concepts of legal institutionalism, legal imperialism, and "Westphalian" sovereignty in the abolition of extraterritoriality in Japan, Turkey, and China. It also offers a preliminary analysis of the transition from British to American forms of legal imperialism in the post–World War II international order. Last, the conclusion provides some suggestions for further research linking legal imperialism, power, and sovereignty in the context of the "American Empire."

1

Positive Law and Sovereignty

Although they differ on many points about the emergence and function of sovereignty in the international system, international relations scholars seem to agree that sovereignty emerged as a product of intra-European thought and practices.[1] This Eurocentric consensus ignores the role Western imperial ideology and the colonial encounter played in the construction of sovereignty.[2] In these encounters, Western state practices and judicial discourses clarified, crystallized, and consolidated the elements of sovereignty doctrine.[3] In particular, jurists defined, identified, and categorized sovereign and nonsovereign entities. Sovereignty criteria then conditioned, shaped, and legitimized Western colonial domination by excluding all non-Western entities from the sphere of sovereignty. In important ways, the articulation of sovereignty is embedded in the domestic legal episteme of the leading imperial state(s). Jurists, statesmen, and diplomats of the imperial states articulated sovereignty norms and practices to deal with legal and political problems the colonial encounter created within the parameters of "law." I call these parameters of law, specifically the collective understandings and discourses determining the scope, application, and underlying values of the laws, legal episteme, and I argue that the nineteenth-century British

[1] For this debate, see Spruyt (1993), Krasner (1998), Philpott (2000), Osiander (2000), Biersteker (2001), Lake (2003), Blaney and Inayatullah (2001), Teschke (2002), and Beaulac (2003).

[2] One major exception is Strang (1995).

[3] My understanding of international law, sovereignty, and positivism is heavily influenced by Anghie (2005) and Simpson (2003).

imperial legal episteme, shaped within legal positivism, is key to the construction of "Westphalian" sovereignty.

Imperialism has been a nonissue for most international relations scholars who study sovereignty. Yet, imperialism has been the most durable, visible, and significant violation of the Westphalian sovereignty of non-Western states. Scholarly neglect of this issue is particularly troubling as the norms and practices of both Westphalian sovereignty and nineteenth-century imperialism emerged around the same time, and international jurists provided the legal framework for both. Western states extended their authority into non-Western states, denying the Westphalian sovereignty of the latter, using two major imperial methods: territorial and extraterritorial imperialism.[4] In territorial imperialism, Western states claimed territorial jurisdiction over non-Western societies and brought them under the hierarchy of the empire. In this process, Western states either destroyed indigenous legal systems or incorporated them into the imperial legal system. In addition to their territorial empires, each Western state also had an extraterritorial empire. In extraterritorial imperialism, Western states rejected the application of non-Western law over Western citizens. Rather, Western states themselves claimed the jurisdiction over their citizens in Asian and African states. For this jurisdiction, Western states developed different strategies. For example, the British government eventually codifed a separate law just for its extraterritorial courts. This extraterritorial law did not extend some rights to British citizens in non-Western countries. It also made them accountable to parts of the non-Western law. While American consular courts in most parts applied federal laws and the District of Columbia Statutes, the Supreme Court rejected extending constitutional rights like jury trial to extraterritorial Americans, putting extraterritorial courts in a unique place in the American legal system.[5]

[4] My terminology is different from that of Doyle (1985: 30–47), but my categories roughly correspond to his distinction between formal and informal imperialism. For conceptual issues surrounding the term "imperialism," also see Abernethy (1999: chapter 2).

[5] For a comparative legal history in the context of imperial expansion see Benton (2001) and Leue (1991). For the workings of American consular courts and their place in the American legal system see Raustiala (2008: chapter 3).

Hegemonic powers, like nineteenth-century Britain and post–World War II America, have the vision, interest, and means to project their authority throughout the international system. The imperialist orientation and processes are embedded in the domestic legal episteme and structures of hegemonic powers. Imperialism must be legalized, because imperialism requires both a domestic legal framework to justify the extension of authority abroad and an international legal framework to deny the domestic sovereignty of a target state.[6] By virtue of motivating and justifying the actions of hegemonic powers, the imperial legal episteme allows hegemonic powers to construct international legal structures and processes including sovereignty norms and practices. Western jurists, statesmen, and diplomats have articulated sovereignty norms and practices to deal with the legal and political problems the colonial encounter created. In particular, the nineteenth-century British imperial legal episteme is behind the construction of Westphalian sovereignty.[7]

Constructivists have rightly observed that sovereignty is not given, but rather is created by ideas and practice. In particular, the practices of state and nonstate actors in conjunction with legal and political ideas are a powerful generative force.[8] Although not a constructivist, Krasner defines sovereignty using nineteenth-century international practices; because I examine nineteenth-century imperialism, I use his definition of Westphalian sovereignty. Westphalian sovereignty is the exclusion of external authority structures from domestic authority structures.[9] Krasner also defines domestic sovereignty as a state's ability to determine its own governing structures. In the nineteenth century, domestic sovereignty (the establishment of law and order, compatible with a positive legal order) was a prerequisite for the great powers in accepting the Westphalian sovereignty of non-Western societies.

This chapter is comprised of three sections. First, I build on constructivist insights to link the legal positivist understandings and

[6] See also Weber (1994).

[7] This is similar to what Koskenniemi (2005: 117) calls "in the image of [their] domestic legalism."

[8] Biersteker and Weber (1996), Biersteker (2002).

[9] Krasner (1999: 21–25). Although "Westphalian" sovereignty is a misnomer and anachronistic, like Krasner, I follow the convention and use it. For my critique of the emergence of this misnomer, see Kayaoğlu (forthcoming).

discourse of law to the international jurists' attempts to construct a sovereignty-centered international jurisprudence. Second, I use a postcolonial approach to examine how the structural power dynamics and positive jurisprudence were coconstitutive in the production of legal imperialism. Third, I relate legal positivism's ascendance to the expansion of British-dominated long-distance international trade and the resulting demand for a state-based legal order to clarify and enforce legal and property rights in the periphery.

THE JURISPRUDENCE OF SOVEREIGNTY AND IMPERIALISM

A positivist legal episteme and the British imperial encounter shaped the "Westphalian" notion of sovereignty. In the words of the eminent historian Eric Hobsbawm, "[n]ever in the entire history of the world has a single power exercised a world hegemony like that of the British in the middle of the nineteenth century."[10] British hegemony and policies shaped the international system starting with the Congress of Vienna (1815). Among these policies were the abolition of the slave trade,[11] the abolition of slavery,[12] the emergence of the gold standard,[13] and the laissez-faire economic system.[14] British hegemony also shaped the development of international law.[15] Britain, for all its influence, was not alone in its legal imperialism. British and French jurists followed similar legal imperial strategies, bringing Anglo-Saxon and continental legal ideas concerning law and sovereignty closer. Similarly, American legal strategies and justifications in its encounter with Asian and African states closely resembled Britain's.[16]

The British example suggests (and as I discuss later Spanish, Dutch, and American examples concur) that an imperial legal episteme contains 1) a set of legal understandings and discourse of law determining the scope, application, and underlying values of law; 2) a great power with a global vision and interest; and 3) regular transnational

[10] Hobsbawm (1997: 365).
[11] Keene (2007).
[12] Keck and Sikkink (1998: 39–51).
[13] Eichengreen (1996).
[14] Ruggie (1998: 66–67).
[15] Grewe (2000: part 4).
[16] For justifications of American extraterritoriality based on British Foreign Jurisdiction Acts, see U.S. Senate (1882).

links between imperial centers and peripheries. Legal ideas provide a framework to turn political positions, self-interest, and normative ideas into arguments and pronouncements, which both raise moral claims and channel the exercise of power in specific ways. Legal experts and scholars produce and, through their scholarship and teaching, spread ideas and ideals of law. They thus shape the broad patterns of legal episteme influencing understandings of the law held by statesmen, diplomats, and the public. The collective understanding of law creates and constrains available choices, but rarely dictates the actual outcome. These background factors shape how imperialism was practiced and, in turn, and even sometimes simultaneously, shape the Western notions of what constituted sovereignty.

In a colonial encounter, imperialists, among other things, like culture, religion, and technology, invoke law. Western extraterritorial groups – merchants, missionaries, settlers, and their supporters at the imperial centers – establish imperial ties between non-Western states and European empires.[17] Lawyers accompany Westerners in non-Western states,[18] providing legal expertise so that Westerners can invoke their home states' law abroad. This pressure for legalization forces Western consular authorities to use their leverage to expand Western legal authority in non-Western states, making colonized and semicolonized societies bear the consequences (such as learning cost, i.e., Gandhi studies law in Britain to practice it in India) of this imposed jurisprudence. In cases where consular authorities are unwilling or unable, lawyers and extraterritorial groups lobby home states' bureaucracies (i.e., foreign ministries and colonial offices) in support of their legal claims. In conjunction with lobbying, sojourners as well as Western media pick and categorize non-Western practices as unjust using Western legal frameworks and their moral underpinnings. An established image of non-Western lawlessness becomes self-reinforcing when Western sojourners feed Western imaginations with more and more stories of non-Western cruelties, injustices, and biases.

Admittedly, even if one disputes the existence of a single standard of justice, reasonable people may agree on what constitutes gross

[17] MacDonald (2004).

[18] For a similar argument for the influence of lawyers in American imperial influences in Latin America, see Dezalay and Garth (2002) and Gardner (1980).

violations of justice and fairness, and there may be instances of them in non-Western societies. However, treating one, like positive standards of law, framework of law as *the* law, and other adjudicative and dispute resolution system as nonlaw or lawless, would be excessive given the diverse methods societies developed throughout centuries. In addition to ethnocentrism, tangible political and economic interest in constructing the image of non-Western lawlessness existed to the Western state rules or Western sojourners such as getting political support for military interventions into these countries or the allocation of more resources to support Western business, cultural, or religious groups in these countries.

The argument that the norms and practices of sovereignty were created within an imperial legal episteme in part to advance colonial domination can be extended to earlier periods. During the Spanish and Dutch hegemonies, these imperial powers and their legal episteme shaped the justification and creation of categories of inclusion and exclusion based on sovereignty. For example, in the sixteenth century, Francisco de Vitoria's conception of sovereignty was a product of the colonial encounter – it was not developed solely within European thought and practice and then later transferred to the Americas.[19] Vitoria's sovereignty emerged out of the Spanish colonial encounter with Indians in the Americas and reflected both the demands of Spanish colonialism and the influence of Thomastic conceptions of natural law. Invoking natural law, Vitoria emphasized the norms of equality and reciprocity between the Indians and the Spanish. Then, he invoked natural law to deny Indians' ability to act according to natural reason, a condition for sovereignty. Idealized natural reason became the universally binding criterion that Indians had to demonstrate in order to claim sovereignty. Meanwhile the Spanish and European inherent entitlement to natural reason, and thus to sovereignty, was assumed. While Spanish military prowess and disease imported from the Old World erased indigenous populations, the standard of "natural reason" erased indigenous law and sovereignty. Once Indian sovereignty and law had been categorically denied, Spanish sovereignty, law, and institutions could legitimately expand into the Americas under the guise of a civilizing mission.[20]

[19] Anghie (2005: 29).
[20] Anghie (2005: 30).

The role of the Spanish colonial encounter in the construction of sovereignty norms and practices is not an isolated example. Hugo Grotius' conceptualization of sovereignty was also closely tied to Dutch self-interest, European colonial expansion, and the dominant jurisprudence of Jean Bodin. While he agreed with Bodin on the indivisibility of sovereignty, he acknowledged colonial realities and offered new political categories that permitted sovereignty to be divided in order to accommodate European colonial interests.[21] In this dualistic system European political order was based on indivisible sovereignty, while non-European order was based on a divisible sovereignty that allowed European individuals and merchant companies to claim absolute (sovereign-like) rights on property and commerce in non-Western states.[22] Essentially, this bifurcated sovereignty facilitated and justified European imperialism.[23] As in the case of Vitorian sovereignty, the European colonial encounter was integral to the construction of Grotian sovereignty.

Positivism and the Domestic Legal Order: Sovereign-Centric Legal Absolutism

Like its predecessors, nineteenth-century "Westphalian" sovereignty reflected the dominant imperial legal episteme embodied in legal positivism and British imperial practices. Natural law, which was the dominant framework for the understandings and discourse of law determining the scope, application, and underlying values of law – or simply legal episteme – prior to positivism, posits that the content of law is set by a transcendental normative source above states. This overarching normative framework facilitates jurists in connecting law, justice, and morality. Natural law jurists offer varying normative sources for this law: nature, human nature, or religion. The transcendental quality of this understanding of law assumed law valid for *everywhere* and *everyone*. Contrary to natural law, positivism argues that law belongs to a specific political community, such as a state. Denying the need of moral justification for law outside of the law itself, positivism

[21] Keene (2002: 44–45).
[22] Keene (2002: 7).
[23] Keene (2002: 119).

reduces the morality of law to law's contractual quality and its instrumental rational foundations. Thus, the form, not the content, validates the law. Essentially, a law is valid if it is legislated and enforced by a sovereign ruler serving the state's utilitarian goals.

Sovereignty was not central to natural law theory.[24] The universalist assumptions of natural law scholars discouraged them from theorizing doctrines such as sovereign recognition and sovereign territoriality.[25] Emer de Vattel's *The Law of Nations*, first published in 1758, was one of the important works bridging natural law and positive law.[26] Deviating from the strictly naturalist "law of nations," Vattel made sovereignty central to international law. Vattel did this by adding an external dimension to Hobbes' and Bodin's conceptualizations of domestic sovereignty.[27] The external dimension of sovereignty entails two qualities: the sovereign state's privilege as the sole representative of a country's population, and the exclusion of what the ruler considers "external" from domestic authority structures. Within this external dimension, which is very similar to the contemporary notion of Westphalian sovereignty, sovereign states became the sole representatives of their populations and the sole subjects of the law of nations.[28] In the nineteenth century, Vattel's notion of sovereignty became widely accepted due to the change in legal episteme, signified by the rising influence of legal positivism, and the instrumental value of Vattel's ideas for British imperialism.[29]

The modern notion of sovereignty as "ultimate" authority is a direct consequence of positivist sovereign-centric legal absolutism.

[24] Alexandrowicz (1967) and Anghie (1999).

[25] Bull (1977: 29–39).

[26] For the influence of Vattel's ideas on the constitution of the modern international system, see Reus-Smit (1999). Also see Krasner (1999: 20–21).

[27] One issue that complicates Vattel's position on sovereignty is the eclecticism of his writings in which he combines positivist and natural elements. Whether Vattel is a positivist or a naturalist is debatable. For a naturalist description of Vattel, see S. Hall (2001). Vattel, for example, continued to carry some universalist ideals of the law of nations, as he claimed that "Nations treat one another as bodies of men and not as Christians or Mohammedans." Simpson (2004: xii).

[28] My account of Vattel's contribution to sovereignty is from Beaulac (2003). For the influence of Vattel on sovereignty, also see Fenwick (1914). Also see Anghie (1999) and Koskenniemi (1989).

[29] Krasner (1993) talks about the importance of Vattel's conceptualization of sovereignty in "Westphalian" sovereignty but does not explain why that particular conceptualization became dominant. Koskenniemi (1989: 89) suggests an interpretation

By the mid-nineteenth century, positivist legal theory dominated Anglo-American philosophy of law. While the intellectual roots of positivist legal theory reach back to Thomas Hobbes (1588–1679)[30] and David Hume (1711–1776),[31] its most systematic development is found in the works of Jeremy Bentham (1748–1832)[32] and John Austin (1790–1859).[33] According to Bentham's and Austin's framework of legal positivism, positive law and legal order were based on sovereign commands backed by coercion. In this approach, sovereignty denotes the source of positive law, distinguishing it from nominal laws such as divine law, morality, natural law, and customary law. Following Hobbes' arguments that laws are coercive commands, Austin suggests that laws are commands[34] "set by political superiors to political inferiors"[35] with the provision of punishment in case of noncompliance.[36] Using law, the sovereign promotes the greatest happiness for the greatest number of people. To fulfill this utilitarian function, all laws should be created deliberately and rationally and be expressed in systematically organized codes so that individuals can adjust their behavior and plan their lives.

This does not mean that all positivist jurists were philosophically committed to utilitarianism or conscious about the utilitarian concerns underlying legal positivism. But they all would agree that a positive legal order is necessary for the rationalization of state and bureaucracy. For a positive legal order, laws should be comprehensive, codified, and sanctioned by coercion.[37] In practice, these requirements of positive law

close to realism when he explains Vattel's popularity among diplomats and statesmen: "It was a 'realistic' book, especially useful for diplomats and practitioners, not least because it seemed to offer such compelling rhetoric for the justification of most varied kinds of State action. Vattel's professed programme is to concretise Volff's abstract theories for the use of sovereigns to whom he expressly writes." Beaulac (2003) alludes to the popularity of Vattel's writings in the Anglo-American world, basing his argument on the numerous printings of *The Law of Nations* and the large number of times the book is cited in U.S. Supreme Court opinions.

30 For Hobbes' views on law, see Hobbes (1969).

31 Milton (1982), Midgley (1975), Bull (1979), and Mackinnon (1966).

32 For Bentham's views on law and sovereignty, see Bentham (1970).

33 For Austin's views on law and sovereignty, see Austin (1832).

34 Austin (1832: 1380).

35 Austin (1832: 9).

36 Austin (1832: 4).

37 Positivist scholars, particularly Austin, were influenced by the Civil Law tradition. For an overview of positivism, see Cotterrell (1989). For Austin's view on

entail state monopolization of the law-making and law-enforcing functions through legislative and judicial institutions. The state's legislature should prepare clear and written laws and publicize them. The judicial institutions should enforce the laws uniformly and adjudicate disputes independently. The positive standards of "law" thereby reduced the law to legislative acts that empowered centralized, modern states and their formal legal institutions.[38] In addition, reducing the law to legislative commands had direct implications for both international and non-Western law. Because the focus of positivism was codified law with a clear enforcer, international law became a conceptual oxymoron.

Positivism and the International Legal Order: The Primacy of Sovereignty

The dominance of positivism over natural law was a mixed blessing for international jurists. These jurists were attracted to positivism's strong methodology but were repelled by early positivists' denial of international "law."[39] In particular, some positivists claimed that because international "law" was neither legislated by a sovereign nor backed by force, international law was not law. Legal positivist Austin is firm in his denial:

> The law obtaining between nations is not positive law: for every positive law is set by a given sovereign to a person or persons in a state of subjection to its author. As I have already intimated, the law obtaining between nations is law (improperly so called) set by general opinion. The duties which it imposes are enforced by moral sanctions; by fear on the part of nations, or by fear on the part of sovereigns, of provoking general hostility, and incurring its probable evils, in case they shall violate maxims generally received and respected.[40]

In the second half of the nineteenth century, jurists such as John Westlake (1828–1913), William E. Hall (1835–1893), Thomas E. Holland

sovereignty, see Dewey (1894) and Eastwood and Keaton (1929). For a contemporary review of Austin's ideas and his influence on nineteenth-century jurisprudence, see Rumble (2005).

[38] Hart (1971).

[39] Alexandrowicz (1961), Anghie (1999).

[40] Austin (1832: 201, 141–142). For Austin's effect on the development of international law, see Nussbaum (1954: 233–234).

(1835–1926), T. J. Lawrence (1849–1920), F. L. Oppenheim (1858–1919), and Thomas A. Walker (1862–1935) devoted the first chapters of their studies of international law to addressing Austin's denial of international law. To substantiate their claims regarding the existence of international law, these jurists modified legal positivism to create a positive international law.[41] The jurists curtailed the law of nations (now called *international law*, a Benthamite construction[42]) to fix international law to sovereignty. It was nineteenth-century international jurists who embraced the formulation of a sovereign-state-centric positive international law, thereby inventing "Westphalian" sovereignty. In this invention, the Peace of Westphalia became a genealogical tool to justify the international lawyers' sovereign-state-centric international law and to reject naturalism in international law.[43] In 1908, Oppenheim, the leading international positivist jurist of his time, stated that "we are no longer justified in teaching a law of nature and 'natural' law of nations."[44] In other words, the positivist critique of international law led the jurists to remove any role for naturalist ideas, such as universal morality, from international law.[45] In this exclusively positivist formulation, state sovereignty became the sole foundation of international law.

To create a sovereign-centric international law, jurists followed two related strategies, both of which excluded non-Western states from the realm of international law. First, they integrated European customary law as the unique source of international law. International law textbooks throughout the last quarter of the nineteenth century assumed that international law was part of European history and civilization.[46] This approach was compatible with the Austinian argument that international law is moral prescriptions applicable among

[41] Anghie (1999). Also see Kennedy (1997), Kingsbury (2002), and Hall (2001). For the most elaborate defense of "international law" see Walker (1893).

[42] For Bentham's use of the term "international" and its implications for sovereignty in this context, see Polat (2000) and Janis (1984).

[43] As examples, see Walker (1893) and Westlake (1894).

[44] Oppenheim (1908: 328). On this issue, compare Anghie (2005: 43) and Koskenniemi (2001: 92).

[45] All major international law books in the second half of the nineteenth century start with Austin's positivist critique of international law. After specifying the critique, the jurists formulate the possibility of international law without resorting to natural law principles. This trend in international-law textbooks continues. See Shaw (2002) and Henkin et al. (1993).

[46] Koskenniemi (2004).

civilized states.[47] Reducing international law to customary European state practices excluded non-Western societies from the realm of international law, as they did not share in European civilization. Second, international jurists modified and qualified a sovereignty doctrine applicable to international law. They argued that international law is positive law because *sovereign* states agree to it through their legislative decisions in the form of treaties. By this formulation, sovereign states themselves became the ultimate source of international legal order.

After affirming treaties as the source of international positive law, jurists faced the problem of how to classify "sovereign states." In response, nineteenth-century positivist jurists created a typology of "sovereign," "semisovereign," and "nonsovereign" entities. Only sovereign states were accorded treaty-making powers in this typology. Non-Western states, labeled either as semisovereign or nonsovereign entities, were disqualified from the treaty-making powers of international law. In their attempts to assert the existence of a sovereignty-based international law in which sovereign states were the sole objects and subjects and to distinguish sovereign states from various nonsovereign entities, legal scholars developed doctrines (territoriality, recognition, and supreme authority) to establish the standards of sovereignty.

Naturalism was compatible with the sovereign authority of nonterritorial entities such as privateers, pirates, and merchant companies.[48] The territoriality doctrine, which tied sovereignty with a fixed exclusive land with clear boundaries, denied the authority claims of privateers, pirates, and merchant companies, because these "private" entities lacked a fixed and properly demarcated land.[49] Furthermore, naturalism did not have a doctrine of recognition. As with the territoriality doctrine, jurists constructed a recognition doctrine. According to the recognition doctrine, a state's claim to sovereignty required other states' explicit recognition of such a claim.[50] Lastly, naturalism was compatible with overlapping authority claims. What naturalism easily

[47] This argument in conjunction with Austin appears in one of the most influential, and avowedly positivist, of the nineteenth century, Wheaton (1845).

[48] Wight (1966).

[49] Thomson (1994) and Horowitz (2005).

[50] Alexandrowicz (1969). Also Anghie (1999: 65–66).

accommodated – nonstate groups', including religious, merchant, and tribal, legal claims – positivists cited as evidence for the lack of "law and order" in non-Western societies. Equating sovereignty with a legal monopoly, positivism asserted that only sovereign states with an institutionalized monopoly of law have the right to claim sovereign authority. While Asian states were *de facto* territorial entities, international jurists did not categorize them as *de jure* sovereign entities because these states fell short on the newly formulated standards of sovereignty: territoriality, recognition, and positive legal authority.

One may question the causal relevance of legal ideas in imperial policy. Was imperial law just a cover to justify a colonial policy that was driven by material concerns? At some level, this is an empirical question that requires an analysis of political contingencies in imperial centers pushing and peripheries pulling for colonial rule. Admittedly, a clear military, economic, and political expediency can force state rulers to act based on logic of consequences to pick a legal interpretation for instrumental reasons, override legal precedents, or establish exceptions to the rule of law.[51] Yet, there are three reasons to suggest that "law" had an independent effect on Britain's territorial and extraterritorial overseas jurisdiction. First, legal reasoning and justifications permeated policy discussions within British governmental agencies, including discussions of colonial issues. Colonial policies, especially the ones that were intimately tied to law and justice, such as extraterritoriality, were articulated within a legal framework. On imperial policy, the British Colonial Office and the Foreign Office often deferred to the opinions of Law Officers.[52] This deference suggests that Law Officers had an important role in British imperial policy. The interdepartmental debates indicate that the first priority of the Law Officers was the "legality" of the suggested policy. They were the ones responsible for setting the problem in a legal framework and defining the available set of legal tools for a particular policy.[53]

[51] For logic of consequences and logic of appropriateness and the conditions under which a ruler acts based on these different logics, see March and Olsen (1999). Schmitt (2005) famously fixes sovereignty with the right to decide on the exception to the rule of law, thereby making the law the exclusive attribute of states, which may at will make and unmake it.

[52] The collective term for three of the highest British judicial authorities, the Attorney-General, the Solicitor-General, the King's Advocate-General.

[53] Johnston (1973: 145).

Second, in significant ways, colonial policy was an issue of domestic rather than foreign policy. For example, in extraterritoriality it was the domestic law of the colonial powers that was applied in non-Western states. As I elaborate in the next chapter, in the case of British extraterritoriality, the Foreign Jurisdiction Acts that empowered British extraterritoriality were perceived to be part of the British constitutional structure for allocating authority among different branches of government. In practical terms this meant that it was easier to change policies rather than constitutional acts. Laws may change in response to policy impediments, but once legislated, laws shape succeeding policies. Third, law also permeated imperial policy through the personnel of the Colonial Office and the Foreign Office who had received intensive legal training. Lawyers often occupied senior positions in the Colonial and Foreign Offices. Some of these senior lawyers were also eminent jurists or had frequent contact with jurists. Law and lawyers have had substantial power in the articulation of the form and substance of legal imperialism.[54]

By the end of the nineteenth century, Western countries expanded and solidified their legal authority in non-Western states. The next section examines the role of legal episteme in constructing and justifying Western legal encroachment into non-Western states and how legal positivism made non-Western societies become categorically lawless and sovereignty-less.

CONSTRUCTIVISM, ORIENTALISM, AND IMPERIALISM

The argument and empirical evidence so far presented are consistent with the constructivist and English School approaches. I have proposed that extraterritoriality has more to do with civilization than power, that the norms and practices of Westphalian sovereignty are embedded in a specific set of legal ideas, legal positivism, and that non-Western states are inducted into the paradigm of Westphalian sovereignty. In these processes, legal scholars and jurists acted as professional norm developers, propagating their ideas and ideals about law, justice, and sovereignty. With their claims to legal expertise,

[54] For a list of eminent nineteenth-century legal scholars working for the British government see Johnston (1973).

lawyers, jurists, and legal advisers often moved from the production and maintenance of the legal episteme to political decision making. When the rules were uncertain, as in international law or constitutional law, rulers and diplomats called on experts "to make authoritative interpretations of rules." Legal professionals themselves "may develop strategies in technical areas which then may become authoritative either directly or indirectly through recognition of those standards by other institutions."[55] The professional and normative consensus for law and sovereignty establishes the framework of sovereignty. In this consensus-building process, lawyers, legal advisers, and jurists "have a political responsibility to justify their decisions so that they appear congruent with decision-making activity (by legislators as well as judges) within the legal system as a whole."[56] In other words, the legal arguments and consensus may often reflect a combination of jurists' professional commitment and political vision as well as the jurists' perceptions of the decision makers' position on a particular issue.

While I agree with most of the observations of constructivist and the English School scholars, I also follow postcolonial scholarship to put a concern of imperialism at the center of legal positivism and its influence on debates about "Westphalian" sovereignty and the place of non-Western sovereignty and law in the nineteenth-century construction of sovereignty. Postcolonial scholars, such as Edward Said, examine the nexus between ideas and material power in the context of imperialism. Said demonstrates the interplay between Western academic studies of non-Western societies and Western imperial involvement. Oriental studies imagined an "Orient" beyond the reach of human progress in the sciences, arts, and commerce. These studies depicted non-Western societies as societies filled with sensuality, despotism, and fanaticism. According to Said, this distorted image of the Orient allowed Europeans to construct a self-image of ethical and intellectual superiority by constructing the image of an inferior "other." Thus, the Orient's image as despotic, stagnant, and backward was propagated and exploited precisely in order to construct Europe's image as enlightened, dynamic, and modern. By creating the Orient as the antithesis of Europe, orientalism provided the rationale

[55] Quotes are from Adler and Bernstein (2005: 304).
[56] Koskenneimi (1989). Compare Finnemore (2003).

and self-confidence for Western imperialism. In the words of Said, "colonial rule was justified in advance by Orientalism, rather than after the fact."[57]

What Said claims for the development of Western cultural, literary, and political perspectives and their relation to the Orient applies to the development of Western jurisprudence as well – in both domestic and international law. The construction of positive law and sovereignty also requires establishing their opposites.[58] Positive law and sovereignty became the institutional frames used by jurists to distinguish Western from non-Western states and to conceptualize both. In this construction, Western societies represented the ideal rule of "law" while Far Eastern and Islamic societies were mired in the rule of "men," "religion," or "custom."[59] In positivist studies, non-Western forms of law established the criteria for what law was not – religious, customary, and unwritten. In short, European, mostly British, positivist jurists constructed the idealized European rule of law together with the image of non-European lawlessness.

While Said did not examine the implications of his arguments in terms of law and sovereignty, his insights suggest that nineteenth-century legal discourse and categories contained an inescapable imperial vision. This imperial vision was ingrained in the worldview of legal professionals, making them committed supporters of their states' imperial aims. In this imperial vision, the positivist legal approach to non-Western law was based on what I call "legal orientalism," wherein Western law and non-Western law were continuously created by scholars in order to legitimate idealized Western notions of law at the expense of non-Western legal orders.[60] More precisely, "legal orientalism" refers to Western jurists and politicians' claims about the ethical and intellectual superiority of Western legal systems. This justified the removal or replacement of the non-Western judicial elite in order to eliminate or significantly limit indigenous legal systems.[61]

[57] Said (1979: 39).

[58] Some international relations scholars explore self–other distinctions in the formation of sovereignty. Among them are R. B. J. Walker (1993), Bartelson (1995), Campbell (1992), and Weber (1995).

[59] Taylor (1997).

[60] Said (1979). Also Macfie (2000).

[61] Schmidhauser (1997), Allain (2004), Ruskola (2002), and Hussain (2003).

The relationship between positivism and Western dominance is not merely sequential but rather substantial: Molding the Western notions of what constituted sovereignty, positivism facilitated and shaped Western colonial expansion.

British legal positivists were heavily involved with imperialism. Many close to Jeremy Bentham, such as James Mill, John Stuart Mill, John Bowring, and John Austin, were supporters and beneficiaries of British imperialism. While Austin and J. S. Mill were employed by the East India Company for a significant portion of their careers, John Bowring's career as a high-level colonial official took him to India, the Ottoman Empire, Thailand, and China. The imperial vision held by these men shaped their encounters with Asian law; their studies of Western and Asian law then shaped colonial politics.[62]

The positivist construction of sovereignty required jurists to construct non- or semisovereign entities. Jurists sorted non-Western states into semisovereign and nonsovereign categories, each granting different rights and entailing different obligations. These categories all rejected the non-Western states' claims to domestic law and excluded them from international law, facilitating and justifying Western colonization of these nonsovereign African states and semisovereign Asian states. In the African case, it largely denied even the existence of states. International positivist jurists were integral to this imperial project. Their textbooks became part of international law, their law classes at Oxford and Cambridge trained a generation of colonial administrators, and their opinions were cited in court proceedings (such as the relationships between the East India Company, Indian local rulers, and the British government) and were solicited by Colonial Office and Foreign Office officials. Numerous references to international jurists appear in the diplomatic correspondence of the late nineteenth

[62] In James', John Stuart Mill's, and John Bowring's writings this influence is explicit. Among the group, Austin wrote the least, one short book, which does not explicitly involve European and non-European law. There is also an ongoing debate about utilitarians and imperialism. The consensus points out a direct link. See Stokes (1959). Also see Majeed (1990). The major exception is Pitts (2003). Pitts claims that Bentham himself was not sympathetic to colonial expansion, but she agrees that other utilitarians were. According to Horowitz (2005), natural law would be incompatible with nineteenth-century imperialism. Also see Anghie (1999) for a similar viewpoint.

century.[63] The jurists' ideas shaped the most important international conferences of the nineteenth century such as Paris (1856) and Berlin (1885). The Berlin Conference is particularly significant, as it was heavily influenced by the involvement of jurists and established the legal foundations for the colonization of Africa.[64]

In sum, idealized Western law and sovereignty were constructed in tandem with the critique of non-Western law and sovereignty. Positivism shaped nineteenth-century legal imperialism through the delegitimization of non-Western law, and thus, non-Western sovereignty. Legal expertise and legal experts were used at every stage of European imperialism. Legal experts used positive law and sovereignty to conceptualize and categorize non-Western legal systems and their authority claims. This taxonomy provided legal resources to Western state rulers in their efforts to extend their authority into non-Western states.

Once non-Western lawlessness had been demonstrated, extraterritoriality emerged as a natural solution to protect the rights of Western subjects, such as merchants and missionaries, who traveled to and lived in non-Western societies.[65] Extraterritoriality was nothing short of legal imperialism. As Paul MacDonald points out, imperial relations are not drawn on a blank slate. In addition to the ideological justifications and resources that legal positivism and orientalism provided, imperialists had equally important economic and political justifications and resources.[66] Mostly established by merchant companies, significant commercial links between the imperial centers and the periphery were already in place at the start of the nineteenth century to support the ever-growing world economy. British hegemony used, and in the process transformed, these commercial links to sustain the increasing volume and complexity of nineteenth-century Western-dominated international trade. Both extraterritoriality and legal institutionalization were important institutions in securing the existing commercial relations between Britain and non-Western countries, and in further opening non-Western markets to British goods and

[63] For the influence of international jurists on policy makers including in the nineteenth century, see Lachs (1987). Also see Kingsbury (2002: 405).

[64] Anghie (1999).

[65] Koskenniemi (2004: 115).

[66] MacDonald (2004).

investment opportunities. European rulers were more disposed to recognize the authority claims of other rulers who were willing and able to institutionalize a legal system and who clarified and enforced property rights within their domains. Domestic legalization was central to the construction of the nineteenth-century, so-called Westphalian, sovereignty.

TRADE, LAW, AND IMPERIALISM

Marc Bloch emphasizes the importance of legal systems when he writes: "[H]ow were men tried? There is no better touchstone for a social system than this question."[67] Bloch's reminder has had few echoes in the literature on sovereignty even though state sovereignty is closely connected to law-making and law-enforcing authority.[68] Although both the traditional state-building literature and constructivist scholarship on sovereignty advanced our understanding of the role of legal institutionalization in the process of state and sovereignty formation,[69] in these accounts, legal institutionalization remains largely internal to the state but a marginal role for the state's external relations. In part, this is because legal theory since Bodin and Hobbes has associated law with the state and the environment beyond it with lawlessness. For example, legal institutionalization occupies a central

[67] Bloch (1961: 359).

[68] See Jupille and Caporaso (2009), Weber (1978), Poggi (1978, 1990), Giddens (1987), and Tilly (1992), who develop a political account of state building emphasizing legal institutionalization. Jessop (1990) offers a Marxist approach regarding the role of legal institutionalization in state building. For a new institutional economics approach to state building and legal institutionalization see North (1990) and Barzel (2002). For a review of different conceptualizations of the state in international relations theory, see Hobson (2000). In my approach to state building I follow Spruyt (1994) and Thomson (1994, 1995).

[69] Weber (1978), Strayer (1973), Poggi (1978, 1990), Anderson (1979), and Giddens (1987). Among the political theory of state building, Tilly (1975) is the only notable exception for his lack of attention to the role of the legal system in the emergence of modern states. Talking on the behalf of the contributors of the edited volume, Tilly (1975: 6) states: "As our work proceeded, the chief omission which the group came to regret was the judicial system. Because courts, judges, and judicial proceedings antedate national states and appear in so many unstately guises, it is easy to forget how large a part certain kinds of courts played in the day-to-day construction of Western states. The issues come up, of course, in papers dealing with taxation, food supply, policing, but the volume as a whole treats the judicial system as much less adequately than we would have liked."

place in the arguments of Max Weber[70] and Douglas North.[71] They argue that state-clarified and state-enforced property rights are the key to understanding the emergence of the modern state. According to Weber and North, both the causes (bargaining between state rulers and bourgeoisies) and the consequences (establishing predictable and calculable market interactions) of state law institutionalization are related to domestic politics. Missing from their arguments are the international implications – both as causes and consequences – of the clarification and enforcement of legal and property rights by the state.

Unlike Weber and North, Gianfranco Poggi and Anthony Giddens acknowledge the international dimension of states' legal institutionalization. Poggi argues that sovereign states create an environment that only sovereign states can populate. Yet, he does not explain *why* sovereign states require other political units to be sovereign. Similarly, Giddens argues that only sovereign states, and not any other type of political entity, mutually empower each other. This mutual empowerment occurs because sovereign states establish a state monopoly over coercion. Yet, Giddens does not elaborate his argument to show *how* a monopoly over coercion empowers sovereign states. In other words, although they attempt to incorporate an international dimension in their account of state building, Poggi's and Giddens' accounts remain underdeveloped because they do not clarify the mechanisms through which domestic authority structures can affect other states' domestic authority structures.

Following the arguments of comparative historical sociology, some international relations scholars acknowledge the role of domestic law in "Westphalian" sovereignty, but its role remains limited in their theories. Friedrich Kratochwil links the revival of private property rights in Roman law to the formation of modern states in Europe.[72] He argues that European state rulers used the Roman notion of property to exclude others from intervening within their respective domains. John Ruggie recognizes the role of state enforcement of laws in the construction of domestic sovereignty.[73] Both for Kratochwil and

[70] Weber (1978).
[71] North and Thomas (1973). Also see North (1981, 1990).
[72] Kratochwil (1995). Also see Kratochwil (1986).
[73] Ruggie (1993). Also see Ruggie (1983).

Ruggie, the revival of Roman law is important for domestic, but not external, sovereignty. They use the analogy of the individuals' private property rights to land in Roman law to state rulers' sovereignty over a territory in the Westphalian system. In the Ruggie-Kratochwil argument, the resemblance between private property and state sovereignty led to the establishment of the mutually recognized, exclusive territorial domains of states. This limited and analogical treatment of the role of domestic law for Westphalian sovereignty overlooks the extensive role of domestic legalization, in particular a positive legal worldview, in Westphalian sovereignty. Domestic legalization established the foundation for territorial jurisdiction and allowed states to coordinate their legal structures facilitating transnational interactions.

After reducing the role of domestic law to domestic sovereignty, these international scholars seek a separate mechanism to explain domestic and international aspects of "Westphalian" sovereignty. Ruggie suggests a theory of social empowerment based on state rulers' recognition of each other as sovereign rulers within their respective territories. In a similar vein, Hendrik Spruyt offers a mechanism of mutual empowerment linking the domestic and international aspects of sovereignty: Mutual empowerment among sovereign states occurs because 1) recognizing clear boundaries eliminates conflicts among authority relations; and 2) state rulers commit themselves to their international arrangements. While I concur with Spruyt that, compared to city-states and empires, sovereign states are better at fulfilling their external commitments, also internally sovereign states' legal institutionalization enhanced their commitment to the clarification and enforcement of legal and property rights. Sovereign states' reciprocal commitment to domestic legalization was necessary for the growing volume and complexity of long-distance trade.

Domestic law has international consequences. First, domestic authority arrangements impact transnational interactions. For example, while some arrangements, such as clear property rights, enable transnational commercial interactions, other arrangements, such as unspecified property rights, discourage them. Second, domestic legal arrangements impact citizens as well as nationals of other states when these foreign nationals reside in another state. Because domestic legal structures affect the lives and properties of foreigners, the home states of the foreigners may become involved with the domestic legal arrangements of other states. Because domestic authority structures influence both transnational interactions and the legal and property rights of foreigners, state rulers hold each other accountable for their domestic legal structures.

This reciprocal legal accountability facilitates transnational transactions. For example, transnational commercial transactions are much more difficult if merchants do not have reliable information about legal and property rights in other countries. These transactions will be precarious if foreign merchants do not trust the enforcement of contracts. The need for legal coordination makes state rulers accountable to each other regarding their domestic legal structures. Like physical boundaries, formal and informal communication among state rulers constructs jurisdictional boundaries. As a result of communications to achieve the coordination of authority claims, state rulers authorize, empower, and demand each other to arrange their legal systems to make the states' domestic legal structures compatible. A particular form of domestic authority structure – the institutionalization of state law – is necessary for the Westphalian system.

The nineteenth century marked a significant rise in the level of transnational interactions between Western and Asian states. The increasing economic, cultural, and political relations among individuals from different countries intensified problems related to the coordination of jurisdiction over transnational interactions. Merchant companies that had regulated trade between Europe and Asia were organizationally and politically unable to deal with the increasing trade. Organizationally, they did not have the infrastructure to support the vast territories they controlled. Politically, the informal and private jurisdiction of merchant communities and mercantile companies became unacceptable for Western state rulers as these rulers accepted ideas such as free trade, state sovereignty, and citizenship.

Domestic legalization – the clarification of rules (codes), the enforcement of these rules (statewide court system), and the creation of a legal hierarchy (appellate system) – reduced these problems. Essentially, it allowed rulers to regulate the transnational interactions by means of accepting each others' jurisdiction over their subjects and citizens as well as the subjects and citizens of other rulers if these subjects and citizens are in their territory. Yet, this right underscored each ruler's responsibility to establish institutions to make and enforce laws that facilitate transnational interactions and moderates the conflict of jurisdictions over transnational transactions. Three conditions are necessary for state rulers to systematically facilitate transnational interactions: internal stability, information about legal and property rights, and enforcement of legal and property rights.[74] First, state rulers utilize state law to pacify their territory. The pacification of the territory decreases the risks for foreigners in contracting with locals. Second, state rulers use state law to provide clear information about legal and property rights. The state's clarification of legal and property rights distinguishes public and private property, commercializes property rights, and specifies state-enforced contracts. Third, the institutionalization of state law designates the state as the actor that is responsible and accountable for clarifying and enforcing legal and property rights.

Although state law institutionalization empowers all states to a degree, it empowers most those states whose citizens engage in long-distance trade. The absence of institutionalized state law means that local customs dominate property rights and their enforcement. This favors local merchants over long-distance traders because customary law creates information and enforcement asymmetries regarding legal and property rights. State law reduces information and enforcement asymmetries by making state rulers responsible for the systemization, standardization, and uniform application of state law.[75] In the next chapter I argue that like the prior gunboat diplomacy that the great powers used to remove Chinese reluctance and Japanese resistance to integrate into international trade, and whose terms the great powers dictated, the great powers used a variety of methods, most importantly extraterritoriality, to facilitate legal reforms in Japan, China, and the Ottoman Empire both for the ideational appeal of a positive legal order and to increase Western merchants' access to markets and investment opportunities in these countries.

[74] For relations between state law and economics, see Barzel (2002) and Dixit (2004).

[75] Spruyt (1994: 168).

2

Extraterritoriality and Legal Imperialism

The rise and decline of Western legal imperialism[1] in the nineteenth and early twentieth centuries suggests a different period and perspective to understand "Westphalian" sovereignty. Essentially, "Westphalian" sovereignty is related to two nineteenth-century developments: the dominance of legal positivism and European colonial expansion. Contrary to the Eurocentric consenus, sovereignty was not developed and consolidated solely within Western thought and practices, but rather in the encounters of Western colonial – particularly British – powers with Asian states. In the process of creating the British Empire's territorial rule in the forms of colonies, dependencies, and protectorates, and extraterritorial rule in the form of extraterritorial jurisdiction over British citizens, subjects, and corporations in Asia,[2] British imperial practices clarified, crystallized, and consolidated the sovereignty doctrine. These practices were embedded in a legal episteme that excluded non-Western entities and understandings from the sphere of law and sovereignty. The conceptual gerrymandering of inclusion and exclusion around normatively powerful concepts

[1] For a comparative legal history in the context of imperial expansion see Benton (2002) and Leue (1992).

[2] While formal/territorial colonization is widely discussed in international relations scholarship, informal/extraterritorial imperialism is less frequently explored. See Doyle (1986: 30–47) and Abernethy (2000: chapter 2); also see Jackson (1990), Kahler (1984), and Snyder (1991). One major exception is Gong (1984), who examines extraterritoriality in the context of the expansion of international society.

such as law, courts, and sovereignty was intimately tied to imperial politics.

This chapter links the rise and decline of extraterritoriality to the rise and decline of positive law and British hegemony from the early nineteenth century to the mid-twentieth century. I develop my argument in three sections. First, I describe the rise of extraterritoriality and the denial of non-Western law and sovereignty. I also discuss how explanations solely grounded on material power and culture overlook the crucial role the legal episteme and domestic legal institutions played in nineteenth-century imperialism. Second, I detail how non-Western hostility toward extraterritoriality replaced the prior non-Western rulers' reluctant cooperation with Western states over extraterritoriality. I also examine why domestic legalization was the best strategy for non-Western states in persuading Western states to end extraterritoriality. Third, I end the chapter with a justification of my research method.

THE RISE OF EXTRATERRITORIALITY

The first entities to feel the effects of this changing legal landscape, brought by legal postivism I described in the first chapter, were merchant companies such as the British East India Company, the Levant Company, and the Dutch East India Company that facilitated much of the trade between Western and non-Western countries until the second half of the nineteenth century.[3] Premodern rulers allowed foreign-merchant communities to self-adjudicate because they perceived that the legal autonomy of foreign merchants facilitated trade.[4] This self-adjudication was also compatible both with natural law and with many local premodern political structures and practices wherein religious and tribal communities, as well as guilds, shared legal authority with the rulers. The prime example of sharing of legal authority between state and nonstate actors was the Ottoman Empire's *millet* system under which the whole society was organized into religious communities. In the religious communities, the religious leaders had quasi-sovereign authority including tax collection, education, representation of their

[3] Thomson (1994). Also Leue (1992).
[4] Greif (1993) and Leue (1992).

communities, and the adjudication of legal disputes. The Ottoman rulers incorporated foreign merchant communities in this environment of legal plurality and allowed them to have legal self-governance. In the system of foreign-merchant self-governance, if a mercantile company existed, the mercantile consul (the highest ranking representative of the company) would have jurisdiction over the merchant community. For example, the British Levant Company operated in the Ottoman Empire and had the power to solve civil and commercial disputes among its employees, British workers in the company factories, and other British citizens residing in the Ottoman Empire.[5] According to the Company's Royal Charter, consuls were to administer to all British subjects "full speedie and expedite justice in all their plaints causes and contencions amongst them."[6] If a foreign merchant community was not attached to a mercantile company, the foreign merchant community would either choose the Levant Company's jurisdiction or they would select a merchant who would act as the consul to adjudicate disputes within their community. Western foreigners enjoyed a high level of communal autonomy before being incorporated into their home-states' public law in the nineteenth century.[7]

Western imperial expansion transformed the non-Western unilateral grants of merchant legal self-governance into the extraterritorial rights of European states in non-Western states. This was a legal process driven by both imperial contingencies and the legal positivist framework of state-centric law. Essentially, the sovereign prerogative of legislating and enforcing the laws that distinguished positive law was incompatible with the merchants' law-making and law-enforcing rights.[8] Western countries transferred the legal rights of mercantile companies and merchant communities to Western state institutions with legislative acts – most of the time without informing or negotiating with the non-Western rulers. For example, in the Ottoman Empire, merchant consuls solved foreigners' legal disputes without

[5] Wood (1935).

[6] For the company's charter, see Epstein (1908: appendix 1).

[7] In China from 1676 (when the East India Company stationed its first agents) to 1833, British citizens were under the jurisdiction of the East India Company. See Keeton (1969: 201).

[8] For the role of merchant companies in the context of state building and sovereignty see Thomson (1994).

interference from their home states until 1825. In that year, the British government decided to "transfer the company's authority over the consuls in Levant to the crown," bringing the Levant consular service under the British government's sovereign authority.[9]

The abolition of the Levant Company caused some constitutional problems. It was not clear how the British legal authority over British citizens in the Ottoman Empire would be carried out. While an act of Parliament abolished the company and transferred its legal authority to the crown in 1825, British Law Officers questioned the legality of the arrangement in 1826. The legal challenge was based on the claim that the crown had the prerogative to enter into treaty relations with foreign governments, but that it did not have the legal authority to administer law on an ongoing basis without a legislative act. In essence, the challenge rested on the fact that the crown cannot make or apply laws without parliamentary sanction.[10]

Legal scholars turned their attention to this ambiguity as the number of British-involved cases in the Ottoman Empire swelled in the 1830s and 1840s (in part because of the influx of a large number of the British Empire's Maltese and Ionian subjects into the Ottoman Empire). In particular, James R. Hope-Scott, a barrister and Queen's Counsel, produced a very influential report that argued that in Christian states territorial sovereignty required Britain to accept the local jurisdiction over British subjects.[11] However, Hope-Scott wrote that in non-Christian states the British government had the right to establish its courts due to the existence of cultural differences regarding views about morality and justice. According to Hope-Scott, any questions about the legality of British jurisdiction were a matter of domestic law, not international law.[12] Ambiguity regarding the legality of the British jurisdiction in the Ottoman Empire, as well as in other Asian and African states, could thus be solved by an act of Parliament clarifying the extent of this right. Hope-Scott recommended the preparation of new legislation to bring the British

[9] Platt (1971: 125).

[10] For discussions of legal justifications of extraterritoriality, see Hall (1894: 5–9, 149–150), Roberts-Wray (1996: 73, 191), and Holdsworth (1956: 81–82).

[11] For Hope-Scott biography and legal career, see Ornsby (1884).

[12] For the text of Hope-Scott's report, see Jenkyns (1902: 243–266).

merchants' legal jurisdiction in the Ottoman Empire under the British Empire's constitutional authority.

Upon Hope-Scott's report, the first Foreign Jurisdiction Act was legislated in 1843, incorporating some of his suggestions verbatim. The act established the legal basis of extraterritoriality by extending British legal authority into the Ottoman Empire. The Act stated that "by treaty, capitulation, grant, usage, sufferance, and other lawful means, Her Majesty the Queen has jurisdiction within diverse foreign countries." This jurisdiction authorized the British government to exercise legal authority in the Ottoman Empire "in the same and in as amply a manner as if Her Majesty had acquired that jurisdiction by the *cessation or conquest of territory*."[13] While the Ottoman Empire had not been conquered or colonized, the British government could extend its laws into the Empire as if it had been. Of course, these laws only applied to British citizens and protégés such as Maltese and Ionians but the effect was much like a sovereign ruling its territory. Thus, in 1844 when British Foreign Secretary George H. G. Aberdeen instructed the British consuls in the Ottoman Empire to implement the act, he was blunt: "as the maintenance of order and repression and punishment of crime are objects of the greatest importance in every civilized community, it is obligatory upon the Christian Powers, standing as they do in Turkey ... *in the place of the territorial Sovereign* to provide as far as possible for these great ends."[14]

While specifically prepared to justify and organize British jurisdiction in the Ottoman Empire, the 1843 Foreign Jurisdiction Act was broadened to have a universal reach. After 1843, each step of British formal and informal colonialism came with an Order in Council decision, which was secured, justified, and legalized within a series of Foreign Jurisdictional Acts (FJAs).[15] FJAs were part of British domestic law. FJAs established the normative framework that defined and justified how the British government would pursue its commercial and political interest within its formal and informal empire.

[13] Italics added. For the text of the Foreign Jurisdiction Act, 1843, see Hertslet (1845: 507–511).

[14] Cited in Spagnolo (1991: 266).

[15] The 1843 FJA was amended in 1865 and 1866. Subsequently new FJAs were legislated in 1875, 1878, and 1890. For the text of the last Foreign Jurisdiction Act, 1890, see W. E. Hall (1894: 287–293).

Constructing imperial policy, FJAs also served as points of reference for the debates among the Colonial Office, the Foreign Office, and the Law Officers.[16] As Thomas E. Holland, a senior law officer and leading international positivist jurist of the nineteenth century, stated, the "Foreign Jurisdiction Act established the legal justification for the British extraterritorial colonization of non-Western countries."[17] Other Western states either followed the British example to justify their extraterritorial courts or claimed most-favored-nation clauses from the non-Western states to substantiate their claims on the basis of British extraterritorial rights in these states; whatever rights a non-Western state' granted to one, Western power granted to all. FJAs established an international precedent and became part of international law to regulate Western states' international relations with non-Western states.

THE NON-WESTERN RESPONSE TO EXTRATERRITORIALITY

In the second half of the nineteenth century, hostility replaced the prior indifference of non-Western elite and societal attitude toward extraterritoriality. This made it difficult for local rulers to acquiesce to extraterritoriality and for imperial powers to persuade them to accept it.[18] There were several reasons for non-Western rulers to regard extraterritoriality with growing antipathy. For one, extraterritoriality severely limited the non-Western rulers' ability to control and tax foreigners. This was especially trying because their revenues were dwindling, the need to raise revenues to sustain reforms and secure the state was intense, and the foreigners' share in the local economies was increasing. Worse, in addition to foreigners, some natives were acquiring extraterritorial protection (either through naturalization or certification of protection, like protégés) to evade taxation and circumvent the government's regulations, thereby undermining the government's capacity to reform.

[16] Jackson (1993: 114–119) compares the Foreign Jurisdiction Act with the General Act of the Berlin Conference (1884–1885) to clarify the normative framework of colonial expansion. Also see Johnston (1973: chapter 6).

[17] Holland (1898: 186).

[18] For the importance of local collaboration imperialism, see Doyle (1986: 38–42). For the Chinese antipathy and resistance to extraterritoriality, see Wong (2005). For the Ottoman resistance, see Ahmad (2000).

Non-Western rulers also disliked the symbolism of extraterritoriality: There was a strong stigma attached to the *unequal* treaties. Earlier generations of non-Western elites had been wary of the unequal rights and responsibilities that were associated with extraterritoriality. However, their skepticism turned into outright antagonism as they internalized the Western norms of territorial jurisdiction and sovereign equality that accompanied their desire to become a part of international society. The growth of nationalist and antiimperialist movements in non-Western societies made the perception of extraterritoriality a more acute symbol of inferiority. These protest movements emerged in the last part of the nineteenth century, gained momentum in the early twentieth century, and became the dominant political current in many non-Western states during the interwar years. Throughout the evolution of these movements extraterritoriality took an important place in the nationalists' framing of their agony and suffering under Western domination. Unanimously and unequivocally, the nationalist movements demanded the abolition of extraterritoriality in the name of justice and national sovereignty.

In addition to the domestic limitations extraterritoriality established and the non-Western inferiority it represented, another reason for the increased non-Western hostility was the perception of an extraterritorial vicious cycle: Growth of Western investment and trade under extraterritoriality justified further Western interest and demands. This, in turn, led to more Western interventions, gunboat diplomacy, and demands of exacting criteria for non-Western reforms.

Extraterritoriality itself and the conditions non-Western states were required to meet in order for extraterritoriality to be abolished made non-Western reforms, regulations, and legalization dependent on foreign approval. Through this dependence, Western states were able to export and impose Western legal forms and ideas to non-Western states.[19] From the mid-nineteenth to the mid-twentieth centuries, in societies with strikingly different legal traditions, non-Western rulers initiated similar large-scale reforms with the goal of domestic legalization. For example, the rulers of the Ottoman Empire, Iran, Japan, Thailand, and China utilized the same three strategies with varying degrees of success: the

[19] Compare it with Badie (2000).

codification of laws, the centralization of the court system, and the establishment of a statewide court structure. In this process, these non-Western states enacted commercial, criminal, and civil codes. They also established state bureaucracies to subordinate and replace religious, communal, and merchant courts with state courts. This reorganization of the court system was accompanied by the numerical and geographical expansion of the state's courts. The union of these three processes – codification of laws, centralization of court structures, and expansion of courts – resulted in the unification of a legal system under the state. In large part, extraterritoriality and the ensuing desire of non-Western elites to be rid of it explain non-Western legalization.

However, the centrality of extraterritoriality in the politics of legal reforms in non-Western states does not mean that non-Western legalization was simply a response to exogenous factors. In important ways these reforms were also the result of internal processes. Under Western imperial advances, non-Western elites were aware of the need to build the state's institutional capacity by implementing new tax codes, centralizing administrative functions, and eliminating the state's internal rivals. In any state-building process, legal systems constitute a crucial step because they are the tools for reorganization. Legal control is integral to political control. Early studies of state building emphasize the role of legal systems. For example, Max Weber analyzes the role of Roman law in the transformation of the feudal institutions that led to the emergence of the modern state and its legal-rational bureaucratic authority.[20] Like Weber, Perry Anderson emphasizes the contribution of Roman law to the emergence of absolutist states: "Roman law was the most powerful intellectual weapon available for their typical program of territorial integration and administrative centralism."[21] Just as their European counterparts did, non-Western rulers were utilizing legal standardization and unification to consolidate their own power.

Paradoxically, extraterritoriality and the Western requirements to end it were equal parts opportunity and constraint for non-Western elites; these conditions became both the catalyst for non-Western

[20] Weber (1978: 839–880).

[21] Anderson (1979: 28).

rulers' legal reforms and their justification. The rulers' attempts at legal unification realigned the domestic groups in their societies. While centralized state rulers and the bourgeoisie supported the states' efforts toward legal unification, traditional authority holders (such as the *ulema* in the Ottoman Empire) and local notables resisted the legal advances of the states. Faced with external demands and internal resistance, these rulers engaged in constant negotiations with Western states and internally with societal groups in the nineteenth and early twentieth centuries. The failed negotiations between some societal actors and the state triggered top-down nationalist revolutions that coercively eliminated societal groups that resisted the state's legal reforms. These revolutions were justified in antiimperialist rhetoric. Overall, the popular desire to end extraterritoriality offered the strongest justification for the reformers' elimination of internal rivals who resisted legal standardization and unification efforts. This dynamic often resulted in the emergence of repressive regimes.

Western states' contradictory demands for non-Western legal institutionalization and for the continuation of extraterritoriality were a formidable obstacle for non-Western rulers' state-building reforms. In response, non-Western elites developed three strategies to persuade Western states to relinquish extraterritoriality: First, they claimed that extraterritoriality violated the principles of state sovereignty and sovereign equality. Second, they claimed that extraterritoriality was inefficient. Third, these elites initiated legal institution-building projects conducive to a positive legal order. Among these three approaches, the last one proved to be the most effective strategy in garnering the abolition of extraterritoriality.

The first strategy was to challenge extraterritoriality on normative grounds. Non-Western rulers claimed that extraterritoriality was a violation of state sovereignty and sovereign equality, and was thus incompatible with international law. Following the Crimean War (1853–1856), the Ottoman Empire used the Paris Conference of 1856 to challenge the normative basis of extraterritoriality. Similarly, China used both the Paris Conference of 1919, and in 1921 the Washington Conference for Disarmament, to raise normative challenges to extraterritoriality.[22]

[22] For the Turkish claims, see Sousa (1933: 177–178). For Chinese claims, see Fishel (1952: chapter 3).

Responding to the Ottoman Empire's claim, European countries confirmed the Ottoman Empire's status as a member of international society. Regarding extraterritoriality, Western states promised to establish a commission to examine the Ottoman judicial system – a promise that was never fulfilled. In other words, despite de jure Ottoman membership in international society, *de facto* inequality based on extraterritoriality continued. In response to the later Chinese challenge to extraterritoriality on normative grounds, Western states established a commission on extraterritoriality to investigate China's legal system. In 1926, the Commission on Extraterritoriality in China, composed of Western diplomats and jurists, rejected the Chinese demands for the abolition of extraterritoriality.[23] Overall, these normative challenges to extraterritoriality were tenuous because international law and sovereignty doctrines had been conceptualized explicitly in order to delegitimize non-Western claims. Western state rulers were able to invoke the norm of protection of their citizens in order to reject the non-Western arguments based on the norm of sovereign equality.

The second strategy was to challenge extraterritoriality on the grounds of legal efficiency and justice. Western states defended extraterritoriality as necessary because of the inefficiency and partiality of the local judicial system. Non-Western rulers replied that extraterritoriality had failed to bring order among foreigners and had led to biased decisions against locals. These complaints about extraterritoriality did not result in the abolition of extraterritoriality but, rather, its reform. Western states reformed extraterritoriality through the establishment of new courts, the clarification of court procedures, the growth of consular codes, and an increase in the number of consular staff. Thus, attempts to bring order and efficiency to extraterritorial rule led to further increases in Western states' authority over their citizens in non-Western states. Labeling this policy "colonizing the colonizers," Eileen Scully argues that the American and British consular court reforms aimed to bring "sojourner nationals under more effective and rigorous metropolitan authority."[24]

The establishment of the U.S. Court for China illustrates how Western countries reformed extraterritoriality to further bring Americans in

[23] Extraterritoriality Commission (1926).

[24] Scully (2001).

China under the rule of American law. Following the Boxer Rebellion (1900), the Chinese government and U.S. entrepreneurs and missionaries complained about the unruly behavior of U.S. citizens in treaty ports.[25] Following a visit by the secretary of state in 1904, Congress passed the U.S. District Court for China Act of 1906.[26] The act introduced a regular inspection mechanism that intensified the federal government's control over Americans and protégés in China. The act also established the U.S. Court for China with "original jurisdiction in most civil and criminal cases where Americans were defendants, and appellate jurisdiction over cases decided first in the U.S. consular courts in China's treaty ports."[27] Overall, the legal efficiency strategy backfired because, rather than abolishing extraterritoriality, Western states strengthened it.[28]

The third – and, ultimately, most successful – strategy of non-Western rulers was to initiate legal institution building in order to fulfill the Western states' requirements for the establishment of a unified formal legal system based on positivist standards. This requirement included the codification of laws, the creation of a statewide court system, and the establishment of a legal hierarchy in the state. Through these requirements Western states effectively engaged non-Western states in shaping the parameters of legal reorganization and changing the characteristics of state-society relations in these states.

EXPLAINING THE ABOLITION OF EXTRATERRITORIALITY

Extraterritoriality emerged quickly and quietly but was eliminated through long, often frustrating, negotiations under public scrutiny and protests. Despite this arduous process and the challenging domestic reforms associated with the abolition of extraterritoriality, starting with Japan in 1899 all non-Western states persuaded Western states to abolish extraterritoriality. What accounts for the abolition of extraterritoriality?

[25] Scully (2001: 90).

[26] Scully (2001: 98). Also see Ruskola (2005, 2008).

[27] Scully (2001: 105–106). Also see Raustiala (2009: chapter 3).

[28] Similarly, the Ottoman complaints resulted in the Hornby Report, which led to the creation of the Supreme Court of Constantinople. Hornby's memoirs detail the process in Hornby (1928).

Domestic Legalization and Extraterritoriality

My approach links the abolition of extraterritoriality to the institutionalization of state law in non-Western states, or, simply, domestic legalization.[29] Domestic legalization includes the codification of rules, the spread of court systems, and the establishment of a legal hierarchy; positive legal scholars deem all three elements to be necessary parts of a legal system that clarifies and enforces legal and property rights. While domestic legalization is critical for the abolition of extraterritoriality, other factors grounded in power and culture are also important in explaining background and enabling conditions in this process.

There are three components of legal institutionalization: the clarification of rules, the spread of the state's court system, and the establishment of a hierarchical system of courts. The clarification of rules is necessary to provide information about legal and property rights. The spread of the state's court system is important to the enforcement of the state's rules. The establishment of a legal hierarchy is required for states to assume responsibility and accountability for the clarification and enforcement of legal and property rights. In other words, domestic legalization *ipso facto* demonstrates the presence of an institutionalized commitment and capacity to clarify and enforce legal and property rights, to reduce transaction costs for transnational commercial relations, and to assure Western rulers about the non-Western rulers' willingness and capability to be accountable for their legal system.[30]

State rulers demand that other state rulers provide information about the legal and property rights within their respective territories. In order to do this effectively, state rulers systemize and standardize the rules. State rulers can rely on court decisions (case law) or legislative codes (civil law) or a combination of codes and cases to systemize and standardize the rules. Through codification, state rulers both replace customary local rules with uniform law and provide information to other rulers. The codification process leads to the preparation of codebooks on different issue areas. The completion of codes on five major areas – civil,

[29] Spruyt (1994) and Thomson (1994, 1995) advance theoretical propositions that link domestic institution formation to explain international politics. The new institutionalism and legalization literatures also explore how clarity, specificity, and enforceability of rules affect the allocation of property rights.

[30] Goldstein et al. (2000) and Abbot and Snidal (2000).

commercial, criminal, criminal procedures, and civil procedures – and the constitution establish "a complete system of legal rules."[31]

"The code" refers to the totality of the five major codes and the constitution. The code, ideally, should be comprehensive and precise and provide clear information about legal and property rights. It should be complete, so that the legal rules cover major social areas (criminal, civil, and commercial) in order to address socio-legal issues of diverse aspects of social life. Furthermore, it should be specific, so that the rules are precise statements rather than broad principles. In other words, the code should be unambiguous in that the rules are consistent and clear. These are ideal typical properties of "the code" rather than empirical and practical. For any legal system, it is impossible to establish complete, specific, unambiguous rules to cover all social interactions in a changing social and political environment. The code thus need to be interpreted by the state officials (judges) in public places (courts), thereby solving empirical and practical problems inherent in any code on behalf of the state.

In addition to the clarification of rules as state law, state rulers are responsible for enforcing state law. Establishment of mechanisms of enforcement is tantamount to enhancing state capacity and power.[32] State rulers do not merely demand that other rulers provide information about legal and property rights; they also demand that these rulers enforce the rules. State courts have been the dominant institution used by state rulers to adjudicate disputes regarding the enforcement of state law. Without courts, individuals would have to select informal means to solve their legal problems. Although other forms of dispute resolution, such as mediation and communal courts, have existed, the state's systemization of legal rules and the creation of state courts created a state monopoly in the area of dispute resolution.

According to legal positivism the state is to have legal monopoly. (Of course, in practice, even in hyper-litigious societies, like the United States, most disputes are solved outside of the legal system.)[33] The state substantiates its claim of legal monopoly through extending its court system in society. State courts, or simply *the* courts, ideally, should be geographically and numerically extensive, independent, occupied by

[31] Shapiro (1981: 126). Also see, on code and codification, Merryman (1969).
[32] Abbot and Snidal (2000: 426–427).
[33] Ellickson (1991).

professionally trained and state-paid judges with no additional state-related administrative duties, and judges should apply the state law uniformly. The geographical and numerical extensiveness of state courts are important for the state's ability to enforce legal and property rights evenly throughout a territory. Independence of the courts refers to the courts' ability to carry out their daily workings separate from interference of other state elements.[34] Because judges adjudicate disputes, they must be trained to interpret state law and must be paid adequately to decrease incentives for corruption. The courts should apply the rules uniformly; the appellate system helps state rulers ensure a high degree of geographical and temporal standardization in the application of law.

The last requirement for the institutionalization of state law is the establishment of a judicial hierarchy. A system of courts of appeal is necessary to make rulers responsible for legal failures and legal changes. First, state rulers are responsible for rectifying legal failures – failures to clarify legal and property rights or failures to enforce them. State rulers bear this responsibility toward other state rulers when the legal failures of the state impact other states or foreigners. Second, state rulers are responsible for legal changes that may affect other states or foreigners. State rulers create a bureaucratic legal hierarchy under the institutional structure of state. The absence of an internal hierarchy in a country may obstruct transnational interactions because it obscures the locus of responsibility for correcting the legal failures.

As Hendrik Spruyt shows, rulers of sovereign states – not the rulers of city leagues or empires, European and non-European alike – took the responsibility to remedy violations of a foreigner's life and property.[35] The state's appellate court structure supervises local courts in order to compel them to apply state laws uniformly. Although, at least as a model, the appellate system already existed in parts of Europe such as in the structure of the Roman Catholic Church as the last surviving element of the Roman Empire, the appellate system reemerged as the dominant tool in Europe for state rulers both to impose state law on local courts and to limit the influence of customary law in early modern Europe.[36]

[34] Shapiro (1981: 20).
[35] Spruyt (1994: 168).
[36] Compare with Shapiro (1981: 39).

In sum, I suggest that legal institutionalization meets an important aspect of Western demands. The institutionalization of state law opens new investment and trade opportunities, reduces transaction costs to regulate the increasing volume of transactions between Western and non-Western states, and allows Western rulers to hold non-Western rulers responsible and accountable for non-Western legal systems. Only after non-Western states have institutionalized state law might Western states give up their claims of extraterritoriality.

However, meeting the demands of a demander and making the demander more willing to agree are not the same thing. Conceding to a demand may bring more demands. Thus, an explanation of the abolition of extraterritoriality must include two additional factors: changing power dynamics and cultural modernization and Westernization of non-Western states.

Power Politics, Legalization, and Extraterritoriality

Legal imperialism is a multifaceted phenomenon. While the domestic legal system is important in explaining changes in legal imperialism, other factors also influenced the great powers' decisions to limit or deny indigenous legal systems. Power is vital to legal imperialism. Focusing on the distribution of power and authority among states, realist theories clarify how powerful states impose domestic authority arrangements on weaker states.[37] Realists would identify three factors in the emergence, maintenance, and ending of extraterritoriality. The first two, power asymmetry and domestic constituencies, are more clearly developed in Stephen Krasner's *Organized Hypocrisy*[38] and the third hypothesis, strategic competition, is developed by neorealist scholars.

Krasner offers the framework of "organized hypocrisy" to explain two seemingly contradictory observations. First, the actions of rulers

[37] For the critiques to the neorealist approach to international relations and the state see Keohane (1986), Cox (1986), Ashley (1984), and Ruggie (1983). Also see the debate between Fischer (1992) and Hall and Kratochwil (1993) on the applicability of state-centric neorealism to medieval Europe for the neorealist conceptualization of the state.

[38] Krasner (1999) distinguishes his approach from traditional and neorealist theories. His emphasis on power asymmetry to explain violations of norms of sovereignty, however, qualifies his approach as a power politics approach. See also Krasner (1989, 1993, 1995, 1999b).

of powerful states often violate sovereignty norms. Second, state rulers always uphold sovereignty norms rhetorically. Krasner argues that organized hypocrisy explains the persistence of sovereignty norms despite their frequent violations. Rulers use diverse and contradictory international norms instrumentally to satisfy their constituencies and remain in power. Following Krasner's approach, one notices that the emergence and maintenance of extraterritoriality required coercion and imposition.[39] In other words, given the non-Western rulers' demands for the abolition of extraterritoriality, Western state rulers could not extract agreements for extraterritoriality if they did not have the necessary coercion. Power asymmetry is thus necessary for the imposition of extraterritoriality.[40] Consequently, the narrowing of power asymmetry between a home and host state could make a home state more likely to concede to the abolition of extraterritoriality.

Krasner argues that because "rulers are calculators" whose purpose is to stay in power,[41] their willingness to use power to impose the wishes of their constituencies on another state will be proportional to the role these constituencies play in helping the ruler stay in power. State rulers determine their interests depending on the interests of their constituencies.[42] State rulers also act to maintain their power; this means that they may pursue a course of action dictated by the domestic logic of appropriateness even if this contradicts the international logic of appropriateness.[43] Krasner, however, does not clarify how constituencies' preferences translate into their rulers' preferences.

Despite the underspecified role of domestic constituencies in Krasner's analysis, the abolition of extraterritoriality offers an easy case for it. In part, this is because nineteenth- and twentieth-century imperialism provided a route of mobility for the professional middle classes of the metropole, especially in Britain and France, and made them proimperialist. As the middle classes in Britain and France are enfranchised in the nineteenth century, these classes became a

[39] Krasner (1999: 12–16). There are four different ways that state rulers can compromise sovereignty norms: conventions, contracts, coercion, and imposition.

[40] Krasner (1999: 37).

[41] Krasner (1999: 41).

[42] Taking state rulers as the main actors in international politics, Krasner distinguishes his approach from the neorealist perspective that views states as rational-unitary actors that he argues in his previous works. Krasner (1978, 1984).

[43] March and Olsen (1999).

powerful proimperialist political force. This was also because the abolition of extraterritoriality is directly related to the interests of two important constituencies in home states: business communities and missionaries. The business community, located in both home and host states, may demand extraterritoriality in order to protect their commercial activities. Missionaries may benefit from extraterritoriality because it may protect their religious activities. One can expect that, given the material and ideological power of business organizations and missionary communities combined with the interest of middle classes, these groups can influence Western state decisions regarding extraterritoriality.

A third power politics factor to consider is the role of geopolitical competition among the great powers.[44] The level of struggle among the great powers in a region may influence rulers' decisions to expand and contract their extraterritorial jurisdiction in that region. If there is a high level of strategic competition, realism expects that great powers will compete to expand their influence over a given state. Because extraterritorial jurisdiction is based on bilateral treaties that allow and legitimize the interventions of powerful states into the domestic authority structures of host states, powerful states will compete to have extraterritorial jurisdiction. In essence, extraterritorial jurisdiction offers a reaping of the benefits of imperialism and expansion of power without undertaking the cost of colonialism.[45] Furthermore, extraterritoriality also informally increases a powerful state's authority over a host state: With the protection of extraterritoriality, the home states' citizens have more incentive to move to the host state for business and missionary activities. In addition to forming part of an expansionist security strategy, extraterritoriality may be part of a balance of power strategy.[46] If states expect that the expansion of extraterritoriality will reduce their security insofar as it threatens other states, provokes an opposing coalition, or endangers the possibility of an alliance with a host state, they may be more likely to give up

[44] For a statement of a contemporary realist (neorealist/structural realist) see Waltz (1979). Also see chapters in Keohane (1986). For a critical, yet sympathetic, review of realist literature, see Donnelly (2000). Snyder (1991) offers a review of realism's account of imperial expansion.

[45] Krasner (2001).

[46] Snyder (1991).

their claims of extraterritorial jurisdiction. A great power may abolish extraterritoriality under high levels of strategic competition to gain a more favorable strategic alliance with a host state.

While realists in general and Krasner in particular stress the importance of power differences in the emergence of hierarchical authority relations in general and legal imperialism in particular, their reduction of power to material capacity and their state centrism prevent them from adequately theorizing the role of legal systems and international legal hierarchies in international politics. This can be seen in Krasner's approach to sovereignty. Krasner isolates four meanings of sovereignty. *Interdependence sovereignty* refers to the ability of public authorities to regulate the flow of goods, ideas, and people across their borders. *Domestic sovereignty* refers to the structure of political authority and the effectiveness of the authorities' control inside the territorial borders of the state. *Westphalian sovereignty* refers to the exclusion of external actors from the authority structures of states. *International legal sovereignty* refers to the international recognition of the legal capacities of political units to act as states, that is, other states recognize the state on the international level. After offering this typology, Krasner argues that we can decouple these aspects of sovereignty from one another. Krasner decouples different aspects of sovereignty to isolate sovereignty-as-authority from sovereignty-as-control. International legal and Westphalian sovereignty are related to authority, domestic sovereignty is related to both authority and control, and interdependence sovereignty is related to control.[47]

Decoupling means more than analytical separation: According to Krasner, change in one aspect of sovereignty does not change another aspect of sovereignty. He argues that "the organization of authority

[47] The distinction between authority (right to rule) and control (capacity to rule) as related to sovereignty was developed by Thomson and Krasner (1989) and Thomson (1995) to reject the liberal interdependence argument that interdependence and globalization reduce state control of transborder activities. Thomson (1995: 216) rejects the conceptualization of sovereignty in terms of state control: "[T]here never was a time when state control over anything, including violence, was assured secure. State control over important external flows has not eroded relative to the state control over internal flows over the past 100 years. In short, it makes no sense to posit that interdependence and/or democracy has reduced state control from a level that was never actually attained. Sovereignty is not about state control but about state authority."

within a state and the level of control by the state are not necessarily related to international legal or Westphalian sovereignty."[48] Removing domestic sovereignty and control sovereignty from his discussion, Krasner's argument reproduces a state-centric approach to international politics in which states, homogenous entities with different capacities, struggle in anarchy. Variation in state capabilities has consequences for the norms of sovereignty, but variation in the other attributes of states, such as authority structures, regime type, and state-society relations does not have any impact on the norms of sovereignty. Such decoupling reinforces the separation of domestic and international authority structures and prevents Krasner from theorizing about how different aspects of domestic sovereignty, such as a state's legal system, may influence international authority structures, such as extraterritorial jurisdiction. My argument repudiates this separation and addresses the tight relationship of domestic legalization and legal imperialism. I explore why and how domestic legal structures in client states pull or push the great powers to extend their legal rule abroad and why and how the great powers intervene to alter the domestic legal system of client states.

The English School, Legalization, and Extraterritoriality

English School scholars have examined the emergence, function, and evolution of the institutions of world politics. (Constructivists have also echoed many of the English School's arguments about the role of cultural and ideational factors in world politics.[49]) Emerging in the 1960s and rising to prominence in the 1970s and 1980s, the English School combines insights from diplomatic history, international law, and historical sociology. Following a diverse and interdisciplinary methodology, these scholars often stress the role of legal ideas and institutions in world politics. Although the English School is theoretically and methodologically diverse,[50] the differentiation of the

[48] Krasner (1999: 12).

[49] For the English School's influence on constructivism, see Dunne (1995), Checkel (1998), Wendt (1999), and Reus-Smit (2002). For the limited influence of the English School in the United States, see Hoffman (1995).

[50] Bull (1996), Singer (1996), and Little (1995). For the development of the English School see Dunne (1998).

international system and international society is one of its core principles.[51] Hedley Bull offers the standard definitions for the international system and international society: States form an international system when "two or more states have sufficient contact between them, and have a sufficient impact on one another's decisions, to cause them to behave – at least in some measure – as parts of whole."[52] States form an international society when "a group of states, conscious of certain common interests and common values, form a society in the sense that they conceive themselves to be bound by a common set of rules in their relations with one another, and share in the working of common institutions."[53] Thus, while all states are part of the international system, only a subset of states composes international society.

States that are part of the international system, but not of international society, can enter international society if they fulfill certain membership requirements. In the case of "Westphalian" international society, the membership criteria established by Western states required non-Western states to engage in Western-style domestic political and social reforms.[54] In addition, states had "to attain an acceptable level of civilization in their activities as members" of international society in order to become members of international society.[55] English School scholars admit that occasionally Western states used the membership requirements instrumentally as a cover for their own aggression. Yet, according to the English School, the membership criteria represented a veritable admissions test that non-Western states *could* and *did* pass. When non-Western states passed the test of admission into international society, Western states abolished extraterritoriality.[56]

[51] For a general introduction to the English School see Bull (1977) and Wight (1991). On the distinction between international system and international society see Wight (1977), Bull (1977), Bull and Watson (1984a), Gong (1984), and Watson (1992). Watson (1987) and Alderson and Hurrell (2000) review Bull's scholarship on international society. Buzan (1993) and Little (1995) discuss international state and international society distinction. For a critical view of the English School's culture-based argument for the expansion of international society see Zhang (1991) and Stivachtis (1998). Using the English School's standards of civilization argument, Donnelly (1998) suggests that international human rights became the contemporary standard of civilization for membership into international society.

[52] Bull (1977: 9).

[53] Bull (1977: 15).

[54] Bull and Watson (1984a: 122–23).

[55] Watson (1992: 273).

[56] Bull and Watson (1984b: 427).

Despite this clear theoretical prediction, the conceptual vagueness of "international society" makes it difficult to derive strong empirical predictions.[57] The international society membership requirements may include state-building practices such as domestic law and order, administrative integrity, the protection of the rights of foreigners, cultural changes such as the internalization of some Western values and ethical standards, and the acceptance of Western economic and commercial practices.[58] Gerrit Gong offers the most detailed conceptualization of the membership criteria required to enter international society. Gong lists five sets of policies that non-Western countries had to accomplish: 1) guarantee basic rights (especially for foreigners) including life, dignity, property, freedom of travel, commerce, and religion; 2) maintain an efficient bureaucracy with a capacity for self-defense of the country; 3) adhere to international law and maintain an efficient legal system with published laws, which guarantee justice for both their own citizens and foreigners; 4) maintain diplomatic relations; and 5) comply with the civilized norms prohibiting practices such as polygamy and slavery.[59]

Gong argues that the standard of "civilization" has an implicit and subjective dimension, making it difficult to measure. Even if a non-Western country accomplishes the necessary reforms in all five areas, the Western countries may continue to perceive it as noncivilized, and thus not a member of international society. Therefore, perhaps it is not membership – but "perception" of membership – in international society that explains the abolition of extraterritoriality. In other words, if home states perceive host countries to be members of international society, then home states will abolish extraterritoriality.

Both the legal institutionalization approach and the English School share a common variable: legal institutions. Yet, there are differences. First, the function of legal institutions differs in the two approaches. The English School emphasizes the role of legal institutions as a prerequisite for non-Western polities to attain legitimacy as civilized states in international society. The role of legal institutionalization

57 Copeland (2003: 427) offers a methodological critique of the English School.
58 Bull and Watson (1984b: 427) and Watson (1992: 273).
59 Gong (1984: 14–15).

in enabling and regularizing transnational interactions is not emphasized. Furthermore, legal institutions are only one of several causal variables the English School uses. Among other variables, the capacity of self-defense, similar to the realist power asymmetry variable, and the abolition of polygamy and slavery are Western cultural standards. Even though legal institutionalization often appears as the most important indicator of the standard of "civilization" in English School studies, the circularity of the argument combined with the ambiguity of conceptual categories like "civilizations" prevents English School scholars from theorizing about the centrality of legal institutions in international politics. English School scholars are unable to provide a robust account of the expansion of international society in the late nineteenth and early twentieth centuries.

NOTES ON THE RESEARCH DESIGN

Nineteenth- and early twentieth-century legal imperialism is mostly related to the British hegemonic power and legal episteme. Because of the centrality of Britain in the history of extraterritoriality, I will define the abolition of extraterritoriality as Britain's decision to accept non-Western jurisdiction over British citizens living in a given state. Britain was a precedent setter whose decisions were often made in collaboration with other Western states and in some cases through joint multilateral treaties. These decisions to abolish extraterritoriality were followed closely, in terms of both timing and content, by other Western states that often subsequently pursued almost identical bilateral treaties with the host state.

This project is a comparative case study based on two research strategies. First, for an initial test of the hypotheses, I use Mill's methods to correlate explanatory variables and the abolition of extraterritoriality. Second, after establishing a correlation between the independent and dependent variables, I trace the process of the abolition of extraterritoriality in each case.

I have three cases (Japan, Turkey, and China) and two observations from each case, for a total of six observations: The Tokyo Conference of 1882 and the 1894–1899 period for Japan; the Paris Conference of 1856 and the Lausanne Conference of 1922–1923 for Turkey; and the Washington Conference of 1921 and the Second World War period for China. One of the observations in each case is a successful effort to abolish extraterritoriality, while the other is a British decision, in collaboration with other Western states, not to abolish extraterritoriality. In each case, I observe how variations on the five factors – power asymmetry, rulers' sensitivity to the extraterritorial groups, strategic competition, perception of host countries' place in international society, and domestic legalization – correlate with the British decisions about extraterritoriality.

Although Mill's methods are useful in finding correlations, they may not detect spurious correlations.[60] This project is susceptible to spurious correlations because I expect that some of the explanatory variables (power asymmetry, institutionalization of a state-based legal system, and perception of civilization) may be correlated with each other. Process tracing offers another set of research tools to eliminate spurious correlations, identify the omitted variables in explanations, and observe interaction effects among different variables.[61] I use intra- and inter-government debates, parliamentary discussions, and reports from the embassies and consuls to assess rulers' motivations. I also use publicly available primary sources such as public declarations, newspaper statements, and memoirs to link and trace the causal variables to abolition decisions.

Four factors drive my case selection: the importance of the host states in world politics, variation on the independent and dependent variables, the ability to conduct within- and across-case comparisons, and the ease with which I could test these cases against alternative theories.[62] First, I selected Japan, Turkey, and China because they are all important actors in world politics. Although extraterritoriality is a forgotten issue in Western countries, it is still common to see references to it in the foreign policy discourses of Japan, Turkey, and China. A study of extraterritoriality contributes both to the foreign policy studies of Japan, Turkey, and China and to scholarship on the state-building processes of these states.

[60] For strengths and weaknesses of Mill's methods see Lieberson (1992, 1994) and Savolainen (1994).

[61] Bennett and George (2004).

[62] For general case selection requirements in comparative case studies, see King, Keohane et al. (1994: 115–149); Van Evera (1997: 49–88); and Geddes (2003: 89–130).

Second, Japan, Turkey, and China provide observations for variation on the five independent variables. I have also opted to examine both successful and failed attempts to abolish extraterritoriality to ensure variation on the dependent variable. Some of these failed attempts came after a major military success and the formation of an alliance (Ottoman Empire, 1856) or only the formation of a military alliance (China, 1921), and some of these failed attempts correlate with significant cultural reforms (Japan, 1882; Ottoman Empire, 1856), which suggest a weakness in the English School's standard of "civilization" hypothesis. Despite my critique of the English School's civilizational approach, my favored explanatory variable, legal institutionalization, is also one of the factors the English School scholars identify in the standard of "civilization," a shared element creating some overlaps between these arguments.

Third, all these non-Western states were "independent" states and not colonies, so the discussion can focus on the diffusion of the Westphalian norm of sovereignty to these non-Western states without the complications and particularities of colonial politics.[63] I exclude formal colonies because of the overdetermination of the outcome. Once a Western country formally colonized a non-Western country where extraterritoriality had previously existed, all approaches will predict the abolition of extraterritoriality. The material strength of the colonizer, as realism predicts, may deter other Western states from continuing to impose extraterritorial rule. Because the colonization of a country may bring that territory into international society, as the English School predicts, Western states may give up their extraterritoriality. Lastly, the colonizer's state-building practices that integrate the legal system into the formal legal hierarchy of the imperial center may lead to the abolition of extraterritoriality, as the legal institutionalization argument claims.[64] Among the noncolonized cases, there are two cases, Iran and Thailand, which I do not discuss extensively. I posit that my legal institutional approach can explain the abolition of extraterritoriality there as well.

[63] I also exclude the informal forms of extraterritoriality that emerged in Latin American states. Benton (2002) argues that imposition of informal extraterritoriality caused legal institutionalization in Latin America.

[64] Liu (1925) provides evidence for the abolition of extraterritoriality in cases of colonization. The evidence he provides suggests that the discussions of the abolition of extraterritoriality in colonial cases focused on the legal system.

I present the case studies chronologically based on the year of abolition of extraterritoriality in order to integrate the transformations in international environment and larger imperial context into my analysis better. The long history of extraterritoriality – from the emergence of British legal imperialism in the 1830s and 1840s to the American legal imperialism in the 1940s – saw some remarkable changes in international environment, such as in the distribution of power, international norms, and political ideas. These changes significantly influenced the debates and negotiations about extraterritoriality. For example, the most intense debates and negotiations in Japan occurred in the 1880s and 1890s when Western states were pursuing imperialist policies, such as the Scramble of Africa. In this period of imperial expansion, the normative claims against imperialism and extraterritoriality were weak, and thus the discussions on extraterritoriality in Japan show hardly any normative argument against imperialism or extraterritoriality. Yet, three decades later, the Turkish elite constantly referred to the norm of sovereign equality at Lausanne in 1923 to challenge the legitimacy of extraterritoriality on normative grounds. Although great powers spurned the Turkish attempts, the normative challenge against extraterritoriality has significantly altered American views about extraterritoriality in China in the 1940s.

Another example of how the international factors influenced extraterritoriality is the change in the distribution of power. The decline of Russian imperialism and the establishment of an antiimperialist Soviet government were important factors for the abolition of extraterritoriality in Turkey and China. For instance, the Soviet Union's unilateral abolition of Russian extraterritoriality in Turkey and its political and military support to the nascent Turkish government bolstered Turkish confidence and resistance against Britain. Britain's inability to dictate the terms at Lausanne and to reimpose extraterritoriality indicates decreasing British power. The British decline was further confirmed in China, where the United States became the leading power on the issue of extraterritoriality in the 1930s and 1940s.

In case studies, I use primary and secondary sources. My primary sources are British and American. My reliance on these sources may create a problem as I argue that my thesis is generalizable to other major home countries' abolition of extraterritoriality. However, I do not expect any systematic bias, because there is no reason to expect that the explanatory variables are sensitive to differences among home states. The only exception to the generalization of British and American abolition of extraterritoriality to the abolition of decisions of other major home states is the Soviet Union's abolition of extraterritoriality. My argument does not adequately explain the Soviet Union's abolition of extraterritoriality in the Ottoman Empire and Turkey following the revolution in 1917. Abolition in this instance occurred as a result of mostly antiimperialist ideological reasons and the new Soviet regime's desire to break its international isolation.

I rely on secondary sources to test some causal variables and to establish the context for my observations.[65] I follow the consensus among historians if one exists. In the absence of consensus, I explain why I chose a particular interpretation over other interpretations. Archival data also allowed me to judge the validity of different historical interpretations.[66]

[65] For how multiple historical interpretations may cause selection bias of secondary sources and suggestions for how to prevent them, see Lustick (1996).

[66] Larson (2001) argues that political scientists should conduct archival research to be able to discriminate between different historical interpretations.

3

Japan's Rapid Rise to Sovereignty

The first Japanese attempt to end extraterritoriality was in the 1870s. The Japanese Iwakura Mission visited the United States and Europe during 1871–1873 and inquired about the possibility of abolishing extraterritoriality in Japan. After a two-year sojourn, the Iwakura Mission returned to Japan in 1873 with much encouragement regarding Japan's reforms and progress toward being considered a modern country, but with no promise from the great powers of abolishing extraterritoriality.[1] Several years later, Japanese overtures directed at home states that had extraterritoriality rights in Japan resulted in the Tokyo Conference of 1882. At this conference, Japan sought to revise the existing treaties to abolish extraterritoriality; despite these efforts, the conference did not result in the abolition of extraterritoriality. Nonetheless, twelve years later, on the eve of the Sino-Japanese War of 1894, Britain and Japan signed the Aoki-Kimberley Treaty to end British extraterritoriality in Japan in 1899. Other home states followed the British lead and signed treaties ending extraterritoriality in Japan. By the end of 1899, extraterritoriality in Japan was over; all foreigners including Western citizens were under Japanese jurisdiction.

Compared to the abolition of extraterritoriality in Turkey and China, the Japanese case is striking because of the short life of extraterritoriality in Japan (Table 2). Extraterritoriality emerged in Japan

[1] On the Iwakura Mission, see Nish (1998).

TABLE 2. *Rise and Decline of Extraterritoriality in Japan*[a]

Home State	Treaties Starting Extraterritoriality	Courts (Mid-1880s)[b]	Treaties Ending Extraterritoriality on July 17, 1899[c]
Britain	August 26, 1858	6	July 16, 1894
United States	March 31, 1854	6	November 22, 1894
Russia	February 7, 1855	5	July 28, 1895
Germany	January 24, 1861	5	April 4, 1896
France	October 9, 1858	4	August 4, 1896
Denmark	January 12, 1867	3	October 19, 1895
Italy	August 25, 1866	3	December 1, 1894
Netherlands	January 30, 1856	3	September 8, 1896
Austria-Hungary	October 18, 1869	2	December 5, 1896
Switzerland	February 6, 1864	2	November 10, 1896
Portugal	August 3, 1860	1	January 26, 1897
Sweden-Norway	November 11, 1868	0[d]	May 1, 1896
Belgium	August 1, 1866	0[e]	June 22, 1896
Hawaii	August 19, 1871	0[f]	April 4, 1894
Spain	November 12, 1868	0[g]	January 2, 1897

[a] See Perez (1999: 188). The table is in order based on the number of consular courts.

[b] All data for the consular court numbers are from Chang (1984).

[c] Except treaties for France and Austria-Hungary, which came into force on August 4, 1899.

[d] Dutch consular (occasionally German and British) courts acted on behalf of Sweden and Norway.

[e] Belgium did not hold any permanent consul in Japan but had honorary consuls in Tokyo, Yokohoma, Osaka, Kobe, and Nagasaki during certain periods in the nineteenth century.

[f] No permanent but one honorary consul.

[g] British consuls acted on the behalf of Spain.

(1856) later than it appeared in the Ottoman Empire (1825) and China (1843). Yet Japan was the first non-Western state to persuade Western states to end extraterritoriality. Japan's success in this endeavor arrived twenty-four years earlier than the abolition of extraterritoriality in Turkey and forty-four years earlier than the abolition of extraterritoriality in China. A second factor that makes the Japanese case different is the relatively low level of Western presence (e.g., few merchants, missionaries) in Japan. The late "opening" of Japan and its effective policy in constraining and controlling Western citizens and trade makes the Japanese case different from the Ottoman Empire and China, where Western penetration and influence were more pervasive. The third factor that distinguishes the Japanese case from others lies with its influence on other cases. The abolition of extraterritoriality in Japan shaped the later debates and negotiations about extraterritoriality in other non-Western states: Western states cited Japanese reforms as examples that the Ottoman Empire and China should emulate; the Ottoman Empire and China accused Western states of double standards for keeping extraterritoriality in their countries while abolishing it in Japan.

Although the influence of increasing Japanese power and Westernization established a favorable context for Western states to end their extraterritorial claims in Japan, a legal-institutional approach best explains the Western states' logic in allowing Japan to extend its legal authority over Western foreigners and commercial interests. Meiji state-building reforms (1868–1912), specifically Japan's legal reorganization to establish a unified legal order compatible with legal positivism, underlie the Western states' agreement to allow Japanese jurisdiction over Westerners. The Western concession of abandoning extraterritoriality in exchange for Japan's legal institutionalization was consistent with Western states' earlier policies toward Japan and other non-Western states. The "opening" of Japan, the imposition of extraterritoriality, and the later demand for legal institutionalization successively served the great powers' aim of expanding opportunities for Western goods and capital in Japanese markets. The Western imperial strategies of keeping extraterritoriality while demanding legal institutionalization were contradictory; Japan, like the Ottoman Empire and China, used its legal institutionalization to negotiate with Western states for the abolition of extraterritoriality. Western states accepted Japanese demands while rejecting Ottoman and Chinese demands because of two factors: Meiji legal institutionalization and Western expectations for ever-larger trade and investment opportunities in Japan.

To elaborate the institutional interpretation, I turn my attention to Japan as compared with other states and to Japan's own internal reforms. Essentially, I examine the foreign policies of Western states, particularly Britain, toward Japan during the Tokyo Conference of 1882 and during the 1894–1899 period. First, I describe the power context among Western powers and between them and Japan to see what, if any, role increasing Japanese power, the Japanese victory over China in 1894, or the British government's need for Japan as an ally against Russia played in ending extraterritoriality in Japan. Second, I link the failure of the early Japanese attempts to abolish extraterritoriality to the early Meiji failures in codification of commercial and civil law. Third, I suggest that the Meiji legal reforms had more weight in Western states' decisions to end extraterritoriality than Japan's Westernization. Fourth, I elaborate how Meiji legal institutionalization led to the abolition of extraterritoriality.

MEIJI STATE BUILDING IN AN INTERNATIONAL CONTEXT

Like all other non-Western state-building projects in the second half of the nineteenth century, Meiji efforts at reorganization and reform were shaped by external pressures, demands, and constraints. Most prominently, the great powers used gunboat diplomacy to demand favorable tariff rates, the removal of trade restrictions, and the imposition of extraterritoriality. The debates and struggles over extraterritoriality were at the center of Western-Japanese interactions. Versions of power-grounded explanations have achieved widespread acceptance for the abolition of extraterritoriality in Japan. Some of these explanations emphasize the increasing Japanese military prowess, and thus its ability to resist Western states. Another version of the power asymmetry claim links the abolition of extraterritoriality to the Japanese defeat of China in 1895 in the Sino-Japanese War. Some historians and political analysts also link the British abolition of extraterritoriality to the British need for an alliance with Japan against Russian encroachment in East Asia.

Material power unquestionably played an important role in nineteenth-century Western-Japanese interactions, such as in the imposition and maintenance of unequal treaties concerning extraterritoriality. Yet important facts question the centrality of power to the ending of extraterritoriality in Japan. Taken together, these facts further illustrate a problem inherent in most theories of international relations: Power is often decoupled from institutions. The material power *versus* institutions dichotomy neglects the role of domestic institutional infrastructure (i.e., legal institutions in a state's power) and conceals the powerful states' motivation in changing a weaker state's domestic institutions and the emergence of extraterritorial and transnational authority relations. Attempts at understanding extraterritoriality are complicated by this lacunae because it occurs at the nexus of power *and* institutions, in particular, power through domestic legalization and power to impose domestic legalization.

Strategic Competition in East Asia

Japan experienced relatively little meddling from great powers, providing it a level of security and autonomy to transform its domestic institutions and develop its economy.[2] For example, unlike in China, Western states did not pursue a policy of spheres of influence over Japan, despite increasing great powers' interest in the region. In the 1890s Great Britain was still the dominant Western military and economic power in East Asia. But France, the United States, and especially Germany and Russia were increasingly challenging British supremacy.[3] Yet surprisingly these struggles did not make extraterritoriality an instrument of geopolitics, and interestingly enough, the abolition of extraterritoriality in Japan occurred with western powers collaborating with each other during a period of increasing great power struggle in East Asia.

Three reasons were behind the renewal of interest in East Asia on the part of the great powers. First, following its defeat in the Crimea (1856), Russia turned eastward to consolidate its authority in Siberia, Central Asia, and East Asia. Unhappy with the conditions

[2] For example, see Moulder (1977).

[3] Great Britain controlled about 65 percent of Chinese trade and about 31 percent of Japanese trade. Langer (1951: 167).

of the Vladivostok Harbor (ice closed it four months of the year), Russia in the 1890s was searching for another harbor in the Pacific from which to base its naval operations.[4] In addition to its attempts to acquire a naval base, Russia started to construct the Trans-Siberian Railway to link its East Asian naval bases to the interior in order to be able to move its military quickly. These policies directly challenged British supremacy in East Asia. Britain took Russia's actions seriously.[5] Before the Sino-Japanese War, when Japan consulted Britain about the possible Japanese annexation of Korea, it was warned and discouraged by Britain that such action could trigger Russian intervention and the Russian seizure of a naval base on the Chinese coast.[6]

The second reason for great power interest in East Asia was Germany's emergence as an imperial power in the 1890s. In the 1880s under Bismark, Germany's competition with Britain in international trade did not lead to an active German colonial policy.[7] Bismark's policy of not competing with Britain over colonial possessions, however, changed with the ascension of Kaiser Wilhelm II. By 1890, Germany had built up an impressive navy to secure its place as a colonial power. Germany was not concerned with the lack of a naval base in East Asia to project its military power until 1898,[8] and the German navy did not attempt to acquire a base in the Far East before the 1880s.[9] However, throughout the 1890s, Germany, like Russia, was searching for a naval base in East Asia. In 1894, Kaiser Wilhelm urged the German chancellor to enter into a secret agreement with Japan to control Formosa after the Sino-Japanese War. The kaiser argued that if the Sino-Japanese War occurred, "we should not permit ourselves to fall short or to be taken by surprise. We also require a base in China, where [our] annual trade is valued at 400 millions."[10] In short, in the 1890s, Germany emerged as a powerful contender in East Asia.

A third factor that contributed to the intensifying strategic competition in East Asia in the last part of the 1880s was the Franco-

[4] Langer (1951: 168).
[5] Langer (1951: 169) and Kennedy (1986).
[6] Langer (1951: 173).
[7] Ganz (1977) and Kennedy (1977).
[8] Marder (1940: 239).
[9] Ganz (1977: 116).
[10] Langer (1951: 177).

Russian naval alliance against the British supremacy of the seas. In March 1889, worried about the Franco-Russian alliance, the British government enacted a Naval Defense Act for a new naval armament program to match the combined French and Russian fleets.[11] A British naval intelligence report of 1895 indicated an equality of naval forces in East Asia between the French-Russian alliance and Britain. Britain had twenty-six battleships and six torpedo boats compared to seventeen battleships and thirteen torpedo boats belonging to Russia and twelve battleships belonging to France. During the same year, the Japanese navy was composed of forty-seven battleships and forty-six torpedo boats.[12]

Japan's victory over China in 1895 in the Sino-Japanese War significantly altered the strategic calculus in East Asia. Gradually, Britain started to see Japan as a future ally against Russia in East Asia. This is evident in Britain's refusal to join the Triple Intervention to make Japan return the Liaodong Peninsula to China.[13] Although the strategic convergence of Japan and Britain was becoming visible,[14] Britain did not abolish extraterritoriality in exchange for an alliance with Japan against Russia. As I show later, a study of British policy does not reveal any evidence that the possibility of an alliance with Japan entered into British discussions on extraterritoriality negotiations. Timing is also a problem; Britain and Japan eventually established an alliance, but this occurred eight years after Britain's decision to abolish extraterritoriality. If alliance hopes had motivated British policy, one would expect to see Britain attempt to maximize its strategic gains and push for a military alliance immediately following a conciliatory policy on extraterritoriality. Britain, however, did not demand any strategic concessions from Japan in return for the abolition of extraterritoriality. Furthermore, although the Triple Intervention provided Britain with an opportunity to cement a strategic alliance with Japan and Japan waited for British support, Britain simply abstained from any participation whatsoever in the conflict. Most importantly,

[11] Kennedy (1986: 179).

[12] Cited in Marder (1940: 238).

[13] Langer (1951: 185).

[14] Britain was also concerned that a Japanese victory and resulting new Japanese armament programs might challenge British supremacy over China. Marder (1940: 239–240).

even if one assumes that strategic calculations can explain British policy, they cannot explain the decisions of other great powers to abolish extraterritoriality.

Given the intensity of the great power struggle in East Asia during the 1890s (particularly compared to the relatively calm 1880s when earlier Japanese attempts to end extraterritoriality had occurred), why did the great powers give up an important means of maintaining and advancing their influence in Japan: extraterritoriality? This is an especially intriguing question because not only were great powers conceding to Japan, but they were also collaborating with each other on extraterritoriality rather than competing. They were intensely consulting each other while engaging in bilateral negotiations with Japan. Interestingly enough, all the bilateral negotiations ended up specifying the same date (July 17, 1899) for the abolition of extraterritoriality. One conclusion to draw from this is that the great powers' policies regarding extraterritoriality transcended the geopolitical struggle among them. Rivals collaborated with one another against Japan. The debates about extraterritoriality should thus be understood within a Western versus non-Western context rather than a state-centric and strategic one.

"Rich Nation and Strong Army"

Although extraterritoriality was not imposed on Japan, like it was imposed on China following a military defeat in the Opium War, and although Japan negotiated extraterritoriality agreements with the imperial powers,[15] the negotiations were shaped by the power imbalances that existed between Japan and the great powers. In this context, the arrival of Commodore Perry in 1853 demonstrated Japanese vulnerability to Western powers, as the Japanese central government did not have a strong army or navy with which to repel Commodore Perry's black ships.[16] In addition to growing external threats, the internal struggle among various *daimyo,* military lords, as well as struggles between the *daimyo* and the shogun, the lord of the dominant Tokugawa domain, increased following Commodore Perry's arrival.

[15] Austin (2004).
[16] Westney (1986).

The heightened external threats and the internal struggles raised the military spending of both the *daimyo* and the Tokugawa Shogunate.[17] When the internal struggle culminated in the victory of Satsuma and Choshu *daimyos* over the Tokugawa Shogunate and the restoration of imperial rule under the Meiji Emperor (1868–1912), "rich nation and strong army" became the promise of the new government.

This promise also supports a realist interpretation commonly offered for the ending of extraterritoriality: A rich Japan with a strong army prevented home states from imposing extraterritoriality.[18] Yet a number of facts about the economic and military disparity between Japan and the great powers refute a simple power explanation. The aggregate statistical data suggest that the variation in Japan's power does not correlate with the abolition of extraterritoriality. Moreover, the data show that Japan's rise to great power status follows – rather than precedes – the abolition of extraterritoriality.[19]

A comparison of Japan with the great powers (these states had extraterritoriality in Japan) reveals a decreasing, albeit significant, power asymmetry between Japan and those states at the time of the abolition of extraterritoriality. These indicators are broadly consistent with other studies that also offer quantitative indicators comparing Japanese and major extraterritorial (home) states' economic and military capabilities. For example, according to John Mearsheimer's calculations (my measurement follows his operationalization and some of the same databases), the Japanese share of world wealth was less than 1 percent until 1920. Additionally, according to Paul Kennedy's numbers based on Paul Bairoch's study, Japan's relative shares of world manufacturing output was a minuscule 2.6 percent in 1860 but decreased to 2.4 percent by 1900. Japanese iron and steel production and its energy consumption remained very small in the last two decades of the nineteenth century.[20]

[17] Observing that the Meiji rulers spent much more money on a central army than on a navy, Westney (1986: 171) argues that this spending pattern was fueled by internal struggles rather than external threat perception.

[18] Foster (1903: 361) and Soyeshima (1910: 107).

[19] For Meiji-era economic development, see Yoshihara (1994), Nish (1968), and Iriye (1986: 758).

[20] For military indicators, see Kennedy (1987: 203, tables 19–20). For economic indicators, see Kennedy (1987: 149, table 7; 200, tables 14–15; 201, tables 16–17).

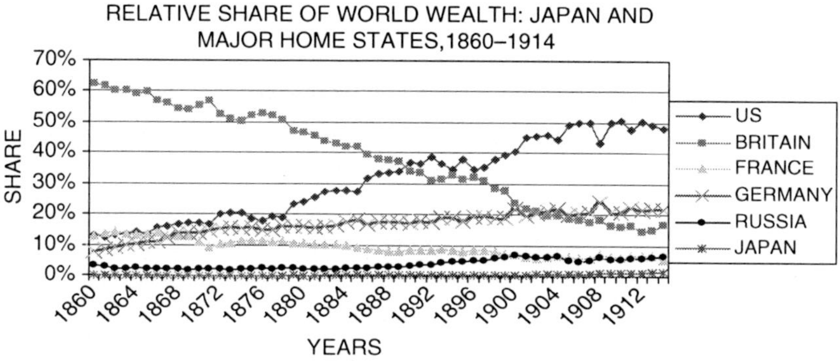

FIGURE 1. Japan's Economic Capacity Compared to Major Home States. For this figure, I am following Mearsheimer (2001: 71) for the conceptualization, operationalization, and measurement. More specifically, like Mearsheimer, I use data from Singer and Small, *National Material Capabilities*. The economic capacity variable is a composite indicator that assigns equal weight to iron/steel production and energy consumption. After determining the total amount of iron/steel that all the major home states and Japan produced for a given year, I calculated the percentage of that total accounted for by each state. I performed a similar calculation for energy consumption and then I averaged together each state's percentages for iron/steel and energy.

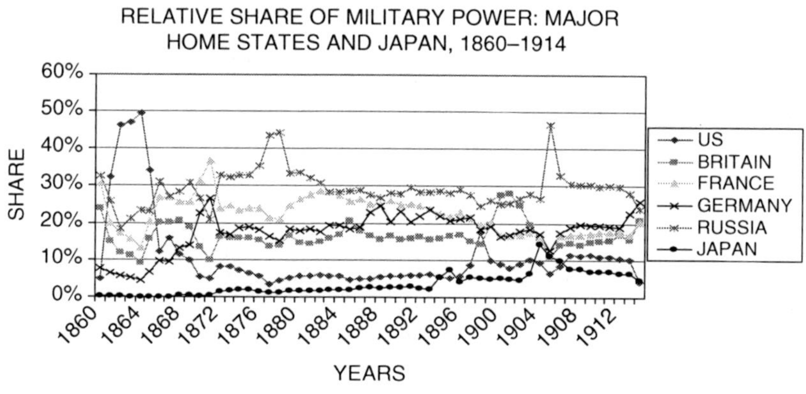

FIGURE 2. Japan's Military Capacity Compared to Major Home States. For this measurement, I use an approach similar to Mearsheimer (2001). Unlike Mearsheimer, I use data provided by Singer and Small, *National Material Capabilities*. The military capacity variable is a composite indicator that assigns equal weight to military personnel and military expenditures. After determining the total number of military personnel of all major home states and Japan for a given year, I calculated the percentage of that total accounted for by each state. I performed a similar calculation for military expenditures. Then I averaged together each state's percentages for military personnel and military expenditures.

Admittedly, an approach based on resources is a weak indicator of power asymmetry and does not provide strong evidence to refute power explanations without assessing the anticipated cost of using these resources versus the benefit. These data, however, suggest that the role of Japan's increasing power on the British government's decision to concede to the abolition of extraterritoriality should not be exaggerated. In January 1894, when Japan asked the British government for the abolition of extraterritoriality (amidst rumors of a possible Japanese unilateral attempt at abolition), a foreign office memorandum by Assistant Undersecretary for Asia Francis Bertie assessed Japan's strength:

> It is possible that no Government may be strong enough to denounce the Treaties with foreign Powers. On the other hand, the exigencies of warfare may drive whatever Government may be in power into denunciation, leaving us with no trade advantages, and without extra-territorial jurisdiction. In such case, we are not locally in a position to enforce our existing treaty rights. The Japanese have a navy nearly as strong as that of China. Their coast defenses are nearly finished, and will be formidable, and their army consist of 70,000 well-armed and well-drilled troops.[21]

The analysis indicates a perception of increasing Japanese power as not enough of a reason to end extraterritoriality but a significant enough factor to inflict a heavy cost on Britain to sustain extraterritoriality without Japan's cooperation. Japan's victory over China also shaped home countries' perceptions of Japan as a powerful state. The Sino-Japanese War changed the balance of power in East Asia since Japan replaced China as the dominant power.[22] According to some military historians, Japan's professional and efficient use of modern weapons – which resulted in quick initial victories over China – produced the Western perception of Japan as a great power as early as September 1894.[23] Offering a power-based argument, Count Taneomi Soyeshima argues that Japan's victory over China "convinced the rest of the Treaty Powers that the time had at last arrived for Treaty Revision."[24] Similarly, John W. Foster links abolition of extraterritoriality to Japanese military

[21] FO 881/6582 (1894: 2).
[22] Soyeshima (1910: 107) and Paine (2003).
[23] Paine (2003: 4).
[24] Soyeshima (1910: 107).

efficiency in the Sino-Japanese War of 1894.[25] However, there are two problems with this interpretation. One is timing: Britain, the leading extraterritorial power, started the extraterritoriality negotiations prior to the war and the treaty for the abolition of extraterritoriality was signed (August 25, 1894) shortly after the war started (August 1, 1894) and well before Japan's victory (April 17, 1895).

The other problem with a focus on Japan's military strength as an explanation for the abolition of extraterritoriality is more substantial: Although Japan defeated China, it could not resist the pressures of the extraterritorial powers of Russia, Germany, and France (Triple Intervention) and returned Liaodong Peninsula to China. The Treaty of Shimonoseki, which was signed on April 17, 1895, to end the Sino-Japanese War, ceded the Liaodong Peninsula to Japan. Six days later, Russia, France, and Germany "requested" that Japan return the strategically located Liaodong Peninsula to China. On May 4th, the Meiji government agreed to return the peninsula to China. Although historians disagree on whether Russia or Germany was behind the Triple Intervention,[26] they agree on Japan's reaction to the intervention. Despite perceiving the intervention as humiliating and unjust, Japan realized it was not powerful enough to ignore the wishes of Western states.[27] Japanese diplomats were certain of a military intervention on the part of Russia, Germany, and France if Japan did not agree to return the peninsula.[28] The Japanese leaders also believed that an already exhausted Japan could not "have resisted the demands of the powers by force."[29] The Russian navy alone or the combined navies of the three states would have defeated the Japanese navy.[30]

Paradoxically, a short time after Russia, Germany, and France coerced Japan into returning the Liaodong Peninsula to China, these major home states signed treaties with Japan (Russia on July 28, 1895; Germany on April 4, 1896; and France on August 4, 1896) to end

[25] Foster (1903: 361).

[26] For historical accounts of the war, see Langer (1951), Inkle (1967), Kajima (1967: 182), and Paine (2003: 288).

[27] Yamagata (1910), Langer (1951), Inkle (1967), Nish (1968), Yuichi (2000), and Paine (2003).

[28] Paine (2003).

[29] Nish (1968: 109).

[30] Paine (2003: 289).

extraterritoriality on July 17, 1899. If the power asymmetry between Japan and major home countries did not prevent the latter from coercing Japan into returning the Liaodong Peninsula to China, it would not have prevented them from continuing to impose extraterritoriality on Japan.

In sum, measured as a relative share of great power economic and military capacity, during the 1890s when extraterritoriality was abolished, Japan was not powerful enough to justify Western states' agreement to end extraterritoriality to solely Japanese power. In fact, aware of its weakness Japan never attempted to abolish extraterritoriality unilaterally but opted for negotiations to convince Western powers. Furthermore, Britain's decision to abolish extraterritoriality before the Sino-Japanese War of 1894 and subsequent coercion by Russia, Germany, and France to make Japan return the Liaodong Peninsula to China show that Japan's victory over China cannot explain the Western states' decision to abolish extraterritoriality. Taken together, these facts suggest that extraterritoriality cannot be reduced to a matter of power politics. Instead of being explained by it, the abolition of extraterritoriality seems to accompany a change in Japan's power. In part, this correlation is due to Japan's mobilization for the Sino-Japanese War; mobilization boosted the power indicators (size of military personnel and budget). But more importantly, one can also reverse the direction of causality: Japanese legal reforms facilitated the growth of its economic and military power. Admittedly, the relationship between Japanese economic and prosperity, the rise of its military power, and its ability to achieve legal institutionalization is a complex and mutually influencing process. However, as I argue later, the Japanese legal institutionalization preceded and fostered the growth of Japanese economic and military power. Moreover, independent of its contribution to the Japanese economic and military power, the legal institutionalization also became a major factor in the British agreement to end its extraterritoriality in Japan.

EARLY MEIJI REFORMS AND EXTRATERRITORIALITY

Following the Iwakura Mission's futile attempt to end extraterritoriality, Japan continued to seek to abolish extraterritoriality. These attempts intensified in the 1880s. Rejecting Japanese demands for the abolition of extraterritoriality in July 1881, the British foreign minister, Earl Granville, suggested to Mori Arinori, the Japanese ambassador in London, that a multilateral conference between Japan and Western states should be held to revise the existing treaties, including the extraterritoriality provision.[31] In every extraterritoriality negotiation, the British government aimed to expand its merchants' access to Japanese markets – by easing Japanese restrictions over Western travel, life, and trade outside of treaty ports – and further clarify legal and property rights in Japan all with minimum concessions on extraterritoriality. The Tokyo Conference was no different. The conference convened on January 25, 1882, with the participation of ten Western states.[32] At the conference, the Japanese government offered two concessions in return for the abolition of extraterritoriality: to hire foreign judges in Japanese tribunals for cases involving foreigners and to allow foreigners to reside in the Japanese interior (as opposed to solely in treaty ports). After sixteen sessions, the conference ended on July 27, 1882, without abolishing extraterritoriality.[33]

Different explanations have been offered for Japan's failure to achieve the abolition of extraterritoriality at the 1882 conference. Alexander von Siebold, a German legal adviser to the Japanese government in the 1880s, concluded that the British government was following the interests of the British community in the treaty ports; these British citizens did not want to be subject to Japanese jurisdiction.[34] In addition, offering an imperialist argument, Siebold suggests that the British government was afraid that the concession of judicial autonomy to Japan would result in a dangerous precedent with respect to the British positions in China and India.[35] Offering a legal institution

[31] See Jones (1931: 98) and Kamikawa (1958: 141).

[32] Britain, France, Germany, Russia, the United States, Austria-Hungary, Italy, Holland, Spain, and Belgium.

[33] See Jones (1931: 99–100) and Kamikawa (1958: 142). There was a second conference in 1886 to discuss the abolition of extraterritoriality. Representatives of Britain, the United States, France, Russia, Germany, Austria-Hungary, Italy, Belgium, Holland (also representing Sweden-Norway and Denmark), Spain, Portugal, and Switzerland participated in the conference at which Foreign Minister Inoue was chairman. The 1886 conference also failed to abolish extraterritoriality.

[34] Siebold (1901: 79).

[35] Siebold (1901: 81). Also see Lane-Poole and Dickins (1894: 270–271) and Perez (1999: 71–72).

explanation, Kamikawa Hikomatsu links the Western, particularly British and French, rejection of the abolition of extraterritoriality to their concern that "fair and just trials could not be expected" from the existing Japanese judicial system.[36] Similarly, F. C. Jones links the failure to abolish extraterritoriality to British skepticism about the completeness and efficiency of Japanese legal reforms.[37] Jones also offers a culture-based argument suggesting that Sir Harry Parkes, the British minister to Japan, was not enthusiastic about "subjecting the English-speaking foreigners in Japan who formed a great majority, to laws which were mainly French and German in origin."[38]

The Japanese legal system is central to most of these interpretations even though each emphasizes different aspects of the legal system. In a similar vein, I suggest that the failure of the early Meiji legal reforms to codify commercial and civil law and Japan's inability to establish a legal hierarchy can explain the failure of early Japanese attempts to abolish extraterritoriality. While the Meiji state-building reforms brought some level of unification and centralization, codification was not one of the priorities of early Meiji reforms. The early discussions about extraterritoriality centered on whether Japan's legal system could protect the present Western trade and investment and create new opportunities in Japan for Western merchants by means of clarification and enforcement of legal and property rights. From a legal imperialist perspective, only such an institutionalized system would supplant extraterritoriality and justify its abolition.

Meiji Legal Reorganization (1868–1912)

Meiji state-building success is distinctive among Asian states. In terms of its scope and transformative influence on politics and society, the Meiji reforms were comparable to Atatürk's reforms in Turkey, Reza Shah's reforms in Iran in the 1920s, and the Guomindang's reforms in China in the 1930s. What makes the Meiji reforms distinctive is their timing and speed. While Meiji state-building reforms happened quickly in the late nineteenth century, the other comparable state-

36 Kamikawa (1958: 142).
37 Jones (1931: 100).
38 Jones (1931: 100).

building reforms in non-Western states extended well into to the twentieth century.

Meiji leaders' state-building projects and legal reorganization constituted a fundamental part of their efforts to create a unified administrative structure in Japan. Prior to Meiji rule, Tokugawa Japan (1615–1868) was composed of semiautonomous domains under the authority of *daimyo* (feudal/regional lords). Even though *daimyo* accepted the political supremacy of the Tokugawa Shogunate, about 250 *daimyo* governed their domains autonomously. The Meiji restoration aimed to eliminate the feudal, semiindependent domains through the creation of a unified administrative structure. While the state-building projects of their contemporaries in the Ottoman Empire, China, and Iran were progressing slowly under external pressures and internal challenges, Meiji leaders advanced the most comprehensive and large-scale state-building project in Asia: The creation of a modern administrative structure was all the more startling because Japan in 1868 possessed a political and administrative system that had more in common with feudalism than with late-nineteenth-century Western states.[39]

A new Japan emerged in the period between 1868 and 1900. Even though they disagree on its sources, scholars on Japan agree about the success of the Meiji rulers in establishing a unified state structure.[40] In 1871, the Meiji government replaced the centuries-old domain system with prefectures, organizing roughly 250 *daimyo* into seventy-five prefectures. Later, these seventy-five prefectures were reorganized into forty-six prefectures.[41] Further reforms from 1871 to 1878 integrated prefectures into a unified and centralized administrative system

[39] Silberman (1993: 159). W. G. Beasley (1989) states that foreign diplomats in Japan, particularly Sir Harry Parkes, the British prime minister, urged Meiji leaders to replace the feudal domain system with a unified administrative structure. Parkes argued that administrative unification would prevent unruly samurais from attacking foreigners and would help Japanese economic development.

[40] For a historical account of Japanese state building, see Beasley (1989). Silberman (1993) puts Japanese state building in comparative study with Western cases. Ward, Rustow, et al. (1964) and Ward, Burks, et al. (1968) compare Meiji rulers' state-building reforms with Turkish reforms. For the influence of Western institutional models on Japanese state building, see Westney (1986, 1987). Ramseyer and Rosenbluth (1995) offer a political economy approach to Meiji state building.

[41] Jansen (1989: 23) and Silberman (1993: 178).

from the emperor down to the smallest village.[42] These administrative reforms included a centralized and unified tax system, conscription, public education, a police system,[43] and a legal system to replace the feudal structure.[44] Changing from domains to prefectures transformed Japan's administrative organization, as Meiji leaders initiated large-scale projects that aimed to establish a bureaucratic structure to oversee the prefectures. This bureaucracy "possessed all of the characteristics of Weber's legal-rational organizational structure,"[45] and it remained largely unchanged until 1945.[46] The legal system included the reorganization of the court structure under the state's legal hierarchy, the codification of laws,[47] and the establishment of a national court system.[48]

Yet the early Meiji state-building reforms failed to effectively codify Japanese law. This failure was partially due to the legacy of Tokugawa Shogunate the Meiji government inherited. Five qualities of the Tokugawa Shogunate's legal system were incompatible with legal institutionalization required by a legal positivist framework: the prevalence of feudal jurisdiction, the prevalence of customary law, the existence of few written rules, the absence of public accessible written codes, and the lack of a court system as a body distinct from other administrative structures of government. To elaborate the first factor, the Japanese judicial system was feudally based: The judicial authority was dispersed among *daimyo*, the imperial court, and the Tokugawa Shogunate.[49] This limited the judicial authority of the Tokugawa Shogunate in both civil and criminal law.[50] Second, the Tokugawa legal system did not provide laws for all aspects of social life. Except for taxes and basic security, village rules (*muragime*) and customs governed the legal and property rights of individuals. Third,

[42] Jansen (1989: 25) and Silberman (1993: 179).
[43] Jansen (1989: 26–32).
[44] Beasley (1989: 634).
[45] Silberman (1993: 221).
[46] Jansen (1989: 31).
[47] Beasley (1989: 642).
[48] See Westney (1987: 42). Westney (1987: 18) also argues that the Meiji rulers' desire to abolish extraterritoriality drove their policies to establish an extensive police system.
[49] Shogunate law was also followed "on the main highways, and certain key cities." It was also sanctioned countrywide on issues such as regulations on foreign relations, Christianity, and currency. Henderson (1968: 399).
[50] Henderson (1968: 397–399).

because of the prevalence of customary law, there were few written rules in the field of civil law.[51] Fourth, the common people did not have access to the written law; only the government officials who administered the law were privy to the laws.[52] Finally, during the Tokugawa period, there were no courts separate from the administrative offices, because courts were understood to be "administrative offices with concurrent power to settle disputes."[53] Even though "law" existed in Japan during the Tokugawa period, these five factors prevented the Japanese judicial system until the Meiji legal reforms from clarifying and enforcing legal and property rights in a manner consistent with the standard of positive law. Meiji legal reforms sought to transform this system.

Meiji government replaced Tokugawa's decentralized, uncodified, customary legal system with a state-based legal system in two steps.[54] In the first stage (1868–1882) Meiji leaders focused on the creation of a central judicial system and the codification of criminal law. From 1882 forward, Meiji leaders directed their attention to the systemization of their prior reforms through a constitution and the codification of an extensive body of law for the entire private law field. In essence, Meiji leaders aimed to wholly replace the regionally diverse customary law; this was an arduous task and customary law continued to operate in some places as late as 1899.[55] Thus, prior to 1882 the Meiji leaders engaged in some codification, but significant codification of laws in Japan occurred only in the second phase of the Meiji legal reforms (1882–1899).[56]

[51] Henderson (1968: 400) argues: "Although the feudal regulatory law was authoritarian, it was not effectively totalitarian, as it did not attempt to penetrate society and displace customary law in the affairs of people."

[52] Hoare (1994: 140).

[53] Henderson (1968: 401).

[54] According to Henderson (1968: 415), the Meiji rulers' state-building project followed the German Rechtsstaat ("state of law") principle. A "state of law" was characterized by the existence of a central authority and a network of general rules guiding the actions of subjects and officials, not lawmakers. Through "state of law," Meiji leaders tried to establish "an orderly system of standards which are made known in advance to the subjects, and which are applied equally by courts or officials to all who come within their purview, however illiberal or discriminating they may be."

[55] Henderson (1968: 416–417) and Ryosuke (1958: 13).

[56] Ryosuke (1958: 14).

While early Meiji reforms led to only modest advancements in codification, court reforms during this period transformed the Japanese court system. During the early Meiji years, state courts and centrally appointed judges replaced the earlier domain courts and judges appointed by the *daimyo*. The Meiji reforms focused on the creation of a separate judiciary without administrative duties. In 1871, the Meiji government established the Tokyo Court of Justice, the first regular court of justice. Public trials were authorized in 1875. After the creation of a separate and transparent judiciary, the Meiji leaders then focused on preventing the interference of judicial superiors or the executive branch in specific trials by prohibiting local governors from acting simultaneously as judges.[57] Despite the work that had been done to create and insulate courts, the newly established courts applied customary law in civil and commercial issues because only criminal law had been codified by 1882. The absence of civil and commercial codes meant that state law had not been sufficiently institutionalized at the time of the Tokyo Conference of 1882. The debates at the Tokyo Conference of 1882 reveal the important role that the lack of commercial and civil codes played in Western (particularly British) decisions to keep extraterritoriality.

Negotiating Extraterritoriality

Against Japanese demands, Britain and Western states responded as a positive development with a tripartite strategy of 1) recognizing Japanese legal reforms, 2) pointing to the shortcomings of these reforms, and 3) demanding ever more legal reforms as a precondition to end extraterritoriality. Western legal standards and demands became more exacting and specific as the Japanese legal reorganization continued.

In July 1881, British Foreign Minister Earl Granville replied to Japan's ambassador in London, Mori Arinori, that the British government could not abolish extraterritoriality "without previous careful examination of the laws of Japan and the constitution and legal procedure of the Japanese Courts." Such an examination was impossible because British government officials "have no means of judging how

[57] Henderson (1968: 423–424).

far the laws which are believed to be under revision and the practice of the Courts, which do not have to be regulated by any positive rules of procedure, have been brought into conformity with the principles received by Western nations."[58] Because of the lack of information about Japan's legal reforms, the British government could not accept the abolition of extraterritoriality. The British government initiated the Tokyo Conference between Japan and Western states possessing extraterritorial privilegesto explore whether the Japanese reforms justified revision of the unequal extraterritorial treaties.[59]

At the conference, the Japanese government proposed that "within five years from the date of the ratification of the proposed new treaties, home states would abolish extraterritoriality," except in certain capital offenses and in matters affecting the personal status of foreigners (e.g., marriage). During the five-year transition period, the Japanese courts, composed in part of foreign judges, would deal with criminal and civil cases involving foreigners. Inoue Kaoru, the Japanese minister of foreign affairs, conceded that if home states were to accept the abolition of extraterritoriality, Japan would have to agree to the expansion rights of residence for foreigners, including the right to reside in the interior, rather than in treaty ports.[60]

Harry Parkes, the British ambassador in Tokyo, raised four objections to the abolition of British extraterritorial rights in Japan. First, there had not been sufficient time to observe the effectiveness of the

[58] From Granville to Jushie Morie, October 12, 1881, FO 881/4763 (1881–1882: 8). Also see Lane-Poole and Dickins (1894: 309–311). Following the letter, Granville contacted other home states (Netherlands, Germany, France, Swiss Confederation, Austria-Hungarian Empire, Portugal) to act together against the Japanese proposal. He also sent letters to chambers of commerce (Incorporated Chamber of Commerce of Liverpool, Birmingham Chamber of Commerce, Yorkshire Chamber of Commerce, and Bradford Chamber of Commerce) to learn their opinion about extraterritoriality. See FO 881/4763 (1881–1882: 5–18) for these exchanges. Granville also contacted the Tokyo Embassy to solicit information about Japanese codes, particularly the Criminal and Criminal Procedures Codes and the Japanese court system. See FO 881/4763 (1881–1882: 18).

[59] Lane-Poole and Dickins (1894: 311). The conference opened in Tokyo on January 25, 1882. The agenda of the conference was broad, including consular privileges, consular jurisdiction, land tenure of foreigners, tariff and commercial questions, and harbor dues. The discussions of the meetings are found in *Protocol Related to the Revision of Treaties* (1882–1896).

[60] FO 881/4763 (1881–1882: 144–158). In his speech, Inoue also gives a detailed distribution of courts in Japan. Inoue's figures are the same as Figure 5. For the American reaction, see FO 881/4763 (1881–1882: 156).

Criminal Code of 1880, which was in force in January 1882. Second, Japan did not have a civil or commercial code. Third, Japanese judges did not have training in Western legal systems and concepts, training that Parkes saw as necessary for the application of the laws adopted from Western legal systems. Fourth, a five-year period was not sufficient time to replace the judges of the old system with new judges to apply the new codes.[61] After the discussions, British and French representatives indicated that they would veto the abolition of extraterritoriality. The conference ended on July, 27, 1882, without the abolition of extraterritoriality.[62]

The discussions at the Tokyo Conference indicate that the abolition of extraterritoriality was tied to questions about the efficacy of the Japanese legal system. Of particular concern were the absence of a commercial and civil code and the application of the criminal codes. While Japanese representatives argued that the Japanese legal system was capable of safeguarding foreigners' legal and property rights, the British representative argued that Britain would not accept the abolition of extraterritoriality because of the lack of codification and qualified judges in Japan.

Could Parkes have used the legal institutions argument to conceal other British motives? Three sets of evidence suggest that Parkes' demands for Japanese legal reorganization were not a cover for strategic calculations, but rather truly reflected his and the British government's genuine concern about the lack of domestic legalization in Japan. First, Parkes continued to establish a direct connection between legal institutionalization in Japan and the abolition of extraterritoriality. When the Tokyo Conference ended, Parkes exchanged opinions with the Japanese delegation. Accepting extraterritoriality only as a temporary system, Parkes told Japanese Foreign Minister Inoue that Britain would accept the abolition of extraterritoriality when "Japan opens the interior to foreigners, and perfects her legal system by promulgating a criminal code, a code of criminal procedures, a civil code, a commercial code, and a code of civil procedure all of which Britain approves."[63] Second, bibliographers Stanley

[61] FO 881/4938 (1883: 166–170).
[62] FO 881/4763 (1881–1882: 238–251).
[63] Jones (1931: 95) and Hikomatsu (1959: 142).

Lane-Pole and Victor Dickins, in their biography of Parkes (based on Parkes' diaries), conclude that Parkes' insistence on keeping extraterritoriality during the Tokyo Conference reflected Parkes' perception of the lack of Japanese legal institutionalization.[64] Third, the British Foreign Office shared Parkes' perceptions. Following the conference, the British Foreign Office published a memorandum agreeing with Parkes' concerns about the Japanese legal system:

> With regard to the proposal laid before the Conference by the president for the establishment of Courts with foreign Judges, having jurisdiction over foreigners, and the eventual abolition of consular jurisdiction, Her Majesty's Government, while they are willing and anxious to give due weight to the views and wishes of the Japanese Government on this question, are unable to express an opinion on the present proposal until the new laws and rules of procedure for the proposed courts are completed and translated.[65]

In sum, the British Foreign Office had rejected the early Japanese attempts to abolish extraterritoriality because of uncertainties related to the functioning of the Japanese legal system. This rejection led to the Tokyo Conference (1882). During the conference, British and French representatives linked their rejection of the abolition of extraterritoriality to the lack of commercial and civil codes in Japan and the absence of qualified judges to apply the laws. The discussions concerning extraterritoriality during the Tokyo Conference indicated that the Meiji rulers' failure to institutionalize state law was the source of Western countries' decision to keep extraterritoriality.

MEIJI MODERNIZATION AND INTERNATIONAL SOCIETY

In one of the steps of their visits, in England on August 21, 1872, Iwakura Mission attended a dinner, hosted by Lord Granville, the foreign secretary. Otto Steenbock from the Swedish Embassy in London, who also attended the dinner, was impressed with the Japanese dignitaries whom he described as "most distinguished personalities who all wore European clothes and in general seemed to have, for Easterners, an unusually high level of culture."[66] Like the members of Iwakura

[64] Lane-Poole and Dickins (1894: 311).
[65] FO 881/4778 (1883).
[66] Cited in Nish (1998: 135)

Mission who believed in the importance of the trappings of westernization in international politics, even on convincing Western states to review extraterritoriality, some of the members of the English School put the westernization of Asian states at the center of these Asian states' relations with the Western powers throughout the nineteenth century.

For these scholars, Japan and the Ottoman Empire offer diametrically opposed paradigmatic cases for nineteenth-century international society. These scholars believe that Japan's nineteenth-century history illustrates a successful cultural transformation, which triggered the expansion of international society; in contrast, as I describe in the next chapter, the Ottoman Empire's interactions with Europe show how cultural differences prevented the Ottoman Empire from becoming a part of European international society. In this cultural interpretation, Japan distinctly demonstrates, and establishes a precedent for, how a non-European state's drastic westernization can allow it to fulfill the standard of "civilization"; that is, Japan became the first non-Western country to gain full recognition as a "civilized" state. In the nineteenth century, Japan succeeded in modernizing and westernizing while other non-Western states failed. Variations of this narrative are common in political science and history. Referring to the Aoki-Kimberley Treaty of 1894 to abolish extraterritoriality, the Japanese Ambassador to Britain and Germany, Shuzo Aoki, declared that with this treaty "Japan has entered the ranks of civilized counties."[67] Sharing Aoki's perspective, the conventional studies of the English School describe Japan's transformation as follows: working "diligently," Japan fulfilled the requirements for the standard of "civilization" with great speed between the coming of Commodore Perry and the abolition of extraterritoriality.[68] In abolishing extraterritoriality, home states upgraded Japan from an inferior status to that of an equal.[69] This narrative can be found in most of the civilization-based arguments for the abolition of extraterritoriality. For example, English School scholars Gerrit Gong and Hidemi Suganami link the abolition of extraterritoriality in Japan to a cultural transformation in which Japan accepted the norms, values,

[67] Jansen (1968: 178).
[68] Gong (1984: 164–165).
[69] Suganami (1984: 197).

and principles of international society. Admittedly, these scholars discuss the role of legal institutions in broader cultural terms. But the actual importance of legal institutions in their account remains marginal compared to external manifestation of culture, like clothing, manners, and gender relations.

This narrative of Japan's accommodation of and gradual acculturation to international standards leading to the abolition of extraterritoriality is not without problems. Both the late establishment of permanent diplomacy in Japan (as a function of Japanese isolation until the arrival of Commodore Perry in 1853) and the existence of the significant level of anti-Western xenophobia in Japan (as shown later) challenge the arguments related to Japan's ability to satisfy some agreed-upon standard of "civilization." There is an additional reason to cast doubt on the claim that Japanese membership in international society is related to the abolition of extraterritoriality: Japan had a very low level of intergovernmental organization (IGO) membership, even compared with that of the Ottoman Empire, a state in a similar international position. Japan joined several international organizations in the nineteenth century: the Treaty Concerning the Formation of General Postal Union (1874), the Universal Postal Union Convention of Paris (1878), the International Telegraphic Convention (1875), the Meter Convention (1885), the Convention of the Red Cross Society (1886), and the Declaration of the Maritime Law (1886).[70] This list reveals only a low level of Japanese involvement with international organizations and thus raises questions about Japan's full membership in international society to justify the abolition of extraterritoriality.

However, Japan's membership in IGOs grew significantly only in the 1900s. In other words, the increase in Japan's membership in IGOs *followed* – rather than preceded – the abolition of extraterritoriality. This rapid increase in Japan's IGO membership is also evident when compared to other non-Western states' membership in IGOs. During the time when home states abolished extraterritoriality in Japan (1890s), the Ottoman Empire had higher levels of membership in IGOs than did Japan. Japan, however, surpassed the Ottoman Empire's membership figure by the early 1900s. This benchmark

[70] *Treaties and Conventions between the Empire of Japan and Other Powers* (1884, 1899).

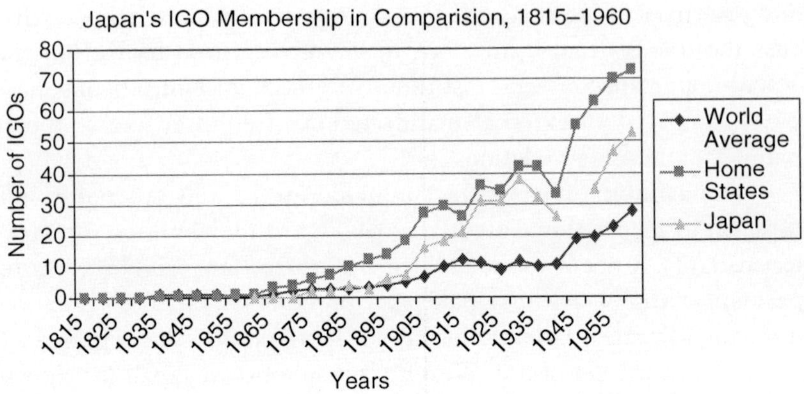

FIGURE 3. Japan's IGO Membership Compared to Home States. All data are from Singer and Wallace, *Intergovernmental Organizations Data.*

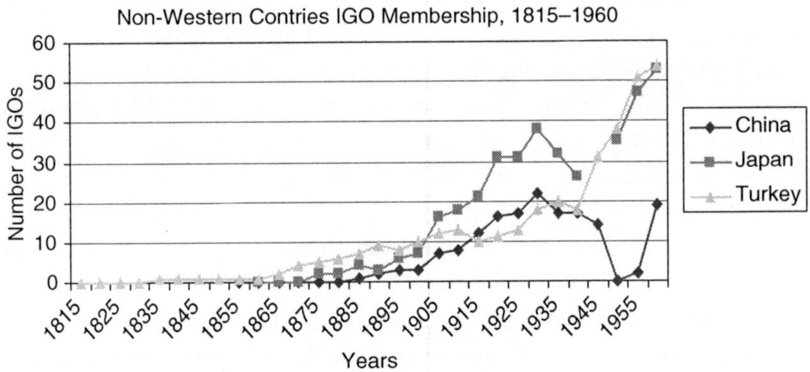

FIGURE 4. Japanese IGO Membership. All data are from Singer and Wallace, *Intergovernmental Organizations Data.*

occurs only after the abolition of extraterritoriality. All of these indicators suggest that Japan followed a policy of seclusion and was slow in integrating into international society until it achieved its sovereign equality and territorial jurisdiction.

In sum, conventional cultural arguments tie the abolition of extraterritoriality to Japan's modernization and westernization through its membership in international society. While these accounts illuminate certain aspects of extraterritoriality and the expansion of Western international society, they are challenged by data regarding Japan's membership in the institutions of international society. The cultural gap between Europe and Japan was wide, anti-Western movements were on the rise in Japan, and Japan was reluctant to join international organizations. On the Western front, despite the claims of Japanese fulfillment of the standard of civilization, in the words of historian Cemil Aydin, "European and American perception of Japan as belonging to the yellow race and thus not equal to the superior Christian and white nations continued, leading to a tension between Japan's legal status in international law and popular Western perceptions of Japanese racial inferiority."[71] All these factors suggest that Western states conceding to Japanese demands on extraterritoriality cannot be explained solely on Japanese "westernization." Rather, as I argue later, one part of this westernization, Japan's legal reforms, was central.

The importance of Japanese legal reforms in contrast to Japanese membership in international society in Japan's anomalous success in ending extraterritoriality becomes even more visible in comparison with the Ottoman Empire. The Ottoman Empire, had a much more salient presence in international society. The difference between Japan and the Ottoman Empire was their success in domestic legalization rather than the difference in their fulfillment of a set of international normative standards of "civilization."

However, there are two caveats to my skeptical conclusion about the standards of "civilization." First, the limited number of IGOs in the nineteenth century makes it impossible to conclusively refute the English School's standard of "civilization" argument. Second, these cultural arguments also emphasize reorganization of Japanese domestic structures along with Western forms.[72] Because domestic legalization can be considered a standard of "civilization," and Japan established legal institutions that were perceived as "civilized," this harmonizes my approach with cultural accounts that explain the abolition of extraterritoriality. I would argue, however, if there was a standard of civilization for non-Western states, legal institutionalization compatible with Western states' understandings of appropriate legal structure, in large part shaped by the positive legal episteme,

[71] Aydın (2007: 40).
[72] Suzuki (2009, chapter 5).

was the most important part of that standard for Western states to agree to Japanese sovereignty over Western citizens and commercial interests.

THE ABOLITION OF EXTRATERRITORIALITY

More than two decades after the Iwakura Mission, Britain accepted the abolition of extraterritoriality in Japan with the Aoki-Kimberley Treaty of 1894. The treaty became effective after a five-year transition period beginning in 1899, and the British decision had a ripple effect, causing other Western states to abolish extraterritoriality in Japan. There are several legal-institutional explanations for the British decision. Gerrit Gong makes a claim akin to mine: Western states recognized Japan as civilized because of Japan's "reformed legal system."[73] Similarly, Frank E. Hinckley suggests that Japan's development of a system of jurisprudence, codification of laws, and improvement in the administration of justice moved Western states to abolish extraterritoriality.[74] I would argue that during the 1894 to 1899 period, Japan's completion of legal institutionalization was *the* determining factor in Britain's decision for the abolition of extraterritoriality.

Meiji Legal Reforms (1882–1899)

Japan's domestic legalization emerged as a fundamental part of Meiji institutionalization. Examining Meiji institution-building patterns in three different institutions (the police system, the postal system, and the press), Eleanor D. Westney concludes: "The 1880s was primarily a decade of reorganization and consolidation in which the organizations so rapidly established in the 1870s were put on a firmer structural basis and extended throughout the country."[75] Although Meiji leaders initiated the establishment of a state-based legal system in the 1870s, they consolidated their legal reforms and extended it throughout the country only in the 1880s and 1890s. Codification of the "Six

[73] Gong (1984: 185).
[74] Hinckley (1906: 183).
[75] Westney (1987: 15).

TABLE 3. *Legal Codification in Japan*

Code	Enforcement
Constitution	1889
Civil Procedure	1890
Criminal Procedure	1890[a]
Criminal Code	1898[b]
Civil Code	1898
Commercial Code	1898

[a] Amended version of 1882 Criminal Procedure Code.
[b] Amended version of 1882 Criminal Code.

Codes" and the inauguration of new courts completed Japan's domestic legalization and ushered in the abolition of extraterritoriality.

Starting with the enforcement of the Criminal Code and the Code of Criminal Procedure in 1882, the Meiji leaders undertook a program of codification.[76]

In addition to the codification of laws, Meiji statesmen established an extensive court structure between 1882 and 1899. This court system further secured domestic legalization in Japan. The 1890 Law of the Organization of Courts established a court system with four levels of courts: a supreme court, appeals courts, local courts, and district courts. Figure 5 describes the increase in the number of courts of first instance (local and district courts) in Japan. Because Japan did not extend its territorial boundaries during this period and did not experience dramatic population growth, an almost 80 percent increase in the number of courts of first instance indicates the increased level of Japanese legal institutionalization. Table 4 shows the number of courts, court staff, and the ratio of population and area per court in 1901. These numbers show that by the end of the nineteenth century, Japan had established an extensive court system.

In sum, following the failure to abolish extraterritoriality at the Tokyo Conference of 1882, Meiji leaders codified legal rules, expanded the Japanese court system, and established a legal hierarchy in Japan. All codes came into operation by 1891, except for the Civil Code

[76] Ryosuke (1958: 19).

TABLE 4. *Courts and Legal Personnel in Japan (1901)*[a]

Type of Court	Number	Number of Judges	Number of Prosecutors	Population per Court	Area of District per Court (sq km)
Supreme	1	25	7	45,193,583	24,998.80
Appeals	7	121	29	6,456,227	3,571.26
Local	49	399	140	922,319	510.18
District	310	557	159	145,786	80.64

[a] Commission (1904: 82).

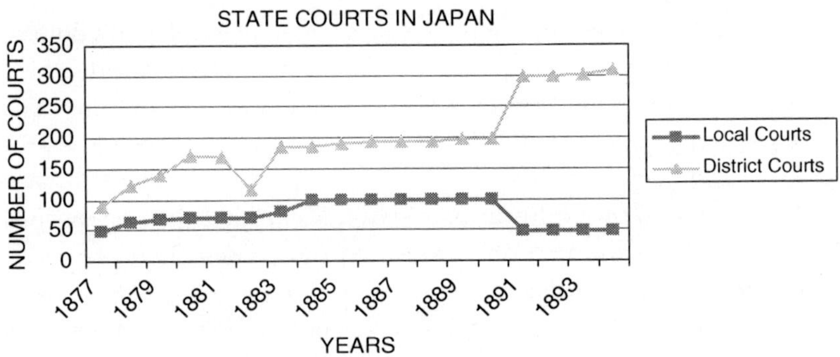

FIGURE 5. Courts in Japan. Note: The supreme court existed in Japan during this period. There were four appellate courts until 1883 when the Japanese government increased the number of appellate courts to seven. Data are from *Tokei Nenkan* (1882–1896).

and the Commercial Codes. The government was unable to implement them due to nationalist criticisms of their incompatibility with Japanese customs. When the government attempted to pass the Civil and Commercial Code in 1893, opponents at the Diet introduced a bill to postpone the implementation for at least four years in order to amend the codes. In response, using a similar nationalist and antiimperialist rhetoric, Prime Minister Viscount Enomoto justified the legal reforms as a means to abolish extraterritoriality. Enomoto failed to convince the Diet not to postpone the implementation of codes. His speech, however, illustrates how popular demands to end extraterritoriality became a tool for reformers to justify legal standardization and unification.

Gentlemen, I appeal to you! Is it not imperative that these Codes – our indispensable weapon of offense, so to speak, against these hated Consular Courts – should be duly carried out into operation from the beginning of next year? At the present moment, when the whole nation is bent upon revising the Treaties, and the operation of the Code is the sine quo non for the attainment of that object, is it not the height of inconsistency to seek to have them postponed? It is not that I maintain that all the 2,826 sections of the Civil and Commercial Codes are absolutely without a flaw – let sections requiring revision be revised by all means, and to this contention I adhere on the ground ... of the intimate connection existing between the Codes and Treaty Revision.[77]

In the early 1890s, Meiji leaders sought the abolition of extraterritoriality. In 1893, Aoki Shuzo, the Japanese ambassador to Britain, presented a draft treaty for the abolition of extraterritoriality to the British government.[78] Disappointed, the British ambassador to Japan, Hugh Fraser, argued that the proposed treaty did not provide any guarantees for the protection of British citizens and their property. The ambassador recommended to the British Prime Minister Lord Rosebery that the "discussion be suspended until after the new Japanese law codes had been in actual operation for at least a year, in order to determine not the nature of the laws, but also the manner in which they were to be implemented."[79] Fraser's reservations regarding the abolition of extraterritoriality reflected his concerns that the legal reforms in Japan had not yet led to the codification of commercial and civil laws.

While their government was negotiating with Japan to abolish extraterritoriality, British citizens in Japan were facing an ever-intensifying campaign against foreigners under the leadership of the Great Japan Society, a powerful nationalist group. The existence of powerful antiforeign groups in Japan cast further doubt upon the cultural claims that the Japanese had internalized "civilized" international values. As in China, Western foreigners in Japan experienced occasional xenophobic campaigns and understood the continuation of extraterritoriality to be a vital component of their security in Japan. Unlike in China, the Meiji leaders suppressed the antiforeign campaigns. In quashing the antiforeign movements, the Japanese government hoped

[77] Jones (1931: 142).
[78] FO 881/6488 (1893: 20–22).
[79] FO 881/6488 (1893:37).

to bolster its ability to contol nonstate violence and protect the legal and property rights of foreigners.[80]

Antiwesternism in Japan resonated only slightly at the extraterritoriality negotiations. Despite the warnings of Fraser, the British ambassador, and the British citizens' concerns about increasing antiforeigner demonstrations in Japan, Britain agreed to discuss the Japanese draft treaty. As a first step and like the Tokyo Conference of 1882, the British government requested information about Japan's law codes. Learning of Britain's insistence on information about the new codes, Mutsu Munemitsu, the Japanese minister of foreign affairs, promised a diplomatic note about the enforcement and publication of the codes. This diplomatic note was to be delivered by the Japanese to the British before the enforcement of the new treaty abolishing extraterritoriality.[81]

On April 2, 1894, the negotiations started. Assistant Secretary for Asia Francis Bertie, who was the British chief negotiator, was disappointed with Japan's inability to provide "full information as to the laws which would be enforceable upon British subjects on the cessation of consular jurisdiction."[82] Later, when Bertie insisted on examining the Japanese codes, Aoki replied that "if any existed they would be in either German or French," as Japan had modeled its codes on German and French codes. Aoki, however, promised to provide translated codes to the British government.[83] Despite the British government's insistence, Aoki did not make a public pronouncement regarding the promulgation of the Japanese codes (due to debates about codification in Japan's domestic politics), but he did assure British officials that if the Japanese government failed to promulgate the codes in the five-year transition period, extraterritoriality would remain in place. British acceptance of Japan's adoption of the civil law traditions of Germany and France, but not Anglo-American common law, was attuned with British insistence of domestic legalization compatible with a positive legal order. Encouraging Japan to develop a system based on common law to replace a system based on customary

[80] For this assessment, see FO 881/6488 (1893:48) and FO 881/6582 (1894: 2–3, 8).

[81] FO 881/6582 (1894: 53).

[82] FO 881/6582 (1894: 62). The other problems related to coastal trade, treaty life, ability of foreigners to hold property, the passport system, and other rights and privileges of foreigners.

[83] FO 881/6582 (1894: 53).

law would have created difficulties for British merchants in Japan. In particular, problems would likely have arisen because customary law would have emphasized local, rather Western principles. Moreover, a legal system emphasizing customary law and a jury system, like common law, would empower local societal actors against the centralized state apparatus, and thus hinder the state's control of its legal system. Ironically, while sponsored by a state with a common law tradition, positive legal order requirements such as codification were more compatible with continental civil law traditions. Like Japan, the Ottoman Empire and China eventually adopted legal systems based on a civil law tradition.

In the last days of negotiation, the British government brought another issue that further illustrates how British concern was motivated by Japanese legal institutionalization and enforcement of property rights. Britain asked Japan to join the International Conventions for the Protection of Property and Copyright to prevent the widespread reprinting without copyrights of foreign books in Japan. The diplomatic note the Japanese government provided regarding the timing of the enforcement of the Aoki-Kimberley Treaty and Japan's acquiescence to joining the copyright convention confirms that Britain was in part motivated by a notion that Japan's Western-style legal institutionalization would open new commercial opportunities for British merchants and secure their property rights. While on the surface the abolition of extraterritoriality put British subjects under Japanese jurisdiction and denied them the protection of extraterritorial courts, paradoxically Japan's new legal system facilitated increasing access of Western merchants to Japan's markets and investment opportunities.[84]

On July 16, 1894, Britain and Japan signed the Aoki-Kimberley Treaty ending British extraterritoriality in Japan. With the treaty, Japan provided a diplomatic note to Britain declaring that the Japanese government would not ask to have the Aoki-Kimberley Treaty enforced until all Japanese Codes were in full operation.[85] In the following two years, 1894–1896, other Western states signed treaties that were

[84] When commenting on drafts and memorandums for treaty revisions, H. G. Berge of the British Board of Trade was less enthusiastic than other British diplomats about the treaty but did not veto the treaty. From Berge to Bertie, June 16, 1894, cited in Perez (1999: 156).

[85] FO 881/6582 (1894: 137).

nearly identical to the Aoki-Kimberley Treaty. In all these subsequent treaties, Western countries gave up their claims of extraterritoriality in Japan.

In sum, the abolition of extraterritoriality in Japan reflects Japan's success in domestic legalization. Meiji leaders completely institutionalized law in Japan in the 1880s and 1890s. Three elements of domestic legalization (legal codification, the establishment of a state-wide court system, the creation of the state's legal hierarchy) took place in Japan during this time. The Japanese finished the codification of commercial and civil codes in 1898, just a year before the abolition of extraterritoriality. Extraterritoriality negotiations show that Japan's legal institutionalization and Western states' abolition of extraterritoriality were related. While Western states' demands for legal reform explain part of the motivation for the Meiji government's legal reforms, legal institutionalization explains the Western states' – particularly Britain's – decision to abolish extraterritoriality in Japan.

Western Foreigners in Meiji Japan

There is one last factor to consider when explaining extraterritoriality in Japan: foreigners on whose lives extraterritoriality had the most direct and drastic influence, and who can lobby to influence their states' policies on extraterritoriality. Unlike the Ottoman Empire and China, much of Japan remained insulated from Western foreigners and merchants in the nineteenth century even after its formal "opening" occurred in 1856. Foreigners were largely restricted to a few treaty ports. This seclusion limited the usefulness of extraterritoriality, the presence of Western interests, and the number of foreigners willing to lobby their governments to continue extraterritoriality provisions. Even when Westerners in Japan demanded the maintenance of extraterritoriality, Western rulers often spurned them. This seclusion became a bargaining tool: The Japanese were willing to offer a relaxation of trade and travel restrictions over foreigners to get concessions on extraterritoriality. While negotiating the end of extraterritoriality, Western rulers were willing to separate their decision from what they perceived to be the narrow demands of anti-abolitionist business and missionary groups. These rulers were inclined to ignore the myopic demands of extraterritorial groups in Japan and to look forward to the long-term benefits of increased access to Japanese markets.

Three factors made this inclination possible. First, there were not many Western citizens in Japan. There were only 1,740 (43 percent of all extraterritorial foreigners) British citizens in Japan in 1893 compared to 14,701 in China (about 6 percent of extraterritorial foreigners) in 1924.[86] The fewer Western foreigners, the less pressure Western rulers faced to satisfy their demands. Japan did not open its doors to Western foreigners until 1854 with the Kanagawa Treaty, which was concluded with the United States. Even then, Japan remained largely inhospitable. For example, foreigners did not have freedom of movement within Japan: They could not reside outside of treaty ports unless they worked for the Japanese government or for Japanese firms. The Japanese government developed a strict passport system to prevent the movement of foreigners to the interior. Another factor that discouraged Westerners – especially missionaries – from living in Japan was that Christianity was illegal in Japan until 1873. These restrictions allowed Japan to engage in state building to strengthen its institutions without the great powers' meddling or intervention.

Second, there was a lack of agreement among the extraterritorial groups over extraterritoriality. Extraterritorial groups failed to lobby strongly against the abolition of extraterritoriality because Japan's willingness to open the interior to foreigners in exchange for the abolition of extraterritoriality divided extraterritorial groups. While certain groups valued extraterritoriality more than the right to reside in the interior, others, especially missionaries, preferred the right to reside in the interior.[87]

Third, the leading extraterritorial power, Britain, was going through an isolationist moment during this period. The Rosebery government (1893–1895) focused on internal policies and was reluctant to support imperialism abroad. The government's narrow majority in the British Parliament and the division of the Liberal Party between Prime Minister Rosebery and the Chancellor of the

[86] The largest extraterritorial group in China in 1924 was Japanese. Out of 231,540 extraterritorial foreigners, 198,206 were Japanese. For complete statistics about the number of foreigners and foreign companies in Japan and China, see Kayaoğlu (2005).

[87] FO 881/4763 (1881–1882).

Exchequer and Leader of the House of Commons William Harcourt forced the government to turn its attention to party politics and domestic politics rather than foreign policy. In 1894, during a time of "splendid isolation," as Rosebery termed it, the government was not receptive to the demands of the extraterritorial groups, and therefore not willing to engage in gunboat diplomacy in order to obtain travel *and* extraterritoriality policies that would please all British groups in Japan.

The British decision to consent to the abolition of extraterritoriality caught Western citizens in Japan by surprise. Upon learning about the extraterritoriality negotiations (through a leaked news story to the Japanese press) between the British and Japanese, the foreigners residing in Japanese treaty ports organized meetings to discuss ways that they might prevent the abolition of extraterritoriality. Among the foreigners, the China Association, the most powerful British interest group in East Asia, was the most vocal. Not only did it organize the foreign community in the treaty ports and pressure the British diplomats in Japan, but it also lobbied in Britain to prevent the government from abolishing extraterritoriality. In their arguments, the China Association cited differences between the Japanese and Western legal systems and antiforeign incidents as reasons for the continuation of extraterritoriality. In a letter sent to members of Parliament, the China Association made a legal-cultural argument against the abolition of extraterritoriality:

> Englishmen are accustomed to a degree of personal and political freedom remote from the conception of an Oriental Government or people. ... The differences are not merely in Code or technical provisions, but in spirit and conception; and nothing but evidence of satisfactory and competent administration of new Codes over a sufficient period will be readily acceptable as evidence of their adequacy to meet the European requirements.[88]

Most British business groups at the imperial centers with commercial ties with Japan were also against the abolition of extraterritoriality on both cultural and commercial grounds. The London Chamber of Commerce, the Manchester Chamber of Commerce, and the Glasgow Chamber of Commerce and Manufacturers raised concerns about the impact of the abolition of extraterritoriality on

[88] FO 881/6582(1894: 153–154).

British firms that traded with Japan.[89] A number of groups, including the masons in Japan, British citizens of Yokohoma, and British missionaries in Japan, organized to prevent the abolition of extraterritoriality. Their efforts were complicated by the fact that the negotiations took place in secret and finished very quickly. This made these British groups angry both because the government had ignored their opinions and because the government had concluded the negotiations in secret. Unable to prevent the preparation of the treaty, the British groups then lobbied to prevent ratification of the treaty. Even at this stage, the British government was unresponsive to their activities. On August 16, 1894, a month after the signing of the treaty, Secretary of State Kimberley replied to a protest letter from the China Association demanding information about the treaty refusing communication: "Before ratification and publication we will not discuss the provisions" of the treaty.[90] This unresponsive attitude drew the ire of the British community to the extent that one British company, Messr. Richardson, Findlay, and Co., lodged a bitter protest that, not without a sense of irony, invoked the most-favored-nation clause by asking the Foreign Office if it "would be willing to send a copy of this to the German Government" so that "Germany (or some other nation) will refuse to surrender so readily the rights and privileges of its nationals, and in this way British traders may be saved from the serious consequences of the Treaty arranged by their own Government."[91] (The most-favored-nation clause guaranteed the continuation of extraterritoriality as long as one Western state kept it.) These pleas did not change the British government's decision to end extraterritoriality.

The failure of the extraterritorial groups to stop the abolition of extraterritoriality shows that one cannot simply reduce Western policies regarding extraterritoriality to citizens' demands. British rulers, in particular, realized that legal reforms in Japan could serve British interests by expanding trade and investment opportunities. Impressed by Japan's legal reforms and eager to have better access to Japan's markets, British decision makers opted to abandon the protections of extraterritoriality. In contrast to the Ottoman Empire

[89] For various protests, see Foreign Office publications about revision of the treaty with Japan. In particular, FO 881/6582 (1894: 167–170), FO 881/5072 (1894: 26, 77).

[90] FO 881/6582 (1894: 148–149).

[91] FO 881/6582 (1894: 161–162).

and China, described in the next chapters, Japan's ability to limit the impact of foreigners with extraterritorial privileges (in taxes, judicial ambiguities, and extending such privileges to native protégés – protected persons) allowed Japan to undertake a series of developmental policies of centralization and rationalization of its legal system without foreign hindrance, meddling, or intervention. Intrusive Western policies and vested Western interests often severely constrained the Ottoman and Chinese rulers from engaging in similar state-building projects.

CONCLUSION

Japan ended extraterritoriality with astonishing speed. This success is often presented in a framework that emphasizes either the role of increasing Japanese power in the 1890s or Japan's rapid westernization. While Meiji reforms changed Japan's economy, military, and culture, none of these factors alone was decisive in the abolition of extraterritoriality. Meiji legal institutionalization was at the center of all of these developments. As detailed in this chapter, the debates and discussions between Japan and Britain, as well as within the British government, focused on Japanese legal reforms. From early on, the British government linked the abolition of extraterritoriality to the Japanese enactment of new codes, establishment of a statewide court system, and implementation of a legal hierarchy through an appellate court system. Admittedly, the Western demands were often elusive, contradictory, and changing, reflecting other imperial concerns and commercial expectations such as opening Japanese markets to Western goods and investment. Amid these imperial contractions, one factor seems to be consistent: Western demands were reflecting the concerns of legal positivism. Positivist legal episteme was shaping the Western expecations from Japan for the former's agreement to end extraterritoriality.

Japan complied. Meiji legal reforms, especially in the 1880s and 1890s, replaced the Tokugawa period's feudal legal structure with a unified and centralized legal system. Advances were made in both codification and the court system. In terms of codification, the Meiji government reforms subjected the Japanese to standardized and systemized codes. In terms of the spread of the court system, the national courts replaced the earlier *daimyo* courts. The Meiji rulers empowered the Ministry of Justice to appoint and supervise judges and to standardize law enforcement with an appellate court system. These reforms were central to the British government's 1894 decision to end its extraterritoriality in Japan in 1899.

4

The Ottoman Empire's Elusive Dream of Sovereignty

Territorial sovereignty was an elusive dream of Ottoman rulers: From the 1856 Paris Conference to 1914, Western states continuously refused numerous Ottoman pleas to end extraterritoriality.[1] The last rejection so frustrated the Ottoman government that they resorted to a policy option that the Japanese government never attempted. The Ottomans gave a memorandum to the extraterritorial powers on September 9, 1914, notifying these powers that extraterritoriality was to be abolished effective October 1, 1914 – a month before the Ottoman Empire declared war on the Allies. The Ottoman memorandum stressed the incompatibility of extraterritoriality with territorial jurisdiction and national sovereignty. The memorandum further enumerated the injustices and humiliation suffered by the Ottoman Empire because of extraterritoriality.[2] The Allies, Austria, and Germany rejected the Ottoman unilateral abolition. It was not until 1917 that Austria and

[1] Major Ottoman attempts occurred in 1862, 1867, 1871, 1881, and 1914. Sousa (1931) offers the best historical account of these attempts. In this chapter, I use extraterritoriality rather than "capitulations," a term preferred by Middle East scholars. One reason for this choice is to differentiate the legal authority of foreign merchant communities and mercantile companies (a form of legal self-rule) from a state's jurisdiction over their citizens beyond state boundaries (a form of extraterritorial jurisdiction). For a similar choice of terminology, see Gönen (2004). For other works on extraterritoriality in the Ottoman Empire, see Hinckey (1906), Liebesny (1955), Platt (1971), Örücü (1992), Soosa (1931), Sousa (1933), Zubaida (2003), and Ahmad (2000).

[2] For the text of the memorandum the Ottoman government sent to the extraterritorial states, see Sousa (1933: 328–331).

Germany accepted the abolition of extraterritoriality in the Ottoman Empire. It would take the Allies several more years; the Lausanne Treaty – the last peace treaty of the First World War – finally ended the extraterritoriality rights of the Allies in 1923.

Similar to discussions in Japan and China, the debates and negotiations about sovereignty and extraterritoriality in the Ottoman Empire/Turkey focused on the Ottoman Empire's legal system. Apart from this similarity, however, the Turkish case offers novel insights about the relationship between sovereignty, extraterritoriality, international society, and domestic legalization. Earlier incarnations of extraterritoriality (under the rubric of capitulations) were developed within Ottoman-European relations; later, Western states reproduced these unequal extraterritorial relations in their encounters with other non-Western states, including China and Japan. Of the non-Western rulers subjected to extraterritorial treaties, the Ottoman rulers were the first among the non-Western rulers to attempt to abolish extraterritoriality. Their first attempt came in 1856, around the same time Western states imposed extraterritoriality on Japan. Ironically, Japan was able to win the abolition of extraterritoriality in 1899 before Turkey's ultimate success in 1923. The time span during which Turkey attempted to abolish extraterritoriality was sixty-seven years longer than the forty-three years that extraterritoriality was present in Japan. The abolition of extraterritoriality in Turkey came as a part of a multilateral comprehensive peace treaty, the Lausanne Treaty of 1923, as opposed to the narrow bilateral treaties that abolished extraterritoriality in Japan and China.

Historians, political analysts, and cultural scholars have proposed various explanations for the abolition of extraterritoriality at Lausanne. Some attribute the abolition to disunity among the Allies. Others argue that the westernization of the Ottoman Empire, leading to the admission of Turkey into international society, accounts for the abolition of extraterritoriality in Turkey. Turkish historiography rejects both these views and suggests that the strength of the Turkish military prevented the Allies' reimposition of extraterritoriality after the First World War. Which of these explanations is valid? Is the abolition of extraterritoriality in Turkey best understood in terms of divisions among the Allies following the First World War, the expansion of international society, Turkish military power, or some other factor?

In order to answer this question I employ two strategies: I first compare the abolition of extraterritoriality in Turkey with the abolition of extraterritoriality in Japan and China; I then compare the Western rejection of Ottoman demands for the abolition of extraterritoriality at the 1856 Paris Conference with the Western agreement to end extraterritoriality at the 1923 Lausanne Conference.[3] The comparisons between Japan and China demonstrate the importance of domestic legalization in the abolition of extraterritoriality; the chronological comparison of Western actions regarding extraterritoriality in the Ottoman Empire/Turkey offers a more refined and complex picture. In particular, two factors explain the abolition of extraterritoriality in Turkey. First the legal concessions guaranteed Turkish legal reforms and protection of the foreigners' legal and property rights during the time of reform. Second, the comprehensive nature of the treaty prevented the Allies from rejecting the Lausanne Treaty in a bid to keep extraterritoriality.

I proceed in four sections. First, I elaborate the place of the Ottoman Empire in nineteenth-century international society. Second, I link the Ottoman Empire's failure to institutionalize state law to Western countries' decision to keep extraterritoriality at the 1856 Paris Conference. Third, in order to establish the historical context, I describe the international changes that occurred in the decade before the 1923 Lausanne Conference. Fourth, highlighting the influence of political bargaining in the process of extraterritoriality, I tie the territorial and legal concessions granted to the Allies by Turkey to the Allies' agreement to abolish extraterritoriality.

THE OTTOMAN EMPIRE IN EUROPEAN INTERNATIONAL SOCIETY

The integral role of the Ottoman Empire in European politics since the Ottoman conquest of Constantinople (1453) makes the Turkish case different from the relatively isolated cases of Japan and China. Extraterritoriality was central to the long history of Ottoman-European interactions. The predecessor of extraterritoriality, capitulations,

[3] Although I focus my argument on these two instances, my evidence and arguments cover the other Turkish attempts to abolish extraterritoriality.

took its most elaborate forms in Ottoman-European interactions dating back to the Ottoman unilateral grant (*ahidname*) for French merchants in 1535 (if not earlier). While extraterritoriality and the earlier capitulations show a significant level of institutionalization in Ottoman-European relations, the exclusivity of these unequal relationships also marks the uniqueness – and, to some scholars, the inferiority – of the Ottoman Empire in the European state system.

How was the Ottoman Empire involved in European politics? Was the Ottoman Empire Europe's eternal enemy whose existence was instrumental for the creation of a common European identity?[4] Or was the Ottoman Empire a European power from the start? Many scholars of international relations would attempt to bridge these seemingly disparate views: The Ottoman Empire was both European and non-European at the same time; it was part of the European system but not part of European society. The distinction between international society and the international system is central to cultural arguments like those advanced by the English School. Specifically, a significant level of interaction between states makes them part of the international system. Yet these same states can fail to be part of international society if they do not share the same norms, values, and institutions. In the evolution of European international society, the Ottoman Empire was the quintessential case for dualism of the international system and international society. The Ottoman Empire was a major military and naval power that Europeans were obliged to take into account. Also, at one time the Ottomans occupied almost a quarter, sometimes a third, of the European continent and controlled trade with the Levant. This trade was an important component of European economies. Although the Ottoman Empire had a significant level of interaction with European states, and the Empire was a de facto actor in European power politics, international society scholars argue that the Empire did not share European norms, rules, and institutions.[5] Thomas Naff summarizes this argument of cultural exclusion: "Even though a significant portion of the Empire was based *in* Europe, it cannot be said to have been *of* Europe."[6]

[4] Neuman and Welsh (1991).
[5] Bull (1979: 13).
[6] Naff (1984: 143).

The debate continues about when – looking at the European Union's relations with Turkey, some *still* may wonder *whether*[7] – European elites started to perceive the Ottoman Empire as sharing European norms and institutions. Diplomatic historians, international jurists, and English School scholars offer different answers. Most diplomatic historians agree that the Ottoman Empire was a crucial part of European politics and institutions. The history of the Ottoman Empire and European diplomatic relations provides ample evidence to suggest the existence of regular and permanent diplomatic interactions between European states and the Ottoman Empire. France, in 1525, was the first Western European state to seek diplomatic relations with the Ottoman Empire and first to send an envoy.[8] In order to facilitate the increasing interactions with the Ottoman Empire, European states opened embassies in Istanbul following the establishment of the British Embassy there in 1583. This unilateral diplomatic institutionalization continued for more than two centuries until the Ottoman Empire established its own embassies in all of the major European capitals, beginning with an embassy in London in 1793. The Empire's involvement with European politics during and after the Thirty Years War and the Napoleonic Wars suggest that it was an important actor in the European balance of power.

Diplomatic and institutional relations between the Ottoman Empire and Europe strengthened in the nineteenth century. In 1836, the Ottoman government established a ministry of foreign affairs to further institutionalize the increasing diplomatic relations with the European states.[9] The existence of permanent diplomatic relations between the Ottoman Empire and major European states in the eighteenth century indicates that the Ottoman Empire was a member of European society much earlier than Japan and China, with whom permanent diplomatic relations emerged only in the late nineteenth century. Ottoman diplomatic historians argue that the Empire became a de facto member of international society in the first half of the nineteenth century; thus, the Treaty of Paris merely codified an existing reality.

Moreover, the Ottoman Empire was the first non-Western country to join intergovernmental organizations. Until the First World War, the

[7] Curley (2009).

[8] Jensen (1985). Even before, the Ottoman Empire had diplomatic relations with the city-states of Geneva and Venice.

[9] For Ottoman Empire–European diplomacy, see Hurewitz (1961), Yurdusev (2003), Kürkçüoğlu (2004), and Berridge (2004).

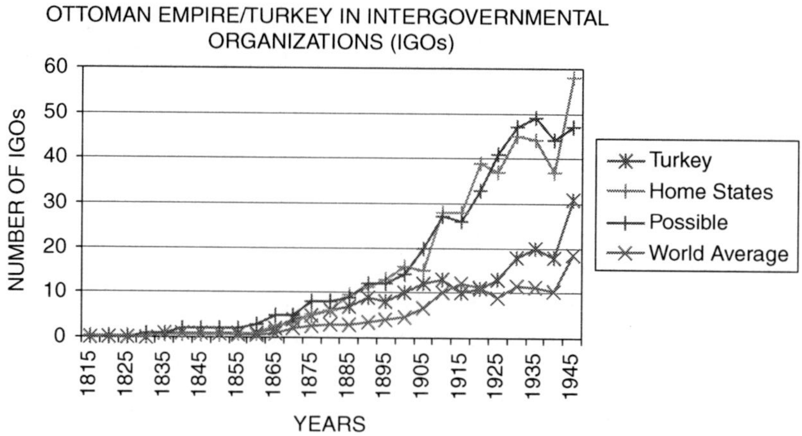

FIGURE 6. The Ottoman Empire/Turkey IGO Membership.

number of organizations to which the Ottoman Empire belonged was very close to the major Western states' average, above the world average, and above the level of both Japanese and Chinese membership. Taken together, diplomatic relations and institutional membership suggest that the Ottoman Empire was part of international society.

Jurists and English School scholars contradict the diplomatic historians' assessment: The Ottoman Empire's military, diplomatic, and institutional linkages with the European states demonstrate its place in the international system *but not* in international society because the empire shared only a few of "Europe's interests, principles, and norms."[10] International jurists have a concrete year for the Ottoman admission into international society: 1856. This year marks the Ottoman Empire's inauguration into European international society because it was when European states declared the Ottoman Empire to be a part of European public law. Specifically, the jurists claim that the empire became a member of international society through Article 7 of the Treaty of Paris in which the Ottoman Empire was included in the Concert of Europe and European international public law.[11] Nineteenth-century jurists claimed that Article 7 made the Ottoman Empire a de jure member of

[10] Gong (1984: 108).

[11] For the articles of the Treaty of Paris see *Parliamentary Papers* (1956 [Volume 61]:19–34). See the discussions in Twiss (1861: section 62) and Hall (1880: section 6) on the Ottoman Empire's role in international law. Wood (1943) offers a more skeptical interpretation of Article 7 and Ottoman de jure admission into international society.

international law, entitling the empire to all the rights and responsibilities that international law conferred on Western states. The Ottoman Empire thus became the first non-Western state to which Western states granted a formal right of participation.

The de jure admission of the Ottoman Empire to European international society poses problems for the cultural arguments advocated by the English School scholars. First, if 1856 is the year that the Ottoman Empire became a member of international society, this membership can hardly be due to the standard of "civilization." According to international jurists, the Ottoman Empire failed to meet the standard of "civilization." James Lorimer, the prominent international jurist of the time, referring to the admission of the Ottoman Empire into European international public law, argued that international lawyers had "bitter experience of the consequences of extending the rights of civilization to barbarians who have been incapable of performing its duties, and who possibly do not even belong to the progressive races of mankind."[12] Lorimer's frustration reveals that membership to nineteenth-century international society was not always dictated by the logic of civilizational fulfillment.[13]

On the contrary, the de jure admission was due to the Empire's weakness and the fear that this weakness would destabilize the European balance of power. The Ottoman Empire remained central to the great powers' struggle throughout the nineteenth century. Yet Western states managed to keep the question of extraterritoriality outside of their strategic machinations. The English-French alliance against Russia in the 1840s and 1850s replaced the English-French rivalry of the 1820s and 1830s. Realizing that weakening Turkey at the expense of a powerful Russia would destabilize the Concert of Europe, Britain and France encouraged Turkey to resist Russian demands for extraterritorial rights over the Ottoman Empire's Orthodox Christian subjects. Acquiescing to this demand would have put the Ottoman Empire under significant Russian influence, reducing British power in the Middle East. Encouraged by Britain, the Ottoman government refused the Russian demands. The result

[12] Lorimer (1883: 101).

[13] For a similar point of importance of strategic concerns in the enlargement of international society, see Stivachtis (1998).

was the Crimean War. Following the war, the 1856 Paris Treaty established a collective mechanism to check Russia's increasing influence over the Ottoman Empire. Western states thus decided to include the Ottoman Empire in the Concert of Europe in order to secure its independence and territorial integrity.

The Crimean War revealed the weakness of the Ottoman Empire because it was unable to defend itself from Russia without help from France and Britain. More telling, it was the European states, not the Ottoman government, that took responsibility for maintaining the independence and integrity of the Ottoman Empire at the Paris Conference following the war. Article 7 of the Treaty of Paris internationalized the concerns about Ottoman survival. The underlying logic of Article 7 was strategic, not cultural. Signatories agreed to respect the independence and territorial integrity of the empire. In addition to the Treaty of Paris, Austria, France, and Britain signed a separate treaty to establish further guarantees for the independence and integrity of the Ottoman Empire.[14] They agreed that they would consider actions against the independence and integrity of the empire as a *casus belli*.[15] The strategic competition between the great powers made a provision in the treaty prohibiting any state from trying to increase its influence over the Ottoman Empire at the expense of another. The security guarantees (which eventually failed) that accompanied the Ottoman Empire's admission to the Concert of Europe and European international public law aimed to sustain a balance of power between Russia and Britain by checking Russian power.[16]

Second, in addition to the overriding strategic rather than cultural concerns that dictated the inclusion of the Ottoman Empire in the Concert of Europe and European international public law, the continuation of unequal treaties in general, and extraterritoriality in particular, further contradicts the cultural arguments. In this sense, the

[14] The Treaty Guaranteeing the Independence and Integrity of the Ottoman Empire: Austria, France, and Britain. Great Britain, *Parliamentary Papers* (1856 [Volume 61]; 444–445).

[15] Even though Russia used extraterritoriality to extend its jurisdiction over Orthodox Christian subjects of the empire, participants in the Paris Conference did not think extraterritoriality prevented their objectives of protecting the independence and territorial integrity of the empire. Capitulations were the basis of foreign intervention.

[16] Stivachtis (1998: 82–88).

admission of the Ottoman Empire into European international society was premature, because it had not yet attained the standard of "civilization" that would allow Europeans to accept Ottoman jurisdiction over Western foreigners. Thus, while being admitted into the European concert, the Ottoman Empire did not merit the status of an equal. Meanwhile, the European states demanded that the Ottomans implement more reforms to conform to European standards. The result was a series of long-term reforms that enabled the Turkish state to modernize and meet the standards set by the European powers.[17]

Making the cultural arguments even more questionable, English School scholars disagree among themselves about when the European states perceived the Ottoman Empire/Turkey to be a member of international society. In the English School's main study, *The Expansion of International Society,* historian Thomas Naff distinguishes between de facto and the formal induction of the empire into international society. He dates 1799 as the de facto membership year due to the Ottoman Empire's alliance with Russia and Great Britain following the French invasion of Egypt. This membership became codified and took a de jure quality in between 1840, when a convention was signed by Britain, Russia, Austria, and Prussia assuring the sultan the protection of the signatory powers against Egypt, to 1856, when the great powers signed the Treaty of Paris.

The paradigmatic case of the Ottoman Empire turns into the most problematic case under further examination. Most significantly, Hedley Bull, whose approach to international society became very influential in the English School, is also unclear about when the Ottoman Empire became a member of international society. Bull agrees with the 1856 date for the de facto statement for the Ottoman admission into the European system. Yet he recognizes that most European leaders and lawyers continued to regard the empire as outside of international society.[18] Nevertheless, Bull thrice cites 1856 as the membership date without much elaboration. He then notes that 1923 may be a better date. The mention of a second date of 1923, which marks the transformation of the Ottoman Empire into the

[17] Lewis (1968).
[18] Bull (1979: 14, 32).

Republic of Turkey, suggests that the Ottoman Empire never was part of international society.[19]

Cultural arguments overstate the Ottoman Empire's exclusion from European international society to justify and explain the continuation of extraterritoriality in the Ottoman Empire. The Ottoman Empire *was* enmeshed in European society beyond just sharing a few interests, principles, and norms. The Ottoman political and diplomatic integration, however, did not cause the abolition of extraterritoriality. Nor did the formal declaration of the Treaty of Paris, in which the Ottoman Empire became part of European international public law, bring about the abolition of extraterritoriality. While European imperialism and hypocrisy were in part to blame for the inconsistency, in one crucial way the Ottoman Empire differed from its European counterparts: It lacked legal institutionalization compatible with a positive legal order. Although the Ottoman conformity with the norms, institutions, and principles of international society in general influenced European public perception of the Ottoman Empire's place in Europe, the Ottoman legal reforms mattered more in European states' policies regarding extraterritoriality.

Likewise, the European power politics was not a determinative force in the abolition of extraterritoriality. Although strategic competition over the Ottoman Empire was intense, one issue remained outside of strategic competition: extraterritoriality. In response to the Ottoman Empire's demands for the abolition of extraterritoriality, Western states united. In other words, strategic differences did not prevent European powers from acting together on the issue of extraterritoriality. European states offered strikingly similar justifications for keeping extraterritoriality: the inefficiency of the Ottoman Empire's legal system to clarify and enforce legal and property rights. At the 1856 Paris Conference they coordinated their demands for legal and administrative reforms as a condition for the abolition of extraterritoriality.[20] This united Western front persisted despite the changed strategic environment facing the Ottoman Empire and European powers. This suggests that extraterritoriality was more a matter of European versus Ottoman interaction than a venue for European interstate rivalries.

19 Bull (1979: 32).

20 Baumgart (1981: 125–128).

OTTOMAN EMPIRE'S DOMESTIC LEGALIZATION

While cultural and strategic elements are important to understand the background conditions of the negotiations and the eventual abolition of extraterritoriality, Ottoman legal institutionalization is the centerpiece. From early on, Western states demanded legal institutionalization in the Ottoman Empire/Turkey as a condition for the abolition of extraterritoriality. This demand was consistent with the precepts of positive law. In addition, state clarification and enforcement of property rights became increasingly important as the Ottoman economy integrated into the world capitalist system.[21] The protection of Western merchants' legal and commercial rights as guaranteed by extraterritoriality was vital for this economic integration. Using extraterritoriality, Western states forced the Ottoman Empire to open new markets and investment opportunities to Western business. Western states would abolish this system only when they were assured that a new system would safeguard Western business interests in the empire while increasing Western merchants' access to Ottoman markets. The Ottoman Empire's legal institutionalization as sanctioned by the Western states would bring additional benefit of further opening of the Ottoman markets.

Legal Reorganization and Reform

The Ottoman Empire attempted to institutionalize state law throughout the nineteenth century. Although some legal reforms, like the establishment of the nascent Ministry of Justice (under the name of the Department of Juridical Ordinances) in 1838 preceded this,[22] modern Ottoman legal reforms started with the Imperial Edict of 1839. The edict inaugurated what Ottoman historians call the Reorganization Period (Tanzimat). The Imperial Edict of 1839 (*Gülhane Fermanı*) and the Reform Edict of 1856 (*İslahat Fermanı*) set forth the principles of the state-building reforms of the period. These edicts stressed legal reforms vital to administrative reorganization. During this period, the first modern Ottoman codes were enacted, and state courts and legal hierarchy were established. Yet, the reforms fell short in legal institutionalization: State, religious, and communal law continued to

[21] Kasaba (1988).
[22] Lewis (1968: 99).

overlap, thwarting the progress of legal reforms based on positivist European models. These persistent legal ambiguities prevented the much awaited rationalization of legal and property rights. Contrary to the reformers' expectations, the reforms had paradoxically furthered legal fragmentation in the empire, rather than ending it.

The Imperial Edict of 1839 listed three broad areas of necessary reforms: the protection of life and property, the establishment of a fair tax system, and a new conscription procedure. The Edict suggested that compiling the existing laws, writing new laws, and then publishing the laws in code books would prevent injustice and disorder. Without new laws to protect life and property, there would be "neither strength, nor richness, nor happiness, nor tranquility for the Empire," the Edict stated.[23] For the protection of life and property, the Edict suggested that all trials would be public and based on a presumption of innocence. More specifically, the state would leave the civil law to religious courts but would establish state courts for commercial and criminal cases. The Ottoman government would publish and distribute commercial codes, penal codes, and procedural codes. The government would also reform the prison and police systems and locate police stations and prisons throughout the empire.

Following the 1839 Edict, the Ottoman rulers intensified their efforts for legal codification. The Ottoman Supreme Council, responsible for codification, published a partial criminal code in 1840 and a partial commercial code in 1850. However, three problems limited the effectiveness of these early attempts at ending legal ambiguities. First, the early Ottoman "codes" were collections of vague precepts rather than precise rules of punishments and procedures. The precepts were not specific enough to adequately clarify legal and property rights. Second, the codification was incomplete. The empire lacked a constitution and a civil code,[24] and the penal code and commercial code

[23] For the text of the 1839 Edict, see Hurewitz (1956: 113–116). For recent discussions on the impact of the 1839 Edict on Turkish political development see Yıldız (1992) and Akyıldız (1993).

[24] The first Ottoman Constitution, the Constitution of 1876, operated for a year and was suspended until 1908. An incomplete civil code (*Mecelle*) was issued between 1870 and 1877. "*[Mecelle]* had the force of law and was applied as the civil code of the Ottoman Empire; however, it was not a code in the strict sense, because it was not a complete and exclusive statement of law as it existed at the time of the codification, but rather a nonexclusive digest of existing rules of Islamic law" (Onar: 295).

remained incomplete, lacking statutes in areas of penal and commercial law that religious law explicitly addressed. Both the unclear and incomplete nature of Ottoman codes echo similar situations in the early attempts at legal codification in Japan and China. However, unlike the early Japanese and Chinese legal reformers, the Ottoman reformers had a unique problem: religious law. The Ottoman codes accepted the supremacy of the (uncodified) religious law. Should the provisions of the codes and religious law conflict, the judges were to follow the latter. Making matters worse, due to the absence of a clear legal hierarchy and appellate system, prospective litigants engaged in venue shopping by taking secular courts' decisions to the religious courts. These religious courts were an especially attractive option for parties that were found liable in secular courts, as the former had the authority to repeal decisions of the latter.[25]

The 1856 Edict repeated the promises made in 1839, which suggests that the earlier promises of reform remained unfulfilled. The 1856 Edict was the outcome of negotiations between the representatives of the Ottoman Empire and its allies during the Crimean War (Britain, France, and Austria). The Ottoman Empire and the Allies agreed on the need for administrative reforms in the Empire. Their goal was to prevent Russia from raising the issue of extraterritorial protections for Orthodox subjects of the empire at the Paris Conference, using the excuse of Ottoman administrative failures. The sultan proclaimed the Edict just prior to the Paris Conference. Despite the involvement of European representatives in the preparation of the 1856 Edict, it is largely a copy of the 1839 Edict, especially the sections regarding the legal and administrative reforms to be made in the Empire.[26] The 1856 Paris Treaty referred to the Reform Edict of 1856, thereby making the Ottoman promises for reforms internationally binding for the Ottoman Empire.[27]

The 1856 Edict reinvigorated the codification movement. The Ottoman Supreme Council used French codes to revise the 1840 Criminal Code in 1858 and the 1850 Commercial Code in 1860. This

[25] The conflicts of religious law and new codes led to the establishment of the Office of Judicial Ordinances (*Divan-ı Ahkam-ı Adliye*). Yet, absent judicial procedures and a constitution, the office tended to follow uncodified religious principles as opposed to a higher state-based law.

[26] For the text of the 1856 Edict, see Hurewitz (1956: 149–153).

[27] Baumgart (1981: 126–128).

codification, however, did not succeed as a legal standardization and systemization due to the fact that religious and communal law continued to operate independently of state law. The Ottoman policy of leaving "local indigenous laws intact"[28] led to a communal system, known as the millet system, in which non-Muslim communities established self-rule.[29] Self-rule included the rights of these communities to establish institutions that organized the education, taxation, and judicial issues of their communities under the authority of each community's highest religious authorities. These communal law systems, particular to non-Muslim communities, survived alongside the *Sharía* laws applicable over Muslims with minimum state control. Taken as a whole, all these problems show that, in spite of all the codification attempts during the Reorganization Period, Ottoman law remained fragmented between the state and various religious and communual entities and the hierarchy between the laws of these different entities remained contested.

The absence of a legal hierarchy further complicated the issue of legal fragmentation. The Empire lacked a formal appellate system and a supervising justice department. During the Reorganization Period, courts of different legal systems worked as courts of first instances applying different rules to solve similar disputes. The first appellate court in the Ottoman Empire was created in 1873 by the Ottoman government to establish the state's formal control over courts and to unify legal interpretations.[30] Its primary jurisdiction was over Islamic and state courts. Yet the role of the appellate court created an enduring conflict between the Department of Juridical Ordinances (the emerging Ministry of Justice) and the office of *Şeyhülislam* (the highest-ranking Islamic authority). This conflict lasted until the abolition of the religious courts in 1924. The absence of an appellate system until 1873 and the ensuing precarious position of the appellate system at the juncture of religious and state authority claims marked the limits of the Ottoman Empire's legal institutionalization.[31]

[28] Örücü (1992: 39).

[29] For the millet system see Bozkurt (1989, 1998) and Eryılmaz (1990, 1992).

[30] Berkes (1998) calls this a "bifurcated legal system."

[31] Aydın (2007).

TABLE 5. *Competing Legal Systems in the Ottoman Empire*

Court System	Jurisdiction	Issues	Highest Authority
Islamic Courts[a]	Muslims	Civil/Commercial/ Criminal[b]	Highest Ranking Ulema (*Şeyhülislam*)
Communal Courts	Non-Muslim Communities (Millets)	Civil/Commercial/ Criminal	Highest-ranking religious authority of each community
Consular Courts	Foreigners	Civil/Commercial/ Criminal	Embassies
Mixed (commercial) Courts (1840)[c]	Mixed	Commercial	Ministry of Commerce
Secular Courts (1870)[d]	Muslims	Commercial/ Criminal	Ministry of Justice

[a] Until the second half of the nineteenth century, the religious courts operated in the houses of the religious judges (*kadis*), not in official buildings. Starting with the relocation of the religious judge of Istanbul in 1837 to state offices, the operation of religious courts in private spaces started to change. See Cin and Akgündüz (1989: 326). Operation of the religious courts in judges' houses as opposed to the state's offices also suggests the lack of state authority over the legal system.

[b] The Ottoman government initiated a series of reforms in 1859, 1867, and 1871 to clarify the jurisdiction of religious courts. See Cin and Akgündüz (1989: 327–328). Yet, the ambiguous boundaries of religious law defied clarification of Islamic, mixed, and secular courts.

[c] Berkes (1998: 161–162) and Liebesny (1955: 328).

[d] The Turkish name of these courts is *Nizamiye Mahkemeleri*.

The impetus for the Ottoman legal reform was not solely – or even primarily – an external one; in important ways the drive to reform was a rational response to stop Ottoman disintegration and decay in the nineteenth century. Frequent European interventions, growing budget deficits, and increasing local and ethnic unrest in the provinces all contributed to the sense of urgency for legal reforms. The Ottomans were aware that the reinvigoration of the Empire depended on modernization of state institutions for increasing state revenues and for bolstering the domestic and international legitimacy of Ottoman rule. The nineteenth-century reformist bureaucrats recognized extensive legal reforms as essential components of modernization. In their quest for legal reforms, the modernizing bureaucrats faced pockets of domestic resistance: Local notables, away from the imperial center, had previously shared legal authority with the central government and did not welcome the central government's legal encroachment; religious communities organized under the millet system feared the legal reforms would erode their communal strength; ethno-nationalist groups perceived the legal reforms as a threat to their goal of having their own state; the *ulema* perceived secularization of law as eviscerating Islamic law and replacing the *ulema* with a new corps of judges. The politics of Ottoman legal reforms reveal three lessons about the relationship between extraterritoriality and legal institutionalization.

The first of these lessons is about the role of ideas: Cultural claims that the Japanese were unique in their ability to internalize the ideas of westernization are flawed. Earlier than their Japanese counterparts, the Ottoman rulers realized both the necessity and desirability of a legal reorganization based on European models. Particularly during the reorganization period, the westernizing elite were the leading force behind legal reorganization. The intellectual history of Meiji and Tanzimat elites reveal some striking similarities. These similarities led historian Cemil Aydın to conclude that the Ottoman and Japanese elites' stances of westernism and antiwesternism were in large part caused by the contradictions and inconsistency of Western policies rather than the cultural or domestic differences of these states.[32] However, in contrast to the Meiji elite, the Tanzimat elite faced greater challenges. These Ottoman reformers inherited structural and institutional, rather than cultural and ideational, constraints on their attempts for modernization.

The second lesson regarding the relationship between extraterritoriality and legalization concerns domestic politics. In their state-building efforts Ottoman reformist bureaucrats had domestic allies as well as rivals. Imperialism and its most salient symbol, extraterritoriality, became a focal point for the development of groups that demanded the Ottoman government end extraterritoriality. Both the earlier liberal Young Ottoman group and later ethnic Young Turk group grew in popularity using the issue of extraterritoriality. The

[32] Aydın (2007).

Ottoman government harnessed these nationalist antiextraterritoriality sentiments to justify its legal reforms based on European models. Thus, the reformers argued that the legal reforms were necessary "to limit the jurisdiction of the foreign tribunals."[33] Framing the issue in this way made it difficult for the state's domestic rivals, who were the immediate targets of the reform, to oppose the reforms. The establishment of the commercial courts, which significantly reduced the *ulema*'s legal power, illustrates how Ottoman rulers framed their legal reforms as necessary acts for the eventual abolition of extraterritoriality.[34] Cevdet Pasha, the head of the Department of the Rules of Justice, argued that adopting European codes was a requirement because European governments were demanding that the Ottoman government "bring forth your code; let us see it and make it known to our subjects"[35] as a condition for accepting Ottoman jurisdiction over their citizens. While legal reformers were often able to reduce the resistance of religious groups, they sometimes needed to compromise. For example, the resistance of the *ulema,* as well as divisions within the reformist elite, prevented the adoption of the French Civil Code. The resulting compromise was the creation of a Turkish Civil Code based on *Sharía,* known as Mecelle.[36]

The third lesson one can draw from the relationship between extraterritoriality and legal institutionalization in the Ottoman case is that the Western influence on the Ottoman legal institutionalization was often negative. In contrast to cultural arguments that tend to embrace the European influence as a "civilizing" one, European involvement in the empire was often harmful for the reforms and

[33] Liebesny (1955: 327–329).

[34] Liebesny (1955: 328) and Örücü (1992: 44).

[35] Berkes (1998: 166–167).

[36] Berkes (1998: 168), also Liebesny (1995, 332). Liebesny links the Ottoman legal development to extraterritoriality: "Historically, however, the capitulations have been an important factor in the legal development of the region once included in the Ottoman Empire. They were one avenue through which Western legal thought and legal procedure were introduced. Also, since the capitulatory rights came to be felt in the nineteenth century as an infringement of sovereignty, they felt a stimulant for judicial reform, since modernization and reform of the judicial system were one way to prove that the capitulations were no longer needed to protect the European merchant from the possible abuses of local courts. The capitulations can thus be regarded as one of the factors which induced the Ottoman Empire and Egypt to adopt continental European codes and procedure and to endeavor to follow European standards in the administration of justice."

Ottoman modernization in large part due to the contradictions in Western policies: While Europeans were demanding legal institutionalization and standardization, they were simultaneously reluctant to give up the legal privileges of extraterritoriality, making it difficult for the Ottoman Empire to raise state revenues and complete its legal institutionalization. From a broader perspective, the Europeans seemed to agree that, while the collapse of the Ottoman Empire was undesirable, so was its revival.[37]

From the Paris Conference to the "Istanbul Conference"

During the Paris Conference, Western states and the Ottoman Empire discussed the abolition of extraterritoriality as a part of the Ottoman Empire's entrance into European public law.[38] Referring to the 1856 Edict, the French Foreign Minister Count Walewski linked the modification of extraterritoriality to administrative, particularly judicial, reforms. The Austrian Foreign Minister Count Buol supported the regulation of commercial relations, but argued that such readjustment should take the acquired rights of the foreigners into consideration. The prime minister of Sardinia, Count de Cavour, argued that the existence of different commercial regulations for different foreign merchant communities made commercial transactions difficult.[39]

The Ottoman representative Ali Pasha also linked the commercial difficulties of the foreign merchant communities to the existence of extraterritoriality. He demanded the revision of extraterritoriality because it limited the Ottoman Empire's jurisdiction over foreigners and commercial transactions. This limited jurisdiction prevented the Ottoman Empire from providing security to foreigners and hindered the development of foreigners' economic rights. Furthermore, Pasha claimed that extraterritoriality "constitutes a multiplicity of Governments within the Government, and, consequently, an insuperable obstacle to all improvements" at which the Ottoman reforms aimed.[40]

[37] Hanioğlu (2008) offers an insightful overview of Ottoman-European relations in the nineteenth century.

[38] Protocols (1856: 13, 39, 58). For a contemporary discussion about the Paris Conference of 1856 within the context of Ottoman-European relations, see Mitzen (2005).

[39] Protocols (1856: 58).

[40] Protocols (1856: 59).

The representatives recognized the "harmful" effects of extraterritoriality for the Ottoman Empire's administrative reforms and indicated that extraterritoriality's circumscription of the Ottoman Empire's jurisdiction was unacceptable. While Western states agreed to modify extraterritoriality in principle, they seem to link it to Ottoman administrative and legal reforms. As one European representative stated, change in extraterritoriality should follow "the reforms which Turkey is introducing into her administration, so as to combine the guarantees necessary for foreigners ..."[41] The representatives also agreed that there should be changes in extraterritoriality with the new position of the Ottoman Empire in international society. But again they emphasized that these changes ought to take the interests of both the Ottoman government and foreign communities into account. They thus decided to convene a multilateral conference on extraterritoriality in the Ottoman Empire.[42]

The conference never took place. Yet, four sets of evidence after the Paris Conference indicate that even if the parties had met, the proposed "Istanbul Conference on Extraterritoriality" would have rejected the abolition of extraterritoriality in the Ottoman Empire because of the Ottoman legal and administrative problems, which in part were caused by extraterritoriality. These four sets of evidence are: British Foreign Office discussions on extraterritoriality, Edmund Hornby's report to the foreign office about the Ottoman legal system, discussions about the Ottoman Land Law and the partial extension of Ottoman jurisdiction over foreigners in 1863–1867, and a U.S. State Department report on extraterritoriality in 1880.

Foreign Office Discussions on Extraterritoriality

In October 1859 and February 1867, Western states collectively gave memoranda to the Ottoman government complaining about the progress of the application of the reforms that the 1856 Edict had promised.[43] The 1867 memorandum included detailed conditions for Ottoman legal reforms.[44] The memoranda indicate both the Ottoman

[41] Protocols (1856: 59).

[42] Protocols (1856: 59). Also see Hinckey (1906: 188) and Soosa (1931: 342).

[43] Since the Treaty of Paris referred to the 1856 Edict, the European states claimed that the promises of the edict were binding on the Ottoman Empire.

[44] Lewis (1968: 119–121).

Empire's failure in carrying out legal reforms and Western states' assertion for the necessity of legal reform in the Ottoman Empire. Yet Western demands for legal reforms were at cross purposes with the desire of these states to retain extraterritorial privileges in the Ottoman Empire. According to the Ottoman rulers, Western insistence on keeping extraterritoriality was a major obstacle in implementing the Ottoman legal reforms.

For instance, when the Ottoman Prime Minister Ali Pasha complained about extraterritoriality limiting Ottoman jurisdiction and subverting its legal reforms, the British Ambassador Sir William Bulwer directly related the abolition of extraterritoriality to the Ottoman government's legal reforms. Bulwer explained this in a letter to Lord J. Russell, British minister of foreign affairs, in 1859. Although Bulwer supported the idea of reforming extraterritoriality, he rejected the possibility of abolishing extraterritoriality given the situation of the Ottoman legal system. He reported that although codes and new tribunals had limited rulers' arbitrary actions somewhat, the judicial reforms had failed to improve the legal system. Bulwer argued that the abolition of extraterritoriality could come gradually, after the Ottoman Empire had established adequate judicial institutions.[45]

In response to the complaints of Ali Pasha, Bulwer, in a separate report to the foreign office, suggested that European countries could initiate reforms in the Ottoman Empire by establishing mixed courts with a single code. These mixed courts could replace the diverse state-specific extraterritoriality. The proposed single extraterritorial system would be a model for Turkey to imitate.[46] Like the earlier reports, this one linked extraterritoriality to Ottoman legal reforms. While it was not implemented in the Ottoman Empire, Western states established mixed courts with a jurisdiction over all Western foreigners in China, Thailand, Iran, and Egypt. Mixed courts were cost-effective alternatives to state-specific extraterritoriality because they reduced the non-Western complaints about extraterritorial inefficiencies, strengthened the Western collaboration on extraterritoriality, and reduced legal transaction costs for cases between extraterritorial foreigners.

[45] FO 881/998 (1859–1861: 1–5).

[46] FO 881/998 (1859–1861).

Edmund Hornby's Reports on the Ottoman Legal System

Wary of the problems extraterritoriality had produced but unwilling to accept Ottoman jurisdiction, the British government decided to reorganize its own consular courts to prevent the abuses about which the Ottoman government had complained. Following the Paris Treaty, the British government appointed Edmund Hornby to reorganize and reform the British extraterritorial system in the Ottoman Empire. Hornby established new procedures for the appointments of consuls. He also suggested the creation of the British Supreme Court at Istanbul. The British government accepted Hornby's plans for reorganization and appointed him chief judge of the British Supreme Court at Istanbul in 1857. Through Hornby's reports, the British judged the Ottoman legal system. Hornby's reports suggested that the practical application of the Ottoman legal reforms was causing more legal fragmentation and ambiguities, rather than bringing legal unification and clarification.[47]

In an 1859 report, Hornby again observed that the Ottoman judicial reforms remained limited in practice and the new codes and courts did not function properly. For example, the religious courts continued to apply uncodified *Sharía*, and the jurisdiction of the new state courts remained unclear. Some courts, such as courts of second instance, which had been established to satisfy European demands, did not have any jurisdictional power at all.[48]

In another report, Hornby complained about the lack of educated judges to apply the codes. Hornby indicated that the Ottoman government's adoption of the French legal system had created some difficulties, as the French legal system required judges with a "refined legal education" to apply the codes.[49] Hornby's assessment of the problems of the judicial system touched on several other areas. He noticed the fragmented nature of the Ottoman judicial system and suggested centralizing the court structure under a new ministry of justice to prevent jurisdictional ambiguities.[50] Hornby also reported on the operation of

47 Edmund Hornby reorganized the British consular courts in the Levant and then reorganized the British consular courts in China and Japan. For his autobiography, see Hornby (1928).

48 FO 881/998 (1859–1861: 6–7).

49 Mr. Hornby to the Earl of Malmesbury, December 6, 1858. See FO 881/981 (1858).

50 Hornby was skeptical of the legal reforms. In his memoir he states: "At the same time, my Lord, it is useless to disguise the fact that Turkish Government will resist

Turkish civil (religious) courts, arguing that "justice is, in fact, administered haphazardly" with the "entire absence of either procedure or rules of evidence" and with prejudice to foreigners:

> In perhaps sixty, or even seventy, cases out of a hundred it is practically administered, but here is no surety of a clear or a just case being adjudicated upon properly. Nobody knows the law which is about to be applied; it is to be found nowhere, because, in deed, it exists nowhere, until the Judge twists a sentence in the Koran, or a clause in the Code de Commerce, or dovetails the one into the other, for the purpose of creating an authority for a decision upon a case which not improbably depends entirely upon a question of fact, or upon the comparative value or testimony, and has nothing to do with either the religious law or the law of commerce.[51]

Hornby also examined new Ottoman commercial courts where Ottoman and Western judges would decide together in cases that involved foreigners if these foreigners opted for Ottoman commercial courts rather than extraterritorial courts. He supported the idea in principle but argued that these courts "have proved failures in a practical point of view, because they lack the essential elements which are necessary to the constitution of all Courts of Justice – namely, a system of laws and procedure, and competent judges to administer them." He thus concluded that these courts were not suitable for commercial transactions between locals and foreign traders. Hornby also examined the criminal law, police, and prison systems, surmising that these systems were inefficient in protecting foreigners in the Empire.[52]

The British ambassador, Sir William Bulwer, and the chief judge of the Supreme Court, Edmund Hornby, linked the abolition of extraterritoriality to Ottoman legal reforms. To justify extraterritoriality

to the last anything like practical reform. They will continue to promise everything. Commissions will be formed; codes will be undertaken, but nothing, however slight in the way of practical change in details, will be voluntarily submitted to. The Turkish Government knows perfectly well that the larger and more comprehensive the change that they promise, the longer will be the delay – the greater the difficulty in rendering whatever, a long lapse of time, may be ultimately accomplished, applicable to the country and people, – and the greater the chances also of exciting a difference of opinion between the Western Powers, and these differences nobody knows better than the Turkish Government how to promote and foster." FO 881/981 (1858: 24).

[51] FO 881/981 (1858: 27).

[52] FO 881/981 (1858: 34).

in the face of increasing Ottoman complaints, the British produced reports identifying instances of abuse, inefficiencies, and delays within the Ottoman legal system. These reports compared the Ottoman legal system with an idealized positivist legal system, and thus concluded that the Ottoman Empire was failing to reorganize and reform its judicial system. The reports of the U.S. State Department were similar to these British reports.

The U.S. State Department Report on Extraterritoriality

A U.S. State Department report, written in 1880 by Edward Van Dyck, a consular clerk of the United States at Cairo, linked the maintenance of extraterritoriality to the failure of the Ottoman government's legal reforms, particularly in the area of commercial law.[53] Even though the Ottoman government had translated and accepted the French Commercial Code in 1860,[54] the Ottoman judges were unable to apply the code because they lacked "knowledge of foreign laws and the application of private international law." Rather than applying the commercial code, the report stated, the Ottoman judges tended to reduce commercial issues to civil law issues and then apply customary and religious law. The American report argued against any transfer of jurisdiction over foreigners to the Ottoman government because such a transfer would sharply curtail foreigners' commercial activities by limiting their access to the Ottoman markets without legal safeguards.[55]

The report then listed five conditions for the abolition of extraterritoriality:[56] 1) a judicial system similar to western legal systems; 2) easily comprehensible; 3) a system of courts for the impartial applications of the codes; 4) well-educated judges; and 5) a stable political order. The report ends with the statement of a British consul: "As soon as ever the Turkish Government really reforms its administration, the [system of extraterritoriality] will fall of [itself]."[57]

Discussions within the foreign office, Edmund Hornby's report, and the State Department's report all agree on two issues. The level

[53] Dyck (1880: 37).
[54] Revised version of the 1850 Commercial Code.
[55] Dyck (1880: 38).
[56] Dyck (1880: 40).
[57] Dyck (1880: 44).

of Ottoman legal institutionalization in the 1860s and 1870s was not sufficient for any transfer of jurisdiction to the Ottoman government. Any transfer of authority over foreigners required further Ottoman legal institutionalization. In addition, discussions about the right of foreigners to acquire real property provides further empirical evidence to suggest that the existence of a land code, which would open the land market to Western merchants, was a prerequisite for Western states' acceptance of Ottoman partial jurisdiction over foreigners.

Ottoman Land Law and Extraterritoriality

In the 1860s, a new land law became the focus of debates and negotiations about the transfer of jurisdiction over Western foreigners from Western states to the Ottoman government. The new law was to address the conditions under which foreigners had the right to acquire real property in the Ottoman Empire. Such laws were of particular interest to foreigners because land markets were the only major part of the Ottoman economy outside of Europeans economic influence. Debate and negotiations surrounding the new land law illustrate one key condition under which Western states were willing to accept Ottoman jurisdiction over Western foreigners. Such jurisdiction must be accompanied by legal institutionalization of property rights.

In the Ottoman Empire, private property rights for land were limited. Ottoman land regulations were based on customary law, and the government held title to commercial lands. The government leased the land to Ottoman subjects for renewable three-year contracts; customary law regulated the transfer of leases. In this system foreigners could not hold any property. Both the Ottoman restrictions and the lack of a land code to regularize the transfer of lands prevented the commercialization of land. The ambassadors of Western states[58] gave a joint memorandum to the Ottoman government in February 1862 demanding the removal of the Ottoman government's restrictions on foreigners acquiring real property. Western states claimed that the Ottoman government had promised the removal of such restrictions at the 1856 Paris Conference.

Unable to resist Western demands for the liberalization of the land market, but not willing to see extraterritorial foreigners' domination

[58] These states were France, England, Prussia, Russia, and Austria.

of the land market with their legal and tax privileges, the Ottoman government linked the removal of the traditional land restrictions to the abolition of extraterritoriality. In a counternote, Ali Pasha argued that the promise made in Paris regarding foreigners' rights to acquire real property was contingent on modifications to extraterritoriality. In response, the Western states argued for the compatibility of foreigners' rights to acquire real property and extraterritoriality. The four-year-long discussions (1863–1867) between the Ottoman Empire and Western states produced the Ottoman Land Code of 1867. The Land Code commercialized the Ottoman land system. The Ottoman government assumed absolute jurisdiction over commercial transactions of real property. The empire would apply the land code as well as land taxes equally to foreigners and Ottomans. The Ottoman government would enforce the land code uniformly in secular civil courts, not in religious courts.[59] In other words, European states accepted partial Ottoman jurisdiction over foreigners in exchange for Ottoman domestic legalization that also expanded Western trade and investment opportunities in the Ottoman Empire.

The extension of partial Ottoman jurisdiction over foreigners was the single success in the Ottoman Empire's elusive quest for sovereignty in the nineteenth century. While similar Ottoman legal reforms of the Reorganization Period led to the emergence of state law, the reforms did not decisively challenge religious and communal legal authority structures. Rather than unifying the legal systems under the state's judicial hierarchy, the legal reforms of the reorganization period introduced an additional legal system, thereby increasing the legal fragmentation in the Ottoman Empire[60] and giving further reason to European powers to maintain extraterritoriality.

WORLD WAR I AND THE CHANGING INTERNATIONAL ENVIRONMENT

Neither Article 7 of the Treaty of Paris nor the earlier agreements among the great powers to guarantee the independence and integrity of the Ottoman Empire restrained the competition over the declining

[59] Gönen (2004).
[60] Örücü (1992: 48–50).

Ottoman Empire. In the political maneuvering prior to the First World War, the empire lost nearly all its territories in the Balkans and North Africa to different great powers and their newly independent allies that seceded from the empire. Yet the great powers continued to act together on the issue of extraterritoriality. When the Ottoman Empire tried to use the abolition of extraterritoriality strategically in its neutrality and alliance negotiations, none of the great powers accepted the Turkish offer. Even when the Ottoman government unilaterally declared the end of extraterritoriality in the Ottoman Empire, not only its enemies (France, Britain, and Italy) but also its allies (Germany and Austria) protested and rejected the Ottoman Empire's right to unilaterally end extraterritoriality.

The empire's survival became threatened following the end of the First World War. The Allies occupied Istanbul in 1919 and the Greek army occupied İzmir and western Turkey in order to make the Turkish nationalists, headquartered in Ankara, accept the conditions of the punitive Sèvres Treaty of 1920.[61] Thwarting the Allies' plans, the Turkish nationalist forces defeated Greece in 1922 and challenged the Allies' forces at the Dardanelles and İzmit (near Istanbul) in what is known as the Chanak Crisis in September 1922. Both the First World War and the ensuing Greco-Turkish war had an enormous impact on the Ottoman Empire. Most dramatically, these wars transformed the multiethnic, multireligious, and multicultural Ottoman Empire into a Turkish nation-state. A decade of war allowed the nationalist Republican elite to consolidate its control over the country and to prepare for its large-scale state-building reforms in the 1920s. Legal reorganization was the centerpiece of these state-building efforts, but the changes in Turkey's international environment were equally drastic.

Turkish historiography argues that the nationalist victory under Mustafa Kemal (later Mustafa Kemal Atatürk) in 1922 against British-sponsored Greek forces caused the Allies to acquiesce to numerous Turkish demands, including the abolition of extraterritoriality.[62] The argument that a powerful Turkey, fresh from defeating the Greeks, deterred the Allies from imposing the Sèvres Treaty of 1920 and thus led to the abolition of extraterritoriality is implausible. To begin, the

[61] Churchill (1929: 373–465), Nicolson (1974 [1934]).
[62] For an example of Turkish historiography, see Eroğlu (1967: 170–176).

Allies dictated the terms of treaty on a number of issues, including reparations, the future of Northern Iraq and eastern Thrace, and the security of and navigation through the Dardanelles and Bosphorus. If the Turkish military were powerful enough to convince the Allies to abolish extraterritoriality, one would expect that Turkey would not have conceded on other issues. Furthermore, Lord Curzon, the British chief negotiator, threatened İsmet Pasha (later İsmet İnönü), the Turkish chief negotiator, with the possibility of war if the Turkish side would not accept the judicial arrangements the Allies demanded. Throughout the conference, there was no instance in which the Turkish side threatened the use of military force if the Allies would not concede.

Despite a perceived weakness of Turkey, several factors limited the Allies' option for military action. The Turkish-Greek War of 1920–1922 and the subsequent Turkish victory coincided with the demobilization of the Allies' armies following the First World War. A war with Turkey seemed to be a real possibility because British Prime Minister Lloyd George had encouraged Greece to occupy western Turkey to impose the conditions of the Treaty of Sèvres. The demobilization and public antipathy toward a new war (antiwar meetings occurred in various British cities) made any potential mobilization seem very costly to the government.[63] The Dominions also did not support the war: Canada, Australia, and South Africa rejected the demands of War Minister Winston Churchill for mobilization. Churchill wrote to Prime Minister Lloyd George of the possibility of war with Turkey that "with military resources which the Cabinet have cut to the most weak and slender proportions, we are leading the Allies in an attempt to enforce a peace on Turkey which would require a great deal and powerful armies and long, costly operations and occupations."[64] The majority of the press and some members of Parliament, including the conservative members of the coalition government, accused Lloyd George and his war minister, Winston Churchill, of bringing Britain to the verge of a war with the Turkish nationalists. The ensuing collapse of Lloyd George's pro-Greek and prowar government in October 1922 and the establishment of Bonar

[63] For a similar argument, see Zurcher (1993: 169).

[64] Churchill (1929: 401).

Law's antiwar government just days before the Lausanne Conference were at least attributable to the public concern about a bellicose foreign policy. Reflecting the public's antiwar position, Bonar Law promised not to use military means to force Turkey to reinstate extraterritoriality.[65]

Given that Turkey had conceded to issues that the War Office claimed were major British objectives in Turkey, such as the demilitarization of the Dardanelles and Bosphorus and preventing Turkish control over Northern Iraq,[66] the British government did not perceive extraterritoriality to be an issue worth the cost of mobilizing an army and fighting a war.[67] This lack of resolve contributed to the Allies' acquiescence to end extraterritoriality in exchange for judicial guarantees from the Turkish government.

Besides a Turkish victory over the Greeks, there is another power-politics argument, which was raised most strongly by Nasim Sousa. He attributes the Allies' decision to abolish extraterritoriality in 1923 to the lack of unity among the Allies.[68] However, contrary to Sousa's arguments, the Western states were united on the issue of extraterritoriality. The First World War changed Turkey's strategic environment. German defeat, the Russian Revolution, American isolation, and the French and Italian alliance made Britain the most powerful country in the Middle East.

The Soviet Union's cooperation bolstered the Turkish nationalist government's confidence against Britain. Starting with the Congress of the Peoples of the East in 1920, the Bolsheviks provided strong political and ideological support for the non-Western struggle against imperialism. The final declaration of the Congress included many praising references to Turkish nationalist resistance against British schemes in Turkey. Russia also financially and militarily contributed to the nationalist resistance.[69] Furthermore, the Bolsheviks were also the first to sign a diplomatic treaty with the Turkish nationalists. With

[65] DBFP (1972: 805–806, 813, 815–816, 829, 839–840).

[66] See the *Memorandum by the General Staff on the Proposed New Treaty with the Allies and Turkey*, October 19, 1922, DBFP (1972: 984–989).

[67] DBFP (1972: 805–806, 813, 815–816, 829, 839–840).

[68] Sousa (1933: 247). Referring to the legal institutionalization in the 1920s, he later observes that the reforms were adequate to protect foreigners' legal and property rights: Sousa (1933: 248).

[69] Zurcher (1993: 160).

the Treaty of Alliance of 1921, Russia abolished its extraterritoriality. The treaty depicted the Bolsheviks and the Turkish nationalists as a unified front by "the common struggle undertaken against imperialism," and it called extraterritoriality an imperialist tool incompatible with national independence and sovereignty.[70] Although Soviet Russia was not an internationally recognized power and thus its influence on other states regarding extraterritoriality remained insignificant,[71] its support to the Turkish government in the early 1920s was important. This rapprochement reduced the Turkish fears about the biggest threat to its survival since the late eighteenth century, allowed the nationalist government to transfer troops from the northeastern front to the western front where a substantial number of Greek forces and a British presence were still threatening, and bolstered the Turkish morale and determination for its resistance against Britain and its demand for the abolition of extraterritoriality.

Extraterritorial great powers supported the British position. As I describe in the next section, the Allies acted together on extraterritoriality, both during the prenegotiation phase and during the negotiations. The British, French, and Italian delegations' prenegotiation consensus was either to maintain extraterritoriality or to replace it with legal guarantees for foreigners in Turkey. During the negotiations, the Allies maintained their prenegotiation consensus. Furthermore, there is no evidence to suggest the existence of bargaining by any one of these states in order to obtain exclusive concessions in return for supporting the abolition of extraterritoriality. Last, not all extraterritorial states in Turkey participated in the Lausanne Conference. These other states would have rejected the abolition of extraterritoriality had the Allies as a group received exclusive concessions from Turkey in return for abolishing extraterritoriality. For example, the American government sent a special mission to Lausanne primarily to prevent the scenario detailed earlier. The special mission's reports to the State Department indicated that the Allies did not attempt to get exclusive concessions from Turkey in return for the abolition of extraterritoriality.[72]

70 For text of the treaty, see Hurewitz (1956 [Volume 2]: 95–97).
71 Sousa (1933: 216).
72 FRUS (1923 [Volume II]: 879–1252).

A third, and the most plausible, explanation identifies the role of powerful interest groups, or the lack thereof, in ending extraterritoriality. Organized efforts on the part of the extraterritorial groups to preserve extraterritoriality did not emerge until the Lausanne Conference. Even then the influence of the extraterritorial interest groups was limited, due to both their diminishing numbers and the political situation following the First World War. In September 1922, on the eve of the Lausanne Conference, the British Chamber of Commerce of Turkey and Balkan States protested some British parliamentarians's calls for the British government to restore complete Turkish sovereignty within the borders of Turkey. The chamber argued that the complete restoration of Turkish sovereignty required the abolition of extraterritoriality, which the chamber believed British subjects needed in order to reside and trade in Turkey.[73] On October 4th, after a two-day joint meeting in Istanbul, the British, French, and Italian Chambers of Commerce in Constantinople sent a memorandum to their respective embassies demanding the maintenance of extraterritoriality because the "security of life and property will immediately become endangered should in the smallest degree the [extraterritorality] be weakened in the protection" with respect "to the administration of justice, the inviolability of domicile and of person."[74] The next day the French Chamber of Commerce of Constantinople issued a separate memorandum, which suggested that "in order to satisfy the pride of the Turks [extraterritoriality] could be declared abolished," but its content ought to be reestablished in a different form until the reorganization of the Turkish legal system.[75]

Despite these vociferous cries, there is no evidence that these demands influenced the decisions of state rulers. Intragovernmental and intergovernmental discussions among the Allies do not reference the demands of the extraterritorial groups. There are two reasons for this absence. The First World War and the Turkish-Greek War reduced the number and influence of business and missionary groups in Turkey. State rulers were able to ignore the demands of these smaller groups. The decreasing numbers of these extraterritorial groups also reduced any potential benefits that might come from reimposition of

[73] Memorandum (1922: 9–11).
[74] Memorandum (1922: 11–12).
[75] Memorandum (1922: 12–13).

extraterritoriality. Additionally, as I discussed earlier, public opinion, especially in Britain, was against a war with Turkey. In October 1922, Lloyd George's coalition government collapsed due in part to the possibility of British involvement in a war in Turkey.

In sum, the Allies *were* united on extraterritoriality. Yet, the demobilization of the Allied armies presented a challenge for these states when they wished to reimpose extraterritoriality in Turkey following the end of the First World War. Without large standing armies, these states lacked a credible way to make threats. Last, the business and missionary communities were insignificant factors in influencing the decisions of state rulers regarding extraterritoriality due to their decreasing numbers in Turkey during and following the First World War.

THE LAUSANNE CONFERENCE

Turkish dreams of putting Western citizens and commercial interest under its jurisdiction materialized with the Lausanne Treaty. The abolition of extraterritoriality came just before the Turkish government embarked on large-scale legal reforms. The debates between the Allies and Turkey on the Turkish legal system and the judicial safeguards that the Turkish government eventually conceded reveal how domestic legalization related to the Allies' agreement to end extraterritoriality. Specifically, the abolition of extraterritoriality was contingent on the judicial safeguards for foreigners that the Turkish government put in place. The combination of the judicial safeguards and the territorial concessions that the Turkish government yielded at Lausanne explain the Allies' decision to abolish extraterritoriality.

This section is composed of four subsections. First, I argue that Turkey completed its domestic legalization in the 1920s. Second, I examine the discussions of the Lausanne Conference, at which, when facing the Turkish side's normative argument based on sovereignty, the Allies had to reconcile two powerful normative claims: extraterritoriality and sovereignty. Third, I outline how the Allies argued for the protection of foreigners' legal and property rights as a condition for abolishing extraterritoriality, countering Turkish claims based on sovereignty norms. Fourth, I examine the discussions over a "judicial declaration" that Western states requested from the Turkish government and the judicial safeguards that the Turkish government promised as a condition for the abolition of extraterritoriality.

Turkey's Domestic Legalization

The Lausanne Conference met after the failure of the implementation of the Treaty of Sèvres of 1920. This treaty was never implemented because of Turkish nationalist resistance. Organized by Mustafa Kemal in Ankara, this resistance demoralized the powers that were involved in occupying Turkey after the war, namely Italy, France, Britain, and Greece. The nationalist resistance effectively thwarted the partition of the remaining Turkish territories into separate Turkish, Armenian, and Kurdish states. As a last resort, the British under Lloyd George decided to throw their influence behind Greek aspirations in Turkey. The Greek army had already occupied Smyrna (the major Ottoman city on the Aegean coast with a heavy Greek population). Goaded by the British, Greek forces moved into interior areas of Anatolia (the Asian part of Turkey) to end Turkish resistance. However, the Turkish nationalist army defeated the approaching Greek forces. This left the Allies with two options: Attack the Turkish nationalist army or negotiate a new treaty to replace the Treaty of Sèvres. The Allies opted for negotiations. These negotiations started in November 1922 in Lausanne, Switzerland.

Just as the Turkish nationalist government sent its representatives to Lausanne, it simultaneously undertook the most extensive top-down state-building project in Ottoman-Turkish history. In particular, the republican government initiated legal reforms to further institutionalize state law in the 1920s. These republican reforms concluded what the Ottoman elite had been dreaming of for a century: all people within Turkey would be subject to the state's codes enforced by state courts through the state's legal hierarchy.[76] Through adoptions and adaptations of European codes, the republican government promulgated the codes shown in Table 6 in the 1920s.

As opposed to the earlier Ottoman legal reforms, the republican reforms did not simply aim to create a body of law alongside the religious and communal law, but rather to eliminate religious and communal law's claims to legal authority. Mustafa Kemal's words best capture this radical replacement of religious and communal law by

[76] Örücü (1992: 52).

TABLE 6. *Legal Codification in Turkey*

Code	Year
Constitution	1924
Civil Code	1926
Penal Code	1926
Commercial Code	1926
Civil Procedure Code	1927
Criminal Procedure Code	1929

the state-based law: "It is our purpose to create completely new laws and thus to tear up the very foundations of the old regime."[77]

Within a year after the Treaty of Lausanne, the Turkish government had abolished the religious courts. In 1926, after the adoption of a revised Swiss Civil Code as the new Turkish Civil Code, the state's courts extended their authority over the communal courts of non-Islamic communities. With the abolition of consular courts in 1923, religious courts in 1924, and communal courts in 1926, the Turkish government effectively achieved legal institutionalization. The legal reforms of the Turkish republic continued the Ottoman legal reforms of the Reorganization Period with one major difference: While the legal reforms of the Ottoman Empire led to a bifurcated legal system divided between state and nonstate formal legal systems, the later Turkish legal reforms aimed to unify the Turkish legal system under the state's legal hierarchy. Part of the reason for these reforms was domestic: The republican government desired to eliminate its domestic rivals, most prominently religious groups. However, the promises and concessions the Turkish government had made to the Allies at Lausanne also created a compelling international reason for the legal reforms. The international impetus was significant as debates and negotiations on the future of the Turkish legal reforms permeated the extraterritoriality negotiations in Lausanne. The following three sections examine these debates.

Extraterritoriality and Sovereignty

Prenegotiation discussions on extraterritoriality indicate the Allies' strong desire to keep extraterritoriality. The British government

[77] Cited in Lewis (1968: 275).

identified the maintenance of extraterritoriality as one of its "essential" objectives.[78] The French government agreed with the British on the need to preserve extraterritoriality. If preservation was not possible due to Turkish resistance at the conference, the British hoped to substitute extraterritoriality with a new regime that would retain the substance of extraterritoriality. For example, such a system might have "a majority of foreign judges sitting as nominally Turkish judges to try mixed civil and criminal cases."[79] The Allies' preconference meeting on November 19, 1922, summarized their objective: "[Extraterritoriality] in some form or other, however, modified, [to be] maintained."[80]

Because it had not declared war on the Ottoman Empire, the American government did not send representatives to the conference. However, it sent a special mission to observe the negotiations. The American secretary of state provided instructions to the U.S. mission at Lausanne:[81] The first item on the list was the preservation of extraterritoriality. If preservation was not possible, the Allies should substitute a system that provided adequate guarantees for Americans.[82] The State Department suggested that Turkey might consider an arrangement like Siam's, in which Siamese courts had jurisdiction in the first instance, but foreigners' cases could be transferred to the consular courts on appeal.[83]

The Turks however would not compromise. The Turkish republican government inherited and advanced the Young Turks nationalism. Extraterritoriality was one area in which the government wanted to pursue the Young Turks' program.[84] The government gave strict instructions to the Turkish delegation not to accept the reestablishment of extraterritoriality, even if such a rejection would prevent the conclusion of a treaty.[85]

[78] DBFP (1972: 273–274).

[79] DBFP (1972: 276–277).

[80] DBFP (1972: 308–317).

[81] The stated aim of the American delegation was to observe the negotiations to guarantee that no party was trying "to obtain a position of special privilege, or to be seeking favors in exchange for concessions in the matter of the capitulations"; see FRUS (1923 [Volume II]: 927). For the attitudes of other extraterritorial countries that were not represented at Lausanne, see FRUS (1923 [Volume II]: 954).

[82] FRUS (1923 [Volume II]: 886–888).

[83] FRUS (1923 [Volume II]: 931–933).

[84] İnalcik (1960), Ahmad (2000).

[85] Sonyel (1975: 188). The conference had broken down mainly on the judicial regime for foreigners, the Turko-Greek reparations, and economic clauses.

The first phase of the Lausanne negotiations focused on two normative issues and one factual point. The two normative issues were the compatibility of sovereignty and extraterritoriality, and sovereignty and the protection of the rights of foreigners. The factual point was the quality of Turkish legal institutions. The normative clashes over extraterritoriality were central to the Lausanne discussions to the extent that they had not emerged until then. Neither Japanese rulers nor the nineteenth-century Ottoman rulers had based their demands for the abolition of extraterritoriality on its incompatibility with the norms of territorial sovereignty and sovereign equality. These terms became the heart of the Turkish agenda at Lausanne.

Yet, Western states had their own normative claims. On the normative issues, both parties agreed that extraterritoriality was incompatible with territorial sovereignty and that territorial sovereignty requires states to establish institutions to protect the rights of foreigners. However, they disputed the relative importance of these normative standards. Any discussion by the Allies of the need to protect the rights of foreigners was met with the Turkish side's stressing the inviolability of sovereignty. The Turkish talking points about sovereignty were, in turn, met by the Allies' arguments about the need to protect the rights of foreigners. Furthermore, the Allies and the Turkish government could not agree on whether Turkish legal institutionalization was adequate for the protection of foreigners' rights.

On the first day of the meeting, December 2, 1922, Italian representative Marquis Garroni, the chair of the Commission on the Regime of Foreigners,[86] conceded the incompatibility of extraterritoriality with sovereignty. Garroni also stated that the abolition of extraterritoriality required a new system to provide guarantees for the life and property of foreigners.[87] The Turkish chief negotiator, İsmet Pasha, agreed with both of these assertions and added that any new regime for foreigners should be considered "on the basis of reciprocity and in conformity with the general rules of international law." İsmet Pasha

[86] In addition to the Second Commission on the Regime on Foreigners, there were two other commissions. The First (Territorial and Military) Commission was on territorial and military issues. The Third Commission was on economic and financial issues.

[87] Cmd. 1814 (1923: 467–468). The Commission on the Regime of Foreigners, in its first day, established a subcommittee to deal with the juridical issues of foreigners.

then argued that, at the negotiations for the 1856 Treaty of Paris the European states had promised to abolish extraterritoriality, contingent on Ottoman judicial reforms. İsmet Pasha further argued that, following the Treaty of Paris, the Ottoman government reformed and modernized its judicial system. Among the improvements to the legal system were the commercial code, the penal code, the codes of civil and penal procedure, and civil codes all "on the model of codes and laws in force in European countries." Given that Turkey had achieved legal institutionalization to protect the legal and property rights of foreigners, the Turkish government could not accept a legal regime similar to extraterritoriality.[88]

After the first day, the discussions about extraterritoriality were moved to the Subcommission on the Judicial Rights of Foreigners. In the subcommission meetings, the Allies presented the Turkish delegation with two sets of judicial demands. The first set of judicial demands required Turkey to institute the following provisions: a guarantee for the protection of foreigners' life and property and rights of residence, the right of foreigners to acquire real property (excluding rural property), military service exemptions for foreigners, and the acceptance of foreign courts' jurisdiction over issues of personal status (excluding inheritance).[89] In the second set of judicial demands, the Allies required the Turkish government to agree to three separate points. First, the Turkish government would hire foreign judges from a list the Permanent Court of International Justice would provide. The foreign judges would work for the courts of first instance of Istanbul, İzmir, and Bursa; the Court of Appeal; and the Court of Cessation. When hearing a case involving an allied national, the foreign judges would be in majority on the bench with a Turkish judge as president. Second, the foreign judges of the Court of Cessation and the Court of Appeal

[88] Cmd. 1814 (1923: 469). İsmet Pasha then stated that "Once our judicial organization and reform had been carried out on the basis of European institutions, the necessity for the suppression of the [extraterritoriality] was again accepted on various dates and on various occasions by the Governments which had already recognized the same necessity at the Congress of Paris. These Governments would thus admit that our judicial organization had become considerably modernized and could guarantee the rights of the foreigners living in our country. They agreed therefore that they entertained no serious objection to the abolition of the [extraterritoriality] regime."

[89] Cmd. 1814 (1923: 502–503). The Commission on the Regime of Foreigners met on December 28 after six subcommission meetings in December 1922.

would be involved in the reform of the Turkish judicial system. Third, in the cities where foreign judges were located, only foreign judges would issue search and arrest warrants for allied nationals. If allied nationals were arrested in other cities, they would be transferred to one of the cities with foreign judges within forty-eight hours, or else they would be released. While the Turkish delegation accepted the first set of judicial demands, it rejected the second set.

The Turks felt that the second set of judicial demands was an infringement of Turkish sovereignty. The rejection of these demands led to the rupture of the conference, ending the first phase of the conference (November 1922 to February 1923). In the next section, I describe how in the second phase of the conference (April 1923 to July 1923) the Allies and the Turkish government eventually agreed on judicial safeguards for foreigners. The discussion of the safeguards, at the Allies' insistence, shows that the Allies required Turkey to carry out legal reforms to protect the rights of foreigners in return for the abolition of extraterritoriality.

Foreigners' Judicial Safeguards and Turkish Sovereignty

After these subcommission meetings, Sir Horace Rumbold of Britain, the chair of the subcommission, concluded that it was impossible to reconcile the Allies' concerns for the protection of foreigners' rights with Turkey's concern for absolute sovereignty. On the issue of the quality of Turkey's legal institutions, Rumbold argued that while the Turkish delegation had repeatedly extolled the satisfactory nature of Turkey's legal system, they did not provide any evidence to support their claims.[90] Rumbold claimed that foreigners in Turkey did not have a sense of personal security. Similarly, Marquis Garroni of Italy, the chair of the Commission on the Regime of Foreigners, concluded: "We disagree, however, on one very important point, namely, the composition of the courts which are to try civil or penal suits affecting foreigners." Garroni continued:

> I am convinced that Turkey will succeed within a short time in creating a system of laws and a bench of judges which will fulfill all modern requirements; but it must be recognized that even under the new regime Turkish justice

[90] Cmd. 1814 (1923: 487–488).

has not yet been able to give proof of its worth, and also that Turkey is still subject to laws some of which are based on religious laws, while others are admitted by Turkey herself to be capable of reform, since they do not harmonize with the requirements of modern international relations. ... One of the requirements of the modern international relations, is to give confidence to foreigners and essential judicial reforms in Turkey would give such confidence to foreigners. Some kind of transitory measures are necessary during the time Turkey is completing its judicial reforms.[91]

Against these criticisms, İsmet Pasha reiterated that hiring foreign judges would infringe on Turkish sovereignty. The Turkish legal reforms, starting with the Edict of 1839, had improved the Turkish legal system by organizing Turkish courts and codes along European lines. İsmet Pasha stressed that "Turkey is requested to furnish guarantees for Allied nationals; but these guarantees already exist in Turkish laws and institutions."[92]

In response to İsmet Pasha's emphasis on Turkish sovereignty and the Turkish legal system's ability to protect the rights of foreigners without any special safeguards, Barrere, the French delegate, stated that without adequate additional safeguards, the French government would not accept the abolition of extraterritoriality. Richard W. Child, the American delegate, developed the most refined analysis to argue that safeguards for foreigners do not infringe on sovereignty:

[S]overeignty, in the sense of the prerogatives of a modern Government, is as often expressed in terms of co-operation with the outside world. ... In the modern world a sovereignty which has its eyes only on its sanctity is a sovereignty of isolation. It is our belief that only those sovereignties are progressive which have the confidence and readiness to arbitrate, to cooperate and to contribute to practical ends. ... The position of Turkey towards the judicial status of foreigners and their property in Turkey, as we are now led to understand it, is that Turkey asserts that she possess a juridical system – including not only laws but their application in her courts – which will satisfy other nations and their nationals. Unfortunately, this satisfaction does not appear at this moment to be the fact. The fact appears to be that other nations and their nationals, no matter how ready they may be for means for cooperation with Turkey, are testifying that Turkey does not offer either the continuance of existing rights or substation for them of a system which will safeguard foreign persons and property in Turkey. The security may exist in mind of

[91] Cmd. 1814 (1923: 483).
[92] Cmd. 1814 (1923: 489–492).

the Turkish Government, but the vital necessity is that foreigners themselves must feel that it exists.[93]

Like Child, Lord Curzon of Britain also developed a theoretical argument for the "true conception of independent sovereignty."[94] Exasperated with İsmet Pasha's references to sovereignty, Lord Curzon retorted:

I am tired of replying to that argument. Cannot the Turks realize that theirs is not the only sovereignty in the world? ... Ismet Pasha repeated the assertion that the judicial system of Turkey is excellent and indeed almost perfect, that Turkey has an admirable code and an excellent bench of judges and magistrates. Unfortunately, everybody knows that this is not the case.[95]

Lord Curzon advanced three concerns about the Turkish legal system: 1) the religious character of the Turkish Civil Code; 2) the inefficiencies due to delays in legal decision making; and 3) the obsolete Turkish Commercial Code. The increasing rift between the Allies and Turkey resulted in an American attempt to mediate. In mid-January 1923, the American mission attempted to intercede in the debates between the Allies and the Turkish representatives. On January 18, İsmet Pasha met with Richard W. Child and the British delegate Lord Curzon.[96] Child stated that extraterritoriality could not be abolished but that it might be replaced by adequate guarantees for the protection of foreigners as "the administration of justice in Turkey is not yet fully developed or perfected." The American mission provided a list of necessary reforms before the full abolition of extraterritoriality: 1) The Turkish government should select the judges properly and pay them adequately to prevent corruption; 2) the Turkish government should complete, revise, and secularize the Civil, Penal, and Commercial Codes; 3) the Turkish government should prepare codes for civil and criminal procedures; 4) Turkish law should protect foreigners against arbitrary searches of domicile; and 5) the Turkish government should modernize and equip Turkish prisons.[97] Similarly, Baron Hayashi of

[93] Cmd. 1814 (1923: 494).
[94] Cmd. 1814 (1923: 495).
[95] Cmd. 1814 (1923: 495–498). İsmet Pasha responded to these criticisms; see Cmd. 1814 (1923: 510–512).
[96] FRUS (1923 [Volume II]: 953) and DBFP (1972: 448–449).
[97] FRUS (1923 [Volume II]: 925).

Japan, drawing on the Japanese example, emphasized legal reform as a precondition for the abolition of extraterritoriality.[98] Baron Hayashi advised İsmet Pasha to follow the example of Japan, where twenty years of judicial reforms resulted in the abolition of extraterritoriality.[99]

The Lausanne discussions on extraterritoriality indicate that the extraterritorial powers perceived that sovereignty had an international dimension, in particular that sovereign state rulers were responsible for establishing appropriate conditions to facilitate transnational cooperation. Among these conditions are the codification and impartial enforcement of the codes. The promises that the Allies demanded from the Turkish government shaped Turkish legal reforms in the years following the conference. The remaining Lausanne debates on extraterritoriality focused on the specifics of the legal reforms that the Turkish government would complete and what kind of legal regime foreigners would obey until these reforms were completed.

Judicial Declaration

On January 27, 1923, at the fourth meeting of the conference, Marquis Garroni, the chair of the Commission on the Regime of Foreigners, argued that hiring foreign judges would not infringe on Turkish sovereignty because the Turkish government would select the foreign judges from a list the Permanent Court of International Justice would present. Moreover, Garroni stressed, these foreign judges would be employees of the Turkish government and would apply Turkish laws without any external interference. The only additional requirement was "a declaration by the Turkish Government undertaking to introduce the suggested reform, and holding good for a transitional period."[100] Arguing that "[I]t is impossible to suppress [extraterritoriality] if adequate guarantees are not given by the Turkish Government,"[101] Garroni then distributed a draft proposal for a Regime for Foreigners, which aimed to reconcile Turkish sovereignty and foreigners' rights.[102]

[98] Cmd. 1814 (1923: 492–494).
[99] Cmd. 1814 (1923: 470–480).
[100] Cmd. 1814 (1923: 523).
[101] Cmd. 1814 (1923: 435–436).
[102] Cmd. 1814 (1923: 790).

While the first article of the draft proposal abolished extraterritoriality, Article 22 included a declaration on the reorganization of Turkey's judicial system.[103] Broadly, these were the same issues – hiring of foreign legal advisers, the role of these advisers in drafting overarching judicial reforms, and the protections granted to foreigners in terms of due process and nationality of the judges ruling their cases – that the allies raised at the start of the conference.

On February 4, 1923, İsmet Pasha stated that the presence of these foreign legal advisers would be another form of extraterritoriality and that the Turkish government would refuse this. This refusal brought Lord Curzon's threats for war.[104] İsmet Pasha offered a counterproposal for a regime for foreigners. The Turkish government's counterproposal was similar to the Allies' declaration, but it had two significant differences. First, the Turkish government would select the European legal advisers from a list composed of judges from states that had remained neutral during the First World War. Second, the advisers would participate in the legal reforms and approve search and arrest warrants for foreigners. They would not, however, hear cases, although they would receive complaints from foreigners about the administration of justice in Turkey and report these complaints to the Ministry of Justice. This system was to be in effect for five years.[105]

When Sir Horace Rumbold of Britain argued that the Turkish declaration did not contain adequate safeguards for foreigners and would not be sufficient for the abolition of extraterritoriality, Rıza Nur of the Turkish delegation replied that the draft declaration contained promises for reforms in Turkish judicial administration and the appointment of foreign advisers.[106] Turkey consented to having foreign legal advisers assist in the reorganization of the legal system and giving these advisers the duty of aggregating complaints from foreigners about the judicial system. However, the two sides could not agree on the selection process for and the exact responsibilities of the foreign legal advisers in the judicial system. Due to these disagreements, İsmet

[103] Cmd. 1814 (1923: 798).
[104] E 1528/1/44 (1923). Also see İsmet Pasha's memoir, İnönü (1987: 88).
[105] FRUS (1923 [Volume II]: 968–969, 995–996, 1012–1013).
[106] İsmet Pasha also argued that the Turkish draft signified the Turkish government's willingness to reorganize its legal system İnönü (1987: 136).

Pasha rejected signing a concluding treaty and left the conference on February 5, 1923, thereby ending the first phase of the Lausanne Conference.[107] The collapse of negotiations for a comprehensive peace treaty over the disagreements about the nature of judicial safeguards replacing extraterritoriality indicates the importance of a legal system in European interactions with the Ottoman Empire/Turkey as well as Turkish attachment to the idea of territorial sovereignty.

On April 23, 1923, the conference resumed. The Turkish government eventually accepted the proposed judicial safeguards for foreigners, with the exception of the requirement that the Turkish authorities obtain permission from the foreign legal advisers before arresting foreigners and searching their residences. The Allies continued to demand this additional safeguard until the end of the conference and then conceded this as a last resort. The British Foreign Office's exchanges with the British delegation, the French government, and the Italian government suggest that while the Allies agreed on the importance of the legal advisers' role in the arrest and searches of foreigners in Turkey, this was not worth another rupture in the conference proceedings.[108]

In the Lausanne Treaty signed on July 24, 1923, European states agreed to the abolition of extraterritoriality in return for Turkey's acceptance of the declaration of judicial safeguards including judicial reforms, foreign judicial advisers, and foreign courts' jurisdiction over foreigners on issues of personal status.[109] The Turkish government agreed to hire four legal advisers for a minimum of five years. If, after five years, the Turkish government failed to carry out the legal reforms it promised in Lausanne, the legal advisers would continue to work in Turkey to supervise the operation of the Turkish legal system in cases involving foreigners and to help the Turkish government carry out its legal reforms. In the end, the Turkish government institutionalized state law within the tenure of these legal advisers and did not need them to stay in Turkey beyond their initial term.[110]

[107] See Sousa (1933: 230) and the memoir of Joseph Grew (1952: 550–552), who presided over the American diplomatic mission at Lausanne.

[108] For the discussions, see DBFP (1972: 805–806, 813, 815–816, 829, 839–840).

[109] For the text of the Treaty of Lausanne, see *The American Journal of International Law* (1924).

[110] According to İsmet Pasha (İnönü 1987: 137), later the Turkish Prime Minister, the legal advisers never participated in the Turkish legal reforms.

The legal reforms in Turkey occurred within the larger framework of the transformation of the Ottoman Empire into the modern Turkish republic. Westernization was inherent in the republican project. According to cultural arguments, most rigorously advocated by the English School scholars, the Ottoman Empire was not a member of international society. Turkey, however, as a consequence of its westernization and thus its fulfillment of the standard of "civilization," was. For example, Gerrit Gong argues that "the Turks had passed a turning-point" when Western countries agreed to abolish extraterritoriality. Like in other cases, Gong reduces the fulfillment of the standards of "civilization" to the abolition of extraterritoriality. Empirically, *apart from the abolition of extraterritoriality,* he provides no evidence to suggest what Turkey *did* to achieve "civilized" status. The only other evidence Gong cites, an editorial from *The Times* written one month *after* the signing of the Lausanne Treaty, argues against the abolition of extraterritoriality on cultural grounds: "Unless the Turks so completely alter their habits as to bring the administration of the law into some sort of harmony with that to which Western Europeans are accustomed, it will be impossible for foreign traders to pursue their calling in security." Without extraterritoriality, *The Times* stated that the safety of foreign residents was in danger. "The treaty will seem a humiliating confession of surrender by the Western powers."[111] Even though Western states conceded to Turkey and agreed to Turkish jurisdiction over Western citizens and commercial interest, a widespread perception for Turkey not belonging to European civilization and inferiority of the Turkish legal system continued in Europe.

In sum, this chapter offers a refinement of the cultural arguments for the abolition of extraterritoriality: The reason why Western states abolished extraterritoriality in Turkey so much later than in Japan lies with Turkey's inability to institutionalize state law. Whereas Meiji state rulers prepared Japanese codes and extended the state's court system under the hierarchy of the Japanese state (1880–1899), the Ottoman bureaucrats of the Reorganization Period (1839–1876) failed to clarify legal and property rights and enforce them through the state's legal hierarchy. While a domestic power struggle and

[111] Gong (1984: 119).

Ottoman modernization were important background factors, the Ottoman Empire's inability to institutionalize state law explains Western states' decision to keep extraterritoriality. Western states opted to retain extraterritoriality until the Kemalist large-scale legal reforms achieved legal institutionalization.

CONCLUSION

The struggles over extraterritoriality between European states and the Ottoman/Turkish rulers were linked to Ottoman/Turkish legal reforms. Both the demands of emergent European international society and the necessities of the empire's survival in an increasingly unstable international environment required the Ottoman rulers to engage in large-scale state-building efforts. Legal institutionalization was the centerpiece of Ottoman reforms. Western insistence on the retention of extraterritoriality and significant domestic resistance of local elite and *ulema* against the legal standardization and unification limited the success of the Ottoman elite's drive for legal consolidation. This failure, in turn, allowed Western rulers to continue to refuse Ottoman pleas for the abolition of extraterritoriality.

The arguments and comparative logic of this chapter show that some broad similarities in the abolition of extraterritoriality in the Ottoman Empire and Japan exist. A condition for the abolition of extraterritoriality was a legal institutionalization that met Western standards; non-Western rulers followed similar strategies for the codification of laws and the consolidation of the state's legal hierarchy. Differences in the experiences of the Ottoman Empire and Japan lay with their variations in state-building capacity. The Ottoman Empire lacked the external and internal factors that facilitated Japan's quick rise to sovereignty, as Japan had been blessed with the relative absence of a dominating Western merchant class and little domestic opposition to legal centralization. The Ottoman Empire, alas, was unlucky on both of these counts. The First World War changed both of these conditions: The economic linkages between Europe and the Ottoman Empire were severed between 1914 and 1923, and domestic resistance against the nationalist demands for legal centralization weakened. These two changes established the favorable conditions for extraterritoriality negotiations and made Western states more willing to accept

Turkish demands. Western states accepted the abolition of extraterritoriality after a series of territorial, legal, and economic concessions.

Law has not only been a tool of imperialism, it has also been a tool of antiimperialism. Ottoman leaders' increasing references to the concepts of law, sovereignty, and equality indicate how the Western states' requirement of legal reform prior to the abolition of extraterritoriality had empowered the Ottoman/Turkish rulers to also make use of legal rhetoric and concepts. The Ottoman claim about the legal inefficiencies of extraterritoriality gave way to Turkish rhetoric about the incompatibility of extraterritoriality with territorial jurisdiction and sovereign equality. In a broader perspective, this rhetorical shift also reflects a normative change occurring at the international level: The standard of "civilization" was losing ground to sovereign equality as more non-European states joined the international system. This normative shift, which seems to have started in the late nineteenth century and gained strength throughout the twentieth century, challenged not only legal imperial institutions like extraterritoriality, but also colonialism. The abolition of extraterritoriality in China is the best example to illustrate the influence of this normative shift regarding the legal imperialism of extraterritoriality.

5

China's Struggle for Sovereignty

Although Mao claimed to have ended foreign imperialism in China in 1949, in fact, the most important imperialist practice in China, extraterritoriality, had been ended by the Guomindang in 1943.[1] China engaged in a long and painful struggle for its territorial sovereignty during the period between the 1842 Opium War settlement and the conclusion of wartime treaties with the United States and Britain in 1943. When comparing the abolition of extraterritoriality in China to that of Japan and the Ottoman Empire, several factors appear different. To begin with, despite a vehement and occasionally violent Chinese nationalist opposition to extraterritoriality, Western states succeeded in maintaining extraterritoriality in China until the comparatively late date of 1943. This lengthy extraterritorial regime ended as a result of an Anglo-American initiative at a time when there was not much Chinese lobbying for its abolition. China is the only case in which the abolition of extraterritoriality occurred during wartime; in Japan it occurred during peacetime and in Turkey as a part of a peace treaty.

Scholars offer different explanations for why the United States and Britain abolished extraterritoriality in China in 1943. One group of historians links the abolition decision to the Allies' support of China. The historian Nicholas R. Clifford suggests that the

[1] For two recent studies on how the sense of humiliation China experienced under extraterritoriality contributed to the rise of Chinese nationalism, see Wond (2004) and Scott (2008).

abolition of extraterritoriality was the United States' and Britain's "gesture of support to their wartime ally."[2] Similarly, another historian, Akira Iriye, argues that the abolition of extraterritoriality was a "symbolic gesture to counter Japanese propaganda about Anglo-American imperialism."[3] A second group of historians ties the abolition decision to the de facto eradication of extraterritoriality during the Second World War. Among these, the historian Wesley R. Fishel claims that it was the "speed and extent of Japanese encroachments in China" that ended extraterritoriality in China.[4] Offering a culture-based argument, political scientist Gerrit Gong claims the United States and Britain abolished extraterritoriality in China because in their view China had "nominally" fulfilled the standard of "civilization."

All these explanations describe important aspects of the background and process of the abolition of extraterritoriality; some of them put the emphasis on long-term trends, like expansion of international society, and some put the emphasis on the immediate causes of the abolition, and wartime conditions severing the transnational imperial connections between China and Western states. In this chapter, I highlight one factor the conventional explanations tend to overlook: the role that Chinese domestic legalization under the Guomindang played in ending extraterritoriality. Similar to the cases of Japan and the Ottoman Empire, the discussions about extraterritoriality in China focused on Chinese legal institutionalization. The later occurrence of Chinese extraterritoriality negotiations, the 1920s to 1943, also provides a nuanced picture of the role that Western lawyers played in legal imperialism and how the international normative context influenced extraterritoriality. To present these complexities, this chapter examines the last two decades of the Chinese struggle with Western states on extraterritoriality. It further focuses on the activities of the Commission on Extraterritoriality in the mid-1920s,

[2] Clifford (1991: 277).

[3] Iriye (1986: 533).

[4] Fishel (1952: 189). Historian K. Chan Chan (1977: 289) argues that Britain and America gave up "rights they could no longer exercise" because of the Japanese control of China, especially after the Japanese invasion of foreign quarters of Shangai (1941–1942). Likewise another historian, Edmund S. K. Fung (1987: 819), argues that the United States and Britain abolished extraterritoriality when extraterritoriality "lost its meaning and usefulness" due to the Japanese occupation of China.

TABLE 7. *Rise and Decline of Extraterritoriality in China*[a]

Home State	Start of Extraterritoriality[b]	Number of Consular Courts in 1926[c]	Dates of the Abolition of Extraterritoriality[b]
Japan	1871	35	1/9/1943[c]
Britain	1843	26[d]	1/11/1943
France	1844	18	2/28/1946
United States	1844	18	1/11/1943
Portugal	1887	7[e]	4/1/1947
Italy	1866	5	2/10/1947[f]
Netherlands	1863	4	5/29/1945
Belgium	1865	4	11/20/1943
Denmark	1863	1	5/20/1946
Sweden	1847	1	4/5/1945
Norway	1847	1	11/10/1943
Total		120	

[a] Not the complete list. Some states like Germany, Austria, and Russia whose extraterritoriality ended after WWI are excluded.

[b] All data are from the commission (1926).

[c] All data are from the commission (1926) unless otherwise stated.

[d] All data are from Tung (1970: 324) unless otherwise stated. The Soviet Union renounced its extraterritoriality on May 31, 1924.

[e] Signed by the Japanese-controlled Wang Ching-wei regime (Chan 1977: 290).

[f] The number includes the Supreme Court located in Shanghai. This figure is from the *China Year Book* (1926).

[g] This figure is from the *China Year Book* (1926: 582).

[h] Fishel (1951: 215).

extraterritoriality negotiations of the 1930s, and the last phase of extraterritoriality in the early 1940s. Comparisons between different time periods in China and among China, Japan, and the Ottoman Empire/Turkey reveal the importance of legal institutionalization. Notably, while the failure of the late Qing and early republican governments to institutionalize state law in China led to the Western states' decision to keep extraterritoriality, I argue that the Guomindang government's legal reforms in the 1930s are mostly responsible for the abolition of extraterritoriality in China in 1943.

This chapter comprises three sections. First, I describe the great powers' struggle in East Asia in the 1920s and examine China's integration into international society in order to provide an account of the international factors shaping the extraterritoriality discussions. Second, I argue that the failure of the late Qing governments and subsequent early republican government, 1911–1927, to institutionalize state law in China prevented the abolition of extraterritoriality in the 1920s. My discussion compares the report of Western lawyers in the Commission on Extraterritoriality to the activities of foreign business and missionary communities in China to argue that the former was more consequential in the American and British decision to retain extraterritoriality. Third, I link the abolition of extraterritoriality in China to the Guomindang government's state-building efforts in the 1930s as well as the changing international context in which the requirement of legal institutionalization lost ground to the norms of sovereign equality, territorial jurisdiction, and newer forms of legal imperialism.

REPUBLICAN CHINA IN THE INTERNATIONAL SYSTEM

Because Western states justified extraterritoriality on the basis of the inefficiency and partiality of the local judicial system, China's initial bid to end extraterritoriality was to challenge it on the basis of the extraterritorial system's inability to provide legal efficiency and impartial justice to Chinese and foreign citizens alike. These complaints about extraterritoriality did not result in the abolition of extraterritoriality. Instead, Western states reformed extraterritoriality as it was practiced in China. The establishment of the U.S. District Court for China illustrates how Western countries reformed extraterritoriality to bring Americans in China further under the rule of American law. In response to Chinese complaints regarding the inability of extraterritoriality to bring law and order among Americans in treaty ports and the subsequent inspection of the secretary of state, Congress passed the U.S. Court for China Act in 1906. This act introduced a regular inspection mechanism that intensified the federal government's control over U.S. citizens and protégés (protected persons) in China.[5]

[5] Scully (2001: 90–98).

The act also established the U.S. District Court for China with "original jurisdiction in most civil and criminal cases where Americans were defendants, and appellate jurisdiction over cases decided first in the U.S. consular courts in China's treaty ports."[6] Overall, the Chinese strategy of making an argument against extraterritoriality based on claims about the lack of legal efficiency backfired because rather than abolishing extraterritoriality, Western states strengthened it in response to non-Western states' complaints about the "abuses" of extraterritoriality.[7]

The Chinese strategy for ending extraterritoriality then shifted to legal institutionalization as Western states linked the possibility of abolition to improvements in Chinese judicial administration. This requirement was formalized earlier in 1902 and 1903 when the United States and Britain promised to abolish extraterritoriality in China if it established adequate judicial institutions to protect the legal and property rights of their citizens. For example, the 1902 Mackay Treaty between China and Britain stated: "China having expressed a strong desire to reform her judicial system, and to bring it into accord with that of Western nations, Great Britain agrees to give every assistance to such reform, and she will also be prepared to relinquish her extraterritorial rights when she is satisfied that the state of the Chinese laws, the arrangement for their administration, and other conditions warrant her in so doing."[8] Fulfillment of this requirement of legalization, shaped within the worldview of legal positivism, proved to be arduous. China had to centralize the legal system, standardize laws through codification, and ensure the efficient and uniform adjudication of disputes.

This requirement was also compatible with the goals of the Late Qing and republican Chinese elites, ruling from the early 1900s to 1949. These elites were similar to their Meiji and Tanzimat counterparts in that they all sought political and administrative reforms to modernize state institutions. In their outcome, the Chinese reforms were closer to the incomplete efforts of the Ottomans than the success of the Japanese: Despite the commitment of the reformers to

[6] Scully (2001: 106).

[7] Similarly, the Ottoman complaints resulted in the Hornby Report, which led to the creation of the Supreme Court of Constantinople (Hornby 1928).

[8] Article XII of 1902 Mackay Treaty. See Fishel (1952: 72).

bureaucratic centralization, administrative efficiency, and economic development in China, the internal and external conditions were not favorable to such large-scale transformations. The vestiges of the earlier imperial institutions that the Republican elite (1912–1949) had inherited made radical change difficult. In the first part of the republican period, the warlord period of 1916–1927, China further disintegrated into localism; under the Chiang Kaishek government, the Nanking period of 1927–1937, it was partially reintegrated; and the Sino-Japanese War of 1937–1945 separated China into local fiefdoms and competing governments.[9] The political fragmentation that precluded Chinese bureaucratic centralization and legalization prolonged the life of extraterritoriality in China.

China's desire for the abolition of extraterritoriality and its implementation of legal reforms were related closely. In the early part of the twentieth century, the Western states' promises regarding the abolition of extraterritoriality motivated the Chinese to reform and modernize their legal system; subsequently, Chinese legal reforms explain the abolition of extraterritoriality. Reorganizing a legal system is hard for a variety of reasons, including institutional inertia and entrenched interests in these institutions. Compounding these problems, in the 1910s and 1920s China lacked the organizational capacity and tax revenues necessary for such a transformation. The Qing rulers' early reforms, the New Government Reforms, suffered a fate similar to Ottoman Tanzimat reforms: They failed when the reformers' goals for the centralization and rationalization of administrative systems led to the alienation and resistance of local nobility. While the desire for autonomy on the part of local nobility and warlords constrained the reformers, the growing nationalism and antiimperialism demanded a strong state that could end imperialist policies over Western states and Japan.[10] In spite of all these external and internal pressures thwarting reforms, the later reformers of the republican period were successful in transforming Chinese legal institutions to bring a legal standardization and unification consonant with Western models.

[9] Strauss (1998: 7).

[10] Strauss's (1998: 8–9) assessment of the Chinese reforms and the difficulties and success of reformers offers striking parallels with those of the Ottomans as described by Hanioğlu (2008: 104–107, 208).

The most important impetus of the reforms was internal: Chinese elites wanted to reinvigorate China in order to end the Century of Humiliation (1839–1949) during which great powers imposed unequal treaties (i.e., extraterritoriality, tariff limitations, Western spheres of influence policies, and treaty ports). China was caught in a vicious cycle in which the policies of the great powers weakened China, and this weakness intensified the competition among the great powers for more concessions from China. However, this competition for concessions did not prevent the great powers from collaborating to the detriment of China. The Washington Conference in 1921 demonstrated the extent of the great power commitment to continue their control over China. One of the purposes of the Washington Conference was to prevent triggering a great power conflict over China. This goal is reminiscent of the 1856 Paris Conference in which the survival of the Ottoman Empire became a point of negotiation among the great powers. At the Washington Conference participants signed three treaties establishing rules for their actions in East Asia. First, the United States, Britain, Japan, and France signed a four-power agreement to act in concert in times of crisis in East Asia. They also agreed not to militarize their Pacific islands. Second, in another treaty, the United States, Britain, and Japan agreed to set their navies (tonnage of armored ships present in East Asian waters) to a ratio of 5:5:3, respectively. These treaties configured power relations in East Asia, but China was not included as an actor in this power game where its future was shaped.

Adding insult to injury, China only appeared in the third treaty in which Italy, Portugal, Belgium, and the Netherlands joined with the United States, Britain, Japan, and France to paradoxically condemn competitive spheres of influence policies in China. These nine powers agreed to maintain the "sovereignty, independence, and territorial and administrative integrity of China."[11] Overall, the great powers promised to avoid further encroachments in China because they feared the reaction of the other great powers, not because of fears related to China's response.[12] This promise of nonaggression

[11] Spence (1990: 379–381).

[12] Home countries were aware of China's weakness. A memorandum by Victor Wellesley, British Superintendent of the Far Eastern Department, confirms China's weakness: "The revolution of 1911 and the disappearance of the Manchu Dynasty

failed, just as similar great power promises in Paris in 1856 regarding the Ottoman Empire had failed.

Unlike in the Ottoman Empire, the First World War did not dramatically alter the international environment that China faced. While some imperial powers left the scene, either permanently like Germany or temporarily like Russia, this vacuum was quickly filled by other imperial powers. Significantly, the United States had emerged as the most important non-Asian great power in the East Asian strategic game. There are different interpretations of the American approach in East Asia during the post–World War I period. Applying Wilsonian idealism to explain American foreign policy, Whitney Griswold argues that by implementing the Open Door Policy in East Asia, the United States aimed to protect Chinese territorial integrity from European imperialists and Japan. In order to succeed, this strategy required the United States to break the Anglo-Japanese alliance and limit the armament of Japan.[13] However, William Appleman Williams argues that the United States was also an imperialist power and sought to preserve its own informal empire against the machinations of Japan and Britain.[14] Akira Iriye argues that the United States wanted to establish a new international order in East Asia – an attempt that eventually failed.[15] Although these accounts vary, they all agree on the existence of strategic competition among Japan, the United States, and Britain in East Asia. Yet in the 1920s, while the great powers fiercely competed for spheres of influence in East Asia, they kept extraterritoriality out of their competition; the issue of extraterritoriality overrode the interstate rivalries. None of these states ever proposed the abolition of extraterritoriality in order to best a rival. As I detail later, the great powers' collaboration in the Extraterritoriality Commission is the quintessential example of such a collaboration.

has left China a legacy of political turmoil and internecine strife, from the throes of which she has not yet emerged. The Central Government is almost impotent, utterly discredited, verging on bankruptcy, and entirely at the mercy of the Provincial Military Governors of the provinces who are the product of the revolution and the real rulers of China." FO 371/6660.

[13] Griswold (1938).

[14] Williams (1988).

[15] Iriye (1988).

China in International Society

According to scholars of international society, Western involvement in China illustrates the civilizing mission that characterizes the expansion of international society. For example, Adam Watson calls the instances of the Western and Japanese collective intervention in China "the most impressive achievement of the international concert: a sustained and developing collective action on behalf of international society."[16] Extraterritoriality was the centerpiece of that civilizing mission: Not only did extraterritoriality force China to accept an influx of Western merchants, missionaries, and educators and provide these Western sojourners a level of legal protection from "chaos" and "lawlessness" in China; extraterritoriality was also a positive factor for China's modernization as the Western-imposed standard of "civilization" triggered Chinese reforms. If one conceptualizes extraterritoriality as part of a much-needed civilizing mission, then any Chinese reaction to and resistance toward extraterritoriality was merely further evidence of China's uncivilized character.

The explanation of international society scholars for the abolition of extraterritoriality is clear: Western states kept extraterritoriality until 1943 because prior to that time China had not met the standard of "civilization." Gerrit Gong argues that Western states established the Commission on Extraterritoriality in order to investigate Chinese progress toward the fulfillment of the standard of "civilization." He further suggests that the commission recommended retaining extraterritoriality because China did not meet the "standards of civilization" at that time. Gong states that the abolition of extraterritoriality during the Second World War "nominally" completed China's efforts to be recognized as a "civilized" state.[17] In other words, as in the cases of Japan and the Ottoman Empire, the abolition of extraterritoriality becomes *the* indicator for Chinese fulfillment of the standard of "civilization."

While I share some of the same concerns with the English School, and this work greatly benefits from the insights the English School scholarship produced, I also believe that the framework of culture and civilization obscures the central place of legal institutionalization

[16] Watson (1984: 31).

[17] Gong (1984).

in international society and prevents this scholarship adequately from theorizing about domestic legal change and its implications for international relations. In other words, while the scholars of international society point to the importance of legal institutions, they offer a limited understanding of legal institutions, mostly creation of the image of "civilized." European legal discourses and understandings of the nineteenth century had a more pervasive role in constitution of "Westphalian" sovereignty and international society than the English School scholars recognize. This role is nowhere more visible than the European interactions with non-Western societies in which non-Western domestic legal institutionalization became constitutive of the membership of these states into international society.

Although the international society approach can also be questioned because it neglects power asymmetry and because of its Eurocentrism,[18] its equating China's induction into international society with the abolition of extraterritoriality is also empirically flawed. Other facts suggest that China was a member of international society much earlier. For example, the diplomatic historian Immanuel C. Y. Hsu examines the establishment of diplomatic institutions between China and Western states and China's use of international law to determine the date when China was accepted into international society. According to Hsu, the 1861 establishment of the Office for General Administration as the central organ for foreign affairs was the first step in forging equal diplomatic relations with Western states and aligning China's foreign policy with international law. Hsu argues that the inauguration of Western diplomatic delegations in China, which occurred between 1858 and 1861, led to China's acceptance of international law, which occurred between 1862 and 1872, and the opening of Chinese diplomatic missions abroad, which occurred between 1873 and 1880, all indicate that China had been integrated into the "world community of nations" by 1880.[19] Historian Yongjin

[18] Callahan (2004), for example, argues that the English School's attempt to show the benefits of Western intervention in China remained ethnocentric without contrasting these views with Chinese views of these interventions as unjust, unequal, and humiliating. For a similar critique, see Suzuki (2009: 17–25). (Also see Kayaoglu 2010 for a critique of Eurocentrism of dominant conceptualizations of international society.)

[19] Hsu (1960: 207).

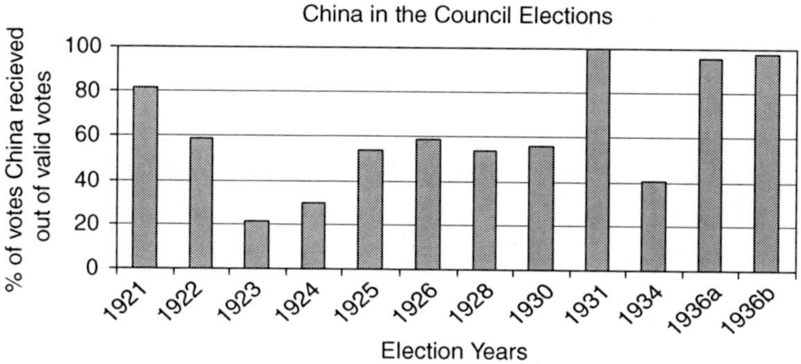

FIGURE 7. China in the League of Nations Council Elections.

Zhang argues that China became a member of international society through its participation in the First World War and the subsequent Paris Peace Conference of 1919.[20]

China's membership in international organizations provides additional support for scholars who claim that China was a member of international society by the 1920s. In 1878, China sent representatives to the Association for the Reform and Codification of the Law of Nations.[21] China attended the Hague Peace Conferences of 1899 and 1907 and adhered to other multilateral conventions related to the law of war and the settlement of disputes.[22] China's participation in international organizations increased following the establishment of the Republic of China in 1911, after which China joined a wide range of international organizations concerning postal exchange, telegraphic and radio services, opium control, patents and copyrights, and the abolition of slavery and the establishment of labor standards.[23]

Finally, Yongjin Zhang suggests that the acceptance of China's full membership into the League of Nations and its election to the League's executive branch, the League Council, as a nonpermanent member in December 1920 confirms "a de facto recognition of China as a full member of the international community."[24] Election records of the nonpermanent members of the League's Council can be viewed

[20] Zhang (1991a).
[21] Hsu (1960).
[22] Gong (1984: 152).
[23] Wright (1939: 114).
[24] Zhang (1991: 147).

as an "index of the popularity of a nation in international society" during the interwar years, according to Yongjin Zhang. This date indicates that China's status was not that of an inferior in the League of Nations. Not only did China compete for the League Council position in all of the elections between 1912 and 1936, it received a decent share of the votes in most of the elections.[25]

During this period, the majority of the League's members were European and Latin American. Thus, the percentage of votes that China received indicates how members of international society perceived China. In the 1921 election, China replaced Greece as a nonpermanent member of the League Council with 81.5 percent of the valid votes. This suggests that these European and Latin American states perceived China to be a part of international society sharing the norms, rules, and principles of international society in the 1920s – well before the abolition of extraterritoriality in 1943. In other words, despite China's inclusion into international society at the level of international organizations, European and American demands for the continuation of extraterritoriality led to tension among Chinese elites between the sense of recognition of China's place in international society as an equal member with a sense of humiliation caused by prolongation of unequal treaties of extraterritoriality. This tension contributed to increasing Chinese nationalism in the 1920s and 1930s.[26]

To the extent that the Western perception of China as "civilized" was based solely on Chinese legal institutions, English School arguments will be compatible with the legal institutionalization approach. Yet even apart from the legal institutionalization standard, the overwhelming evidence suggests that China was a member of international society in the 1920s. If this is the case, then the function of extraterritoriality in China should be different from the standard of "civilization" required for membership in international society. China *was* a member of international society during the time extraterritoriality existed there. The reduction of extraterritoriality to a standard of civilization conceals its role as a tool of legal imperialism. Through extraterritoriality the great powers denied China's laws and forced China to replace them with a new legal system that would further

[25] Quan (1939: 37). 1936a and 1936b are due to two elections in the same year.
[26] Scott (2008: 220–222) and Wong (2005: chapter 4).

increase the great powers' access to Chinese markets. It is thus not surprising that each stage of reforms China undertook in order to rid itself of extraterritoriality was supervised and judged by Western states.

LEGAL REFORMS AND THE COMMISSION ON EXTRATERRITORIALITY

The first major Chinese effort to end extraterritoriality came in the years following the First World War. Like the Ottoman Empire, China's participation in the war was partly motivated by its desire to end extraterritoriality. However, rather than fighting the Allies, China joined their efforts. In declaring war on the Central Powers, China wanted to abolish German and Austrian extraterritoriality in China and then convince the Allies to take some steps with regard to their extraterritorial regimes in China.[27] To the disappointment of the Ottomans and the Chinese, neither fighting against nor fighting with the Allies had much effect on the Allies' decisions regarding extraterritoriality: At the Paris Conference of 1919, China found the great powers unsympathetic to its desire to end extraterritoriality.

Undeterred, China brought the abolition issue to the Washington Conference in 1921. On November 25, 1921, Wang Ch'ung-hui presented the Chinese arguments for the abolition of extraterritoriality to the delegates at the Washington Conference.[28] The Chinese representative's argument responded precisely to the Western rationale for the necessity of extraterritoriality in China. Offering a legal institutionalization plea, Wong argued that the codification of Chinese laws and Chinese judicial reforms had made extraterritoriality unnecessary as Chinese judicial institutions were now adequate for the protection of foreigners and their property.[29] What were the conditions of Chinese legal reforms in the early 1920s? Had China institutionalized its legal system through the codification of its law and the establishment of a statewide court system?

[27] Zhang (1991).
[28] Pollard (1933: 217).
[29] Proceedings ... (1921–1922: 932–934).

The Late Qing and Early Republican Legal Reforms

I must make an important caveat before proceeding to my argument about Chinese legal institutionalization, which I understand to be the codification of laws, the spread of a court system, and the establishment of a legal hierarchy. Namely, I wish to stress the existence of significantly systematic and effectively enforced law in China prior to the establishment of the modern codes. As Martin Shapiro states, "China had a very long, very detailed code of laws created by imperial decree" and "the Chinese had a very hierarchical, disciplined judicial bureaucracy to enforce that code."[30] The Tang Code, promulgated in 652 AD and modified in subsequent centuries, established a legal tradition in China.[31] It is one of the significant achievements of legal orientalism when the Western legal positivist jurists were able to categorically deny Chinese law as "law." When wholesale denial of Chinese law was untenable given the long legal tradition in China, Western jurists created a fiction of the Chinese legal system as irrational, instrumentalist, arbitrary, and similar to so-called *kadi* justice, and then compared it with another fiction: idealized European positive law.[32]

Relying on legal orientalist knowledge, Western states discredited Chinese laws on a categorical basis. China lacked *positive* law, the only type of law acceptable to Western states. Chinese laws did not fulfill the positive standards of law for three main reasons. First, until 1911, the Chinese codes were not publicly accessible. Without knowing the legal codes, the public, particularly foreigners, had little idea of their legal and property rights. Second, the traditional Chinese Codes were not provisions to clarify the legal and property rights of individuals, but were administrative regulations sent by the central government to provincial authorities to solve disputes. Chinese codes covered criminal issues extensively, but remained notably incomplete on issues about commercial and civil interactions. Third, China did not have a judicial system separate from its administrative structure.

30 Shapiro (1981: 161–162).

31 Chen (1999: 6). Other sources suggest that the Tang Code was enacted in 654 AD. See Roscoe (1954–1955).

32 For examples of legal orientalism in Chinese context, see Ruskola (2002; 2005; 2008).

Magistrates who were both administrators and judges in their districts conflated their judicial and administrative roles. With the dual role of magistrates and the lack of appeal mechanisms, it was impossible for the public to gain reliable knowledge about their legal and property rights. For these three reasons, the traditional Chinese codes, as a prominent American legal scholar observed, were "not a code of law in a modern sense but rather a compilation of ethical precepts as to the relations of individuals to the family and to the government."[33] In this modern understanding and discourse of law, in large part shaped by nineteenth-century legal positivism, law cannot provide the utilitarian benefits that are a hallmark of positivist law if law is not clearly specified.

Modern legal reforms started in China at the turn of the twentieth century, although these early Chinese attempts to institutionalize state law under the state's hierarchy failed mostly because of the fragmented political system under the warlords. The first step of the legal reorganization was the establishment of the Law Codification Commission in May 1904 following the 1902–1903 British and American declarations linking the abolition of extraterritoriality to state law institutionalization.[34] The commission drafted the Civil Code of 1911 based on the Japanese Civil Code, which, in turn, had been based on the German Civil Code. However, the Chinese Civil Code of 1911 was never promulgated due to "strong conservative resistance" among Chinese elites.[35] Chinese codification attempts failed until the Guomindang came to power. Legal historian Philip Huang claims that "despite the vigorous drafting activities of the legal reformers, little was actually accomplished in civil judicial reform until the 1930s."[36] Similarly, the late Qing and early republican leaders' attempts to replace the Tang Code with civil, criminal, and commercial codes failed until 1930.[37] Without having codified their laws, the early republican governments could not clarify property rights either for their own citizens or for increasingly influential foreigners.

[33] Pound (1954–1955: 227).
[34] Chen (1999: 19).
[35] Huang (2001: 29).
[36] Huang (2001: 29).
[37] Pound (1955–1955: 229).

The early republican government's attempts to consolidate the Chinese legal hierarchy had to overcome the very intricate legal system of the late Qing period. During the late imperial period China was divided into twenty-two provinces. Each province was composed of several prefectures, with each prefecture administered by a single prefect. Each prefecture was divided into several districts; and in each district, a local magistrate and his staff carried out the administrative and judicial responsibilities for about two-hundred-thousand people. This fragmented political system created a fragmented legal system. On the one hand, the central government had little control over the magistrates and the magistrates' courts. Yet, many judicial disputes were not even officially adjudicated through the magistrate, but were solved through mediation or adjudication using customary law, or by unofficial mechanisms such as village elders, clan leaders, or guild heads. Using Confucian ideals about harmony, the central government encouraged people to use mediation to alleviate the judicial burden on the district magistrate. The limited ability of the central state to solve legal disputes and the uncertainties about legal rules and procedures created "a very definite and very strong pattern of avoidance of litigation."[38]

An early republican legal reform to establish "modern courts" to revoke the judicial responsibilities of local magistrates was ineffective. By 1926, the government had established only ninety-one courts of the first instance.[39] The number of Chinese courts under this legal hierarchy is startling when compared with Japan, where three-hundred-fifty courts operated at the time Western states abolished extraterritoriality; the difference is even more striking given Japan's smaller geographical size and population. In the remaining areas of China, where "modern courts" did not exist, magistrates continued to adjudicate legal cases and people continued to use unofficial means to solve their legal disputes. In addition to the lack of "modern courts," between 1916 and 1927, the warlords maintained significant military and administrative control within their territories, meaning that these territories functioned independently of the policies of the central government.

[38] Shapiro (1981: 182).
[39] Extraterritoriality Commission (1926: 100).

In sum, despite various attempts, the late Qing and early republican governments failed to consolidate the central government's legal hierarchy in China in the 1910s and 1920s. The failure to institutionalize state law explains why the Chinese were unsuccessful in abolishing extraterritoriality in the 1920s. China's inability to accomplish legal institutionalization showed ipso facto that it had failed to fulfill the American and British prerequisites for the abolition of extraterritoriality. This American and British prerequisite under the rubric of a modern legal system was a demand for a legal order characterized by positivist legal understanding and discourses about the scope, application, and underlying values of law. More than just trappings of civilization, Western jurists and state rulers seemed to believe that legal standardization and institutionalization were the only acceptable legal order in protecting and advancing Western legal and property rights in China. The Chinese representative at the Washington Conference recognized these requirements when he claimed that extraterritoriality should end because China completed its legal institutionalization, a claim falsified by the facts on the ground.

Further conclusive evidence links the abolition of extraterritoriality to the establishment of a positive legal order: the Commission on Extraterritoriality. The activities and the report of the Commission on Extraterritoriality played a critical role in the Western, particularly the American, decision to keep extraterritoriality. Skeptical about the Chinese claims of legal institutionalization, Western states agreed to establish the Commission on Extraterritoriality to evaluate the Chinese judicial system. After deliberating, the conference decided to establish an international commission to investigate law and judicial administration in China in order to determine the possibility of abolishing extraterritoriality.[40] After a postponement of four years, the commission finally met on January 21, 1926, in Peking.[41] Composed of Western lawyers and jurists, the commission recommended that

[40] Proceedings ... (1921–1922: 1000). According to the resolution, each of the signatories of the conference and other states with extraterritorial rights would send one member to the commission. The following states sent representatives to the commission: the United States, Belgium, Britain, China, France, Denmark, Italy, Japan, the Netherlands, Norway, Portugal, Spain, and Sweden. Commission (1926: v).

[41] Although the resolution asked for establishment of the commission within three months, Dr. Sze, the Chinese minister in Washington, asked for a postponement of the first meeting of the commission to allow China more time to translate all

the Western states retain extraterritorial privileges until China fully codified its laws and consolidated its legal authority.

Before I detail the activities of the Commission on Extraterritoriality, there is one more factor to consider for the politics of extraterritoriality: the role of foreigners in China. A careful consideration of the role of foreigners on extraterritoriality is important because these powerful groups' lobby, rather than Chinese legal institutionalization, may have influenced the great powers' decision.[42]

Foreign Business and Missionary Communities and Extraterritoriality

It is a truism that the British and American governments were aware of the concerns of business and missionary groups in China and these groups were instrumental in expansion and maintenance of Western legal authority in China. These governments regularly contacted and solicited information from business and missionary groups in the 1920s. For example, anticipating possible Chinese demands for the abolition of extraterritoriality, the State Department asked American consuls in China to assess American business and missionary opinions about the Chinese judicial system.[43] Prior to the first meeting of the Commission on Extraterritoriality, the institutionalized contacts between extraterritorial groups (missionary and business groups) and the State Department became more frequent; the State Department and these groups found that they needed each other.

Western communities during the same period were also quite active. The American business and missionary communities convened conferences, published pamphlets, and contacted their governments in order to influence the American government's position on extraterritoriality. The American Chamber of Commerce in Shanghai lobbied both through American consuls in China and their headquarters in

of the Chinese codes. Britain supported the idea of postponement of the meeting. See Fishel (1952: 75–78). Due to a currency disagreement with China over Boxer indemnity, the French reluctance to sign the resolutions of the Washington Conference also contributed to postponement of the commission. For the establishment of the commission, see Fishel (1952).

42 The historian Robert Bickers (1999: 116) links the failure to abolish extraterritoriality to a lack of British resolve in the face of expatriate resistance.

43 Fishel (1952: 54–57).

Washington, D.C.[44] Similarly, the Associated American Chambers of Commerce of China was especially concerned about the increasing warfare among the warlords and was suspicious of the recommendation of the Commission on Extraterritoriality. They issued a declaration with a clear position on extraterritoriality: "any consideration of a revision of the system of extraterritoriality now existing in China should be indefinitely postponed."[45] The U.S. secretary of state sent an extensive response to the Chamber of Commerce and acknowledged the Chamber of Commerce declaration as *the* view of American business groups in China.[46] The State Department's point-to-point immediate and high-level reply to the Chamber of Commerce's declaration indicates that the department was concerned with the interests and opinions of American business groups in China.

Like the business groups, missionaries were also very active in trying to influence the American government. A State Department document states that American missionaries "keep their Boards at home informed of the very dangerous trend of Chinese affairs and bring [these issues] to the attention of the Department through various agencies."[47] The proactive attitude of the missionaries "has suggested to the Department the desirability of obtaining a measure of direct cooperation with these interests in matters relating to the direction of their policies in China."[48] The State Department decided to collect the views of the missionaries about extraterritoriality.[49]

Although rulers were sensitive to the demands of extraterritorial groups, the influence of these groups on extraterritoriality remained insignificant due to conflicting interests of these groups. A State Department document reports a "strong and growing movement among the missionaries in China against any reliance upon such

44 Fishel (1952: 101). Similarly, on November 4, 1925, the New York State Chamber of Commerce Executive Committee adopted a resolution to call on the United States to maintain extraterritoriality. See Borg (1947: 75).

45 FRUS (1924 [Volume I]: 588). For the whole report, see FRUS (1924 [Volume I]: 580–594).

46 The State Department agrees: "The businessmen who had adopted the sixteen resolutions contained in this report presumably represent the leadership of American business in China." FRUS (1924 [Volume I]: 595).

47 FRUS (1924 [Volume I]: 599).

48 FRUS (1924 [Volume I]: 599).

49 FRUS (1924 [Volume I]: 599–600).

social privileges as extraterritorial rights."[50] John V. A. MacMurray, chief of the Far Eastern Affairs Division of the State Department, met frequently with representatives of the missionaries to discuss extraterritoriality.[51] MacMurray and the Far Eastern Affairs Division were hopeful that communications about extraterritoriality would "prove of value in assuring sympathetic cooperation between the missionary interest and the various agencies of the Government charged with the protection of American interests in China."[52] However, the emergence of pro-abolition sentiments among some influential missionary groups after the Washington Conference damaged the relationship between the Far Eastern Affairs Division and the missionaries. Mutual suspicions replaced what had initially been sympathetic contacts.

The missionaries' pro-abolition stand was driven by both normative and pragmatic concerns. They perceived extraterritoriality to be insulting to the Chinese and, thus, an impediment to the progress of Christianity in China. In 1923, the Foreign Missions Conference declared the missionaries' support for the abolition of extraterritoriality in China.[53] In the same year, James L. Burton, the secretary of the American Board of Commissioners for Foreign Missions, asked the State Department if missionaries could individually waive their extraterritorial privileges.[54] MacMurray's response was negative:[55]

> It has been repeatedly held that a citizen cannot by his independent act control the right of his government to intervene or afford protection in an appropriate case. With reference to the exercise of extraterritorial rights, Congress has, furthermore, enacted legislation extending to American citizens in China the laws of the United States. No American citizen in China, so long as he remains such, can waive the application to his person or property of such laws by the claim of a preference to be subject to the laws of China.

Although the State Department had regularly consulted representatives of the missionaries in the United States and requested that American consuls solicit the opinions of the missionaries in China, these contacts did not change the opinions of the majority of State

[50] FRUS (1924 [Volume I]: 600).
[51] Warg (1958: 200).
[52] FRUS (1924 [Volume I]: 600).
[53] Borg (1947: 68).
[54] FRUS (1924 [Volume I]: 600–601).
[55] FRUS (1924 [Volume I]: 602–603).

Department personnel who felt extraterritoriality to be necessary. Furthermore, State Department personnel knew that there were Americans, including missionaries, in China who had different opinions regarding extraterritoriality.[56] Responding to missionaries' demands for the abolition of extraterritoriality, a State Department document states: "To such an attitude, Mr. MacMurray made it clear that the Department is unreservedly opposed; in the interest of all our residents in China, and in the interest of China itself, it is felt to be necessary to hold the Chinese Government to as rigorous fulfillment as we may of the obligations due to foreigners."[57]

MacMurray believed some of the missionaries were endangering American interests in China by supporting their parochial interests without paying attention to the larger political situation in China. Failing to find support in the Far Eastern Affairs Division, the pro-abolitionist Federal Council of Churches of Christ in America appointed a committee in 1925 to present a statement to Secretary Frank B. Kellogg that conveyed the support of some missionaries for the abolition of extraterritoriality.[58] Kellogg responded more favorably to the demands of the missionaries than to his own Far Eastern Affairs Division. In addition, pro-abolition missionary groups found another important supporter in Congress: Senator William E. Borah, chairman of the Foreign Relations Committee. Borah entered into bitter arguments with the representatives of the Chamber of Commerce about the need for the abolition of extraterritoriality.[59]

The pro-abolition stand of the American missionaries[60] and their dispute with the State Department challenges the arguments that stress

[56] The State Department was correct about the existence of different opinions about abolition among the American missionaries in China. The abolition issue divided American missionaries. While the National Christian Council and the Peking Missionary Association supported abolition, the anti-abolition China Inland Mission resigned from the National Christian Council because of the pro-abolition campaign of the group. Borg (1947: 82–91); also see Fishel (1952: 102).

[57] FRUS (1924 [Volume I]: 600).

[58] Borg (1947: 68).

[59] Fishel (1952: 105).

[60] Compared to the American missionaries, British missionaries were more supportive of keeping extraterritoriality. One influential British missionary, Rev. G. G. Warren, stated: "I make bold to assert three things: (1) the present abandonment of extraterritoriality would inflict a wrong on those who now possess it. (2) the retention of it for the time being is no wrong either to China as a Republic or to any individual Chinese. (3) the retention means the retention of the best lever there

the role of domestic interest groups and cultural differences between China and the West in the American decision to retain extraterritoriality. According to scholarship about the role of the interest groups, the rulers of great powers violate the sovereignty of other states with arrangements like extraterritoriality to satisfy the demands of their domestic constituencies. Then, the rulers instrumentally invoke another international norm such as human rights norms to justify the violation of the sovereignty norms. But the debates between missionary and business groups and the impact this had on the State Department suggest that rulers' domestic constituencies often have different, and sometimes even contradictory, foreign policy preferences. Who should the rulers listen to when the preferences of significant domestic interest groups clash?

Kellogg's initial stand in favor of abolition and the activities of Senator William E. Borah, whose pro-abolition stand alienated the representatives of the Chamber of Commerce, suggest that the business lobby was not very effective in setting the American policy on extraterritoriality. One might argue that the power of the business lobby explains why Kellogg retreated from his pro-abolition stand. However, as I show in the next section, Kellogg held firm in his pro-abolition opinions until the publication of the *Report of the Commission on Extraterritoriality*. This report, which recommended retaining extraterritoriality because of the Chinese failures in legal institutionalization, persuaded Kellogg to change his mind. It was not the influence of the business lobby, but the judgment of Western lawyers and jurists that China lacked a positive legal order, which explains why Kellogg agreed to keep extraterritoriality.

The demands of missionaries also reveal another reason to be skeptical about the cultural argument linking the Western states' decision to keep extraterritoriality to China's failure to reach the standard of "civilization." If such criteria of civilization existed, missionaries – rather than business groups – ought to be more sensitive to such cultural differences because their interactions with the Chinese were in the realm of ideas, values, and worldviews. Missionaries embodied, symbolized, and represented significant elements of Western

is at present working to raise the Chinese people to our level; its abandonment is more likely than any other movement to confirm the Chinese on their present level" (Fishel 1952: 104).

civilization in non-Western countries. Furthermore, as opposed to business groups that clustered in treaty ports, the missionaries often worked in rural areas and small towns in the interior where the state's ability to establish law and order was more unreliable. Thus, the civilizing agents, the missionaries, who were working in hostile and insecure areas, ought to have been more united and active in favor of retaining extraterritoriality. But this was hardly the case. It was not cultural differences but the desire to retain legal, and thus economic, privileges such as exemption from local taxes, that explains the business groups' strong position in favor of extraterritoriality.

The Commission on Extraterritoriality

The most decisive strike to China's struggle for its complete sovereignty by ending extraterritoriality came with the Commission on Extraterritoriality. The United States, Japan, and ten European states established the commission to investigate the Chinese claims at the 1921 Washington Conference. These extraterritorial powers were to decide whether Chinese legal institutionalization met the Western requirement for the abolition of extraterritoriality. The commission did not meet until 1926. From the Washington Conference to the first meeting of the commission, Western states collected information about the Chinese judiciary. A 1923 State Department document shows the American exasperation with China's failure to establish adequate legal institutions: "The fact is that the Chinese have made virtually no serious effort, as did the Japanese and the Siamese, to create a situation in which the Powers might find it safe to relinquish their rights. Practically nothing has been accomplished towards that end except the drafting of certain codes by the Law Codification Commission. ... There has, moreover, been very little attempt on the part of China to build up a judiciary." As long as no efforts were made to reform the judicial system to protect foreigners, the State Department argued that Western home states "must insist on a condition precedent to an abandonment of the jurisdiction over their nationals."[61] The State Department's concerns suggest that American

[61] Cited in Fishel (1952: 78–79).

officials directly linked the abolition of extraterritoriality to the institutionalization of a Chinese judiciary.

Although the extraterritorial powers also met and discussed Japan's progress toward legal institutionalization at the Tokyo Conference of 1882, the Commission on Extraterritoriality in China was unique in one important respect: While Western representatives at the Tokyo Conference were all diplomats, important Western representatives at the Commission on Extraterritoriality in China were lawyers and jurists, a further indication of the legalization of imperial relations. Silas H. Strawn, from Winston & Strawn, was the president of the Chicago Bar Association and later became president of the American Bar Association.[62] The French representative G. Ch. Toussaint was the general prosecutor for the French extraterritorial court at Hanoi, French Indochina, or Vietnam. Sir Skinner Turner, the judge of the British Supreme Court at Shanghai, represented Britain.[63] The commission selected the American representative Silas H. Strawn as chairman and the French representative as vice chairman.[64] Like some eminent lawyers and jurists of the nineteenth century with their efforts to justify development of extraterritoriality, some lawyers became an integral part of twentieth-century imperialism with their efforts to maintain extraterritoriality.

Admittedly, not all lawyers were equally independent in their investigations. Frank B. Kellogg, the American secretary of state, encouraged Strawn to explore Chinese law without any prior commitment to keep extraterritoriality. However, the British representative was under strict orders to work for the continuation of extraterritoriality to prevent the surrender of British interests to the collective decisions of states that did not have similarly extensive interests in China.[65] The commission's report proved that British fears were unfounded because other Western states shared Britain's interest in keeping extraterritoriality, and because their lawyers and jurists were committed to standards of positive law that were impossible for the Chinese to fulfill.

The commission was, in the language of Judge Turner, to "test" the Chinese legal system including its codes, finances, independence,

[62] For Strawn's view on extraterritoriality in China, see Strawn (1926).

[63] For Turner's view on extraterritoriality in China, see Turner (1929).

[64] Extraterritoriality Commission (1926: 4).

[65] Trotter (1984: 33–38).

personnel, bars, and prisons. Based on an ideal type implied by positivist legal standards, this was a test that China would fail – as any existing legal system likely would. In addition, finding a legal system that would fulfill not only the ideal positivist standards, but would also satisfy a lawyer (Strawn), a prosecutor (Toussaint), and a judge (Turner) seems difficult. Furthermore, Turner accepted that some of his reservations and his difficulty with China's legal system was its civil law character, as China had adopted aspects of civil law systems from Japan, France, and Germany. Turner questioned himself about the fairness of expecting China to satisfy both common law and civil law traditions.[66]

While preparing the final report, Silas H. Strawn, the American representative on the Commission on Extraterritoriality, sent an individual report to Secretary of State Kellogg on April 16, 1926. The report enumerated the five reasons for the commission's impending recommendation that extraterritoriality in China be maintained: the lack of a central government in China recognized by all the provinces; the warlords' absolute and arbitrary control over governmental activities; the absence of constitutionally prepared laws; the lack of competent, trained, and independent judges; and the absence of funding for the judiciary.[67] Strawn thus linked his suggestion to keep American extraterritoriality in China to the central government's inability to institutionalize state law in China. Strawn's arguments appear in detail in the more comprehensive report, which was published soon after his individual report.

The Report of the Commission on Extraterritoriality in China is the clearest expression of the Western judgment about the Chinese judiciary and the description of the Western requirement of legal reforms in accordance with the legal positivist worldview as a necessity for the abolition of extraterritoriality in China. The report had four parts: Practice of Extraterritoriality; Laws and Judicial System of China; Administration of Justice in China; and Recommendations. The first part described the efforts of the Chinese Law Codification Commission and evaluated its efforts. The second part evaluated Chinese codification. It pointed out two problems with Chinese

[66] Trotter (1984: 260–268).

[67] FRUS (1926 [Volume I]: 971–973).

codification: The Parliament enacted very few of the codes as laws, and Chinese courts did not apply the codes. Offering a strictly positive understanding of law, the report argued that, lacking legislative sanctioning, Chinese "laws" were not proper laws but were either mandates of the president or orders of the Ministry of Justice. Furthermore, the report indicated that in addition to being improperly prepared, Chinese laws were incomplete because China lacked a civil code, a commercial code, bankruptcy law, and patent law.[68]

The third part of the report described the conditions of law enforcement. The report stated that the increasing disorder, linked to the weakening authority of the central government after the death of President Yuan Shikai, prevented the courts from enforcing the laws. Absent a strong central authority, the warlords retained administrative, legislative, and judicial functions. The independence of the courts was also compromised by their financial dependence on the warlords.[69] In addition, the number of courts was inadequate. According to the report, in 1926, there were one-hundred-thirty-nine modern courts of all levels (ninety-one of them courts of first instance) in China. Given the large Chinese population, this meant that there was one court of first instance for every 4,400,000 people.[70] The third part of the report concluded by noting that China had not achieved legal institutionalization.

After identifying problems in the codification of the laws and the consolidation of judicial authority in China, the fourth part of the commission's report detailed the five reforms that Western states expected from China in order for extraterritoriality to be abolished. First, a civilian judiciary should independently adjudicate civilians' cases without any interference from other branches of the government. Second, China should complete and promulgate the following laws: civil code, commercial code, bankruptcy law, patent law, land expropriation law, and a law concerning notaries public. In addition, China should revise its criminal code. Third, China should establish

68 In Part II, the commission also reported the conditions of prisons and detention houses. The modern prisons and detention houses were in satisfactory condition, but they constituted only a very small percentage of the prisons and detention houses in China.

69 Commission (1926). Also see FO 881/6317 (1926).

70 Commission (1926, 100).

and maintain a uniform system for the regular enactment, promulgation, and revision of laws to prevent uncertainties regarding its laws. Fourth, China should expand the system of modern courts, prisons, and detention houses and eliminate the magistrates' courts and the old-style prisons and detention houses. Fifth, China should make adequate financial provisions for the maintenance of courts, detention houses, and prisons, and their personnel.[71]

These recommendations tied the abolition of extraterritoriality to legal reorganization in China. Ultimately, the report demanded legal institutionalization compatible with a positive legal order: China should institutionalize state law through the codification of laws, the establishment of a statewide court system, and the creation of a government-supervised legal hierarchy. Only after such reforms would home states feel comfortable in abolishing extraterritoriality.

The commission was not an appeasement instrument to satisfy Chinese demands, but a quasi-independent body offering policy prescriptions. The commission's report shaped the Western states' policies, including American policy. The report changed Kellogg's pro-abolitionist position. Kellogg had indicated his preference before the Commission met: "It has been my hope that we could give up extraterritoriality in China within a reasonable time."[72] In another message, he wrote: "It has been my desire to renounce extraterritoriality in regard to China and everywhere else as soon as such action is compatible with the requirements of protecting American lives and interests."[73] Kellogg also specified the conditions that must be present prior to abolishing extraterritoriality: "[I]deal conditions are not expected by us, but we must have assurance of courts that American citizens will be fairly protected by the Government."[74] Despite his pro-abolitionist inclinations, Kellogg waited for the report from the commission to develop a policy for extraterritoriality. Kellogg wrote to Strawn: "I wish first to have your honest judgment of the situation."[75] After receiving the final report, the United States followed the recommendation of the report and did not abolish extraterritoriality.

[71] Commission (1926: 107–109).
[72] FRUS (1926 [Volume I]: 976).
[73] FRUS (1926 [Volume I]: 978).
[74] FRUS (1926 [Volume I]: 977).
[75] FRUS (1926 [Volume I]: 978–979).

Kellogg's change of heart following the publication of the report indicates the impact of this report on Kellogg's decision making.

The British government also claimed to view the report with great importance. On December 18, 1926, Britain stated that it would implement the recommendations of the report of the commission.[76] This statement was hypocritical given the British commitment to retain extraterritoriality, no matter the findings of the commission. However disingenuous, the statement further increased the authority of the report, thereby creating a Western framework to deal with China's demands for the abolition of extraterritoriality in the coming years.

The creation of the Commission on Extraterritoriality, its activities, and its report all show that Western states as a group demanded Chinese legal reorganization around positivist standards as the condition for the abolition of extraterritoriality. Like their imposition on Japan and the Ottoman Empire, Western states imposed legal conditionality grounded on positivist jurisprudence on China. Western states established the commission to examine the Chinese judiciary and to assess its capacity to protect individual and property rights. After examining Chinese codes, courts, and prisons, the commission concluded that the Chinese government lacked the institutional structure to protect individual and property rights. Based on these findings, the commission recommended that China continue its reforms to institutionalize a state-based legal system. This institutionalization was a condition for the abolition of extraterritoriality. Following the commission's report, the Western states kept extraterritoriality.[77]

To conclude, in the 1920s China started to make some modest progress in its struggle against extraterritoriality. While it capitalized on wartime conditions to unilaterally end German and Austrian extraterritoriality in the First World War, and the Soviet Union unilaterally renounced its extraterritoriality in 1924, it could not prevent the negative judgment of the Commission on Extraterritoriality. The next major Chinese attempt to end extraterritoriality came in 1928 under the Guomindang's Nanking government (1927–1937).

[76] Louis (1971: 153–154).

[77] For the influence of the report on the United States decision to keep extraterritoriality, see FRUS (1926 [Volume I]: 978–979). For its influence on Britain's decision, see FO 371/11646 (1926) and FO 371/11647 (1926).

THE GUOMINDANG LEGAL REFORMS

Starting with Guomindang's consolidating its power, China's struggle for its sovereignty intensified. To that end, along with the legal reforms, China also engaged in a series of bilateral negotiations with minor powers (Belgium, Italy, Denmark, Portugal, Spain, Switzerland, Norway, and the Netherlands). These powers had agreed to end extraterritoriality only if all signatories of the Washington Conference (i.e., the great powers of United States, Japan, France, and Britain) also ended theirs.[78] Realizing that convincing the major powers was key to ending extraterritoriality, in November 1928, China presented a memorandum entitled "Present Administration of Justice in China." This memorandum outlined the achievements of the Guomindang government such as promulgation of codes, growth of the number of modern courts, and securing the independence of the judiciary. These reforms meant that China had met most of the recommendations included in the *Report of the Commission on Extraterritoriality*, and China then asked for the abolition of extraterritoriality. China was also willing to accept foreign legal counselors who would observe the Chinese legal system, receive complaints from the foreign community, and make recommendations to the Ministry of Justice.[79] This arrangement of foreign legal observers was similar to the observer provisions to which Turkey had agreed at the 1923 Lausanne Conference.

China's renewed attempts to end extraterritoriality were based on the state-building reforms it had carried out during the Nanking period (1927–1937). Although Chinese reformers during the republican period had shared similar goals for legal institutionalization, none were as successful as the reforms carried out during Chiang Kaishek's Guomindang government. After establishing the national government in Nanking in April 1927 and capturing Beijing in June 1928, the Guomindang initiated a series of state-building projects. It was during this period that the Chinese reformers made their greatest, but still incomplete, efforts for the centralization and modernization of the Chinese administration. In addition, the Chinese Legislative Yuan revised the earlier draft codes and compiled new codes.[80] These

[78] Fishel (1952: 145–149).

[79] Fishel (1952: 151–153).

[80] Chinese Civil Code (1931: xiv). The National Government transferred the responsibilities of the Codification Commission to the legislative organ of the government,

TABLE 8. *Legal Codification in China*

Code	Enforcement
Criminal Code	1930–1931
Criminal Procedure	1928
Civil Code	1929–1930
Civil Procedure	1931
Commercial Code	1931

activities swiftly produced five major codes for China (Table 8). In large part, the success of the Guomindang regime did not lie with their superior ideas about the reforms, but rather with their military success in establishing a central government that allowed and sustained these institution-building reforms. Like the Meiji rulers in Japan and the Tanzimat statesmen in Turkey, the consolidation of the government's legal authority was integral to the state-building process.[81]

In addition to codification, the Guomindang reorganized the judiciary to strengthen the central government's legal hierarchy; this was only a partial success. The Organic Law of 1931 put the Chinese judiciary under the control of the Judicial Yuan. The Judicial Yuan's most important responsibility was to standardize interpretations of the law and to see that these interpretations were applied throughout the country. The Law of Organization of the Judiciary of 1932 divided the courts into three different levels: the District Courts in districts, the High Courts in provinces, and the Supreme Court in Nanking. According to statistics released by the Chinese Ministry of Justice, under the Judicial Yuan, the number of "modern courts" grew from 139 in 1926 to 406 in 1937. Of these 406 courts, 298 were District Courts, 107 were High Courts or Branch High Courts, and one was the Supreme Court in Nanking.[82] The activities of the Judicial Yuan from 1928 to 1937 show that the Guomindang worked to consolidate

the Legislative Yuan. The Yuan established five commissions for codification: The Commission on Civil Codification, the Commission on Commercial Codification, the Commission on Land Legislation, the Commission on Labor Laws, and the Commission on Local Administration Laws.

[81] Chen (1999: 23).

[82] Ch'ien (1950: 132–133).

the state's legal authority to enforce codes. Although these steps seem insufficient, as only about a quarter of districts had "modern courts" and the judicial presence of the state in the rural areas was low, the central government's reforms indicate a strong trend toward the further consolidation of the state's legal authority.

Extraterritoriality Negotiations

In April 1929, confident in its reforms, China reiterated its demand to the great powers to start negotiations that would lead to the end of extraterritoriality in China. The Chinese based their request on the completion of Chinese legal reforms.[83] The ambassadors of the great powers disagreed with the Chinese government on the effectiveness of these legal reforms. They sent almost identical reports indicating their disappointment that many of the reforms existed only on paper and that China had failed to carry out the recommendations made in the *Report of the Commission on Extraterritoriality*.[84] Despite the report, acting together with Britain, France, and Japan, the United States gave the Chinese government a note consenting to a possible, albeit gradual, abolition of extraterritoriality, "provided that such gradual relinquishment proceeds at the same time as steps are taken and improvements are achieved by the Chinese Government in the enactment and effective enforcement of laws based on modern concept of jurisprudence."[85] Later, Britain and France also provided similar notes.[86]

More worrisome to the great powers than the Chinese government's demands for the abolition of extraterritoriality was the rising nationalism and antiimperialism in China. The vociferous nationalist and antiimperialism movement was forcing the Chinese government not to accept Western conditions and to cease collaboration with Western states.[87] Between the unresponsive Western states and the nationalist and antiimperialist demands to end extraterritoriality, the Chinese government initiated a plan for its unilateral abolition as of

[83] FRUS (1929 [Volume II]: 559–561).
[84] FRUS (1929 [Volume II]:562–563).
[85] FRUS (1929 [Volume II]: 596–599).
[86] Fishel (1952: 163).
[87] For extraterritoriality and its influence on Chinese nationalism, see Fung (1987).

January 1, 1930. The Chinese government was going to justify this action on the basis of the completed legal reforms and the incompatibility of extraterritoriality with Chinese sovereignty. Publicity surrounding this plan led to a strongly worded report from the British ambassador in Peiping, accusing that the "spirit of accommodation" shown by Western states had emboldened the Chinese government. Short of gunboat diplomacy, the ambassador believed that only a "very solemn warning" to China would prevent China from presenting the West with a fait accompli.[88]

Not everyone was as reactionary as the ambassador; in January 1930, the United States and Britain started separate negotiations with China. Extraterritoriality negotiations were a subject of popular and tense debate in China. In a rhetorical competition, the nationalist and antiimperialist rivals of the Guomindang, most significantly the communists, accused the party of being soft on extraterritoriality, while factions of the Guomindang accused each other of the same behavior. In the summer of 1930, the split within the Guomindang became more visible when the powerful left-wing groups under the leadership of Wang Ching-wei abandoned the party.[89] Paradoxically, the nationalist split had contradictory implications for American and British extraterritoriality policies. One option was to postpone negotiations due to questions about the authority of the central government and its ability to continue the reforms. The other option was to give concessions to Chiang Kaishek's nationalist government in order to increase the government's domestic prestige and legitimacy and to further its collaboration with Western governments.

With this situation in mind, in October 1930, the Department of State delivered a draft treaty to China for the gradual abolition of extraterritoriality. The gradual abolition of extraterritoriality was conditioned on a set of legal safeguards that China would implement and exemptions China would grant. The draft included the continuation of extraterritoriality in special areas, including Shanghai, for a period of ten years. The draft treaty also included the retention of American jurisdiction in China on major criminal cases in which Americans would be defendants. Furthermore, it introduced

[88] Fishel (1952: 170).

[89] For the debates of extraterritoriality in the nationalist-communist split in the 1930s, see Wong (2005: chapter 4).

the principle of evocation, which gave the American government the right to withdraw cases from the Chinese courts. In terms of legal safeguards, the draft required China to establish special chambers attached to high courts and district courts of the twelve largest cities. In these chambers, while the judges would be Chinese, there would be a number of foreign legal advisers who would supervise the proceedings, receive complaints, and validate the judgments of cases involving Americans.[90] In response to these provisions, in February 1931, China indicated it would accept the special chamber and foreign legal advisers but would not allow the advisers to interfere with any judgments. China also rejected the evocation clause, the exclusion of criminal cases, and the continuation of extraterritoriality in special areas like Shanghai.[91] The State Department then made some minor concessions, such as dropping the evocation clause.[92]

While the negotiations were in progress, seething nationalists met at the National People's Convention (May 5–17, 1931) and declared on May 13 that China would no longer recognize any "unequal treaties." The similar views on extraterritoriality held by the Guomindang's factions did not unify these factions; in particular, the left-wing clique moved further apart. Under the leadership of Wang Ching-wei the left-wing members of the Guomindang established a new government at Canton. Complicating the situation even more, the Japanese occupation of Manchuria began in September 1931. Given these uncertainties, on October 26, 1931, the State Department decided to suspend the extraterritoriality negotiations.[93]

When the negotiations were halted, the United States and Britain had already agreed to the abolition of extraterritoriality, subject to legal safeguards and exemptions. The Japanese invasion of the rest of China in 1937 downgraded the importance of the extraterritoriality negotiations in China's relations with the United States and Britain. The American and British authorities would return to the issue of extraterritoriality in China when their plans for a new international order became clear.

[90] FRUS (1930 [Volume II]:471–480).
[91] Fishel (1952: 179–181).
[92] FRUS (1931 [Volume III]: 726).
[93] FRUS (1931 [Volume III]: 917).

Extraterritoriality in a New World International Order

Extraterritoriality in China ended when China was struggling for its survival rather than its complete sovereignty. As the Japanese army occupied Eastern China (1937–1945), China slipped into further disarray. The Guomindang moved to the Western provinces and established itself in Chongqing. This move deprived the Guomindang of its industrial and financial base. China's weakness became more evident as it proceeded to fight the Japanese. The Chinese were able to slow the Japanese advance, but they were not able to stop it. Japanese-controlled puppet states in the east and south, the Chinese Communist Party in the northwest, and the Guomindang in the west competed for greater control and legitimacy in China. The survival of the Guomindang came to depend to a large extent on Western military and economic aid; this relationship of dependence also explains the low priority that China gave to advocating for the end of extraterritoriality after 1931.

Surprisingly, it was the Allies who initiated negotiations for the first time. The problem of extraterritoriality resurfaced in Britain and the United States in the early 1940s. Intradepartmental debates show splits within both the British Foreign Office and the U.S. State Department regarding the abolition of extraterritoriality. John Brenan of the British Foreign Office and Ashley Clarke, the head of the Far Eastern Affairs Division, advocated for the immediate abolition of extraterritoriality so that Britain would receive credit for it. The British Foreign Minister, Anthony Eden, initially favored abolition: "I personally believe it to be a good policy to abolish extraterritoriality now, and I should like to do it in such a manner that China knows that initiative is ours, not American. I am not afraid that gesture would be regarded as one of weakness."[94] However, Maurice Peterson, the superintendent undersecretary of the British Far Eastern Department; Alexander Cadogan, the undersecretary of the Foreign Office and the former British ambassador to China; and W. E. Beckett, the acting counselor of the Diplomatic Service, were all concerned that abolishing extraterritoriality would be seen as a sign of weakness during wartime.[95] Winston Churchill concurred with the

[94] FO 371/31657 (1942).
[95] FO (371/31657). Also see FO (371/31660) and (371/35679).

latter group.[96] After concluding an informal agreement with the United States in which both states agreed that neither state would act alone on the issue of extraterritoriality, the Foreign Office decided not to initiate the abolition of extraterritoriality.[97]

The State Department also had extensive internal discussions regarding extraterritoriality in March and April 1942. On March 19, 1942, in a memorandum, Walter A. Adams of the Far Eastern Affairs Division offered five arguments about extraterritoriality in China. First, Japanese occupation removed the extensive American economic and cultural presence in China that extraterritoriality substantiated. Second, the State Department should find a way to show China that the Americans appreciated China's war efforts. Third, on several occasions during the war, American officials, including Secretary of State Cordell Hull, assured the Guomindang of America's intention to abolish extraterritoriality after the defeat of Japan.[98] Fourth, despite Chiang Kaishek's state-building efforts to unify China, it was likely that China would experience internal disorder after the end of the war due to the struggle between Chiang Kaishek's forces and the communists. Extraterritoriality could be useful in such anarchy to rebuild American interests in China. Fifth, there was no popular demand in China for the abolition of extraterritoriality. After highlighting these American concerns regarding extraterritoriality in China, Adams concluded, favoring the retention of extraterritoriality for the time being, noting that "there is more to be lost than gained by abolishing extraterritoriality now." He acknowledged the possibility of abolition based on the conditions in China after the defeat of Japan.[99] On March 27, 1942, agreeing with the overall conclusions of the Adams report, the chief of the Far Eastern Affairs Division, Maxwell M. Hamilton, raised two concerns that diverged from earlier legal and instrumental arguments. These concerns challenged extraterritoriality on a normative basis: Extraterritoriality was contradictory to the "manifestation of the war aims of the United

[96] Prime Minster Office Files (1942: file number 3740).
[97] FO (371/31657).
[98] FRUS (1942 [Volume China]: 269). (Note that for 1943, the diplomatic exchanges related to China are contained in a single volume labeled "China" rather than with a numerical identification.)
[99] FRUS (1942 [Volume China]: 268–270).

Nations," and it was an anachronism in that "the extraterritorial system is bound to go."[100]

However, in May 1942, the Foreign Office and the State Department decided to retain extraterritoriality and to act together in the event of Chinese demand for abolition. Yet Hamilton's normative critique against extraterritoriality gained momentum.[101] In July and August 1942, American policy started to shift. On July 11, 1942, Secretary of State Cordell Hull wrote to the American ambassador in the United Kingdom that the United States would abolish extraterritoriality "at the earliest moment."[102] Hull's message did not offer any reason for his decision. But later in August, in a letter to John G. Winant, the American ambassador to Britain, Hull referred to the American public's desire to abolish extraterritoriality but added that there was no "strong concentrated pressure." Although no urgent practical reason to abolish extraterritoriality existed, Hull concluded that extraterritoriality was not compatible with "modern international practices," "general norms in international relationships," and "generally accepted principles of modern international law."[103] In another letter to Ambassador Winant a week later, Hull enumerated three objectives that the abolition of extraterritoriality might accomplish: "(a) some psychological and political benefit to the cause of the United Nations which would be of concrete assistance to China and thus tend to strengthen the determination of that country in its war effort; (b) the wiping out once and for all of an existing anomaly in our relations with China; and (c) the achievement of agreement in principle to regularize in China the usual rights normally acquiring to American and British nationals in friendly foreign countries."[104]

In October 1942, anticipating that the new Chinese ambassador, Wei Tao-ming, would demand the abolition of extraterritoriality, the State Department informed the British Foreign Office of the American intention to abolish extraterritoriality.[105] The State Department then sent a draft treaty abolishing extraterritoriality to the British Foreign

[100] FRUS (1942 [Volume China]: 270–273).
[101] FRUS (1942 [Volume China]: 276–278).
[102] FRUS (1942 [Volume China]: 281).
[103] FRUS (1942 [Volume China]: 282–285).
[104] FRUS (1942 [Volume China]: 287–288).
[105] FRUS (1942 [Volume China]: 297).

Office so that the British government might review this document.[106] The Foreign Office agreed with the State Department on the major points of the draft but asked to include "an exchange of notes containing additional assurances concerning the treatment" of British and American citizens after the abolition of extraterritoriality.[107] On October 10, 1942, the British and American governments notified China that they would abolish extraterritoriality.

One can draw two conclusions from these State Department and Foreign Office documents. First, the American and British policymakers seemed deeply interested in laying the foundations for a new postwar international order. Second, American and British policymakers believed that extraterritoriality did not belong in this postwar order. American and British policymakers made numerous references to extraterritoriality as an "anomaly" and an "anachronistic" system and their conviction that the extraterritorial system "is bound to go" and "has no place in international law." These references in interdepartmental documents indicate a normative shift regarding the appropriateness of extraterritoriality in the international system. In the words of the chief of the Far Eastern Affairs Division, Maxwell M. Hamilton, "It would seem desirable not to envisage the re-emergence of a system which in a broad sense no longer conforms to modern concepts."[108]

While strategic competition between the Allies and Japan in East Asia during the Second World War was high, such competition did not influence the extraterritoriality policies of these states. America and Britain did not abolish extraterritoriality with the goal of strengthening China against Japan. The argument that the Allies' goal in abolishing extraterritoriality was an instrumental one of shoring up China against Japan has problems. The wartime alliance between the Allies and China dates from long before the abolition of extraterritoriality in 1943. An agreement to end extraterritoriality was not the glue in the Sino-Western alliance. The strategic justification for the alliance between China, the United States, and Britain (to combat Japanese aggression) was itself a factor in the formation of a Sino-Western

[106] FRUS (1942 [Volume China]: 298–301).
[107] FRUS (1942 [Volume China]: 301–302).
[108] FRUS (1942 [Volume China]: 270–273).

alliance. Furthermore, the asymmetry of dependence between China and the Allies – China desperately needed America and Britain for its survival – suggests that China would not have left the alliance over the issue of extraterritoriality. Japanese aggression and occupation provided China with all the incentives it needed to maintain its alliance with the Americans and British.

Although I reject the instrumentalist logic of strategic competition in favor of a normative framework of sovereignty and equality, I still believe Chinese legal institutionalization was important in American and British decisions to end extraterritoriality. This is because the American and British governments had been observing the Guomindang legal reforms, and American and British officials' references to these reforms suggest that these Chinese reforms (both as implemented and as promised) were significant factors in the decision to abolish extraterritoriality. The American and British governments received assurances of continued legal institutionalization and of the protection of American and British citizens and their property. For example, on the same day that extraterritoriality was abolished in China (January 11, 1943), the State Department and the Foreign Office gave a statement to the Chinese ambassadors. The content and timing of the statement suggest the existence of a causal relationship between the abolition of extraterritoriality and the Chinese judiciary:[109]

> This Government has been following in recent years the progressive steps which the Chinese Government has taken in matters relating to the administration of justice. This government has noted the spirit which the Chinese Government has shown in adopting new civil and criminal codes, in establishing modern courts of justice, and in building improved prisons. It is believed that it is the intention of the Chinese Government that this progressive program shall be extended throughout the territory of the Republic of China and that as areas of Chinese territory now under Japanese military control are restored to Chinese jurisdiction modern courts of justice will be re-established and modern prisons will be restored or be built in such areas.

The statement continued to announce that the American government received assurances from the Guomindang that:

> [F]oreign nationals who are parties to civil or criminal cases shall be subject to the jurisdiction of the modern Chinese courts of justice only; that in the

[109] FRUS (1942 [Volume China]: 418).

case of police offences foreign nationals shall be tried either by the modern Chinese courts of justice or by the police tribunals acting in accordance with duly promulgated laws, ordinances, and regulations; and that foreign nationals who may be detained or arrested or imprisoned by the Chinese authorities shall be held only in prisons designated by the Ministry of Justice for the detention of foreign nationals.

By abolishing extraterritoriality in China a century after its formal imposition, Western states recognized China's sovereignty over Western foreigners in 1943. This recognition came unexpectedly – and paradoxically – when the Guomindang's territorial authority was limited to eastern China. China's *internal* incapacity to institutionalize a legal system compatible with a modern legal order shaped by expectations of legal positivist understandings and discourses of law explains the late abolition of extraterritoriality in China. The establishment of the Commission on Extraterritoriality and its reports provide conclusive evidence that Western states maintained extraterritoriality in China due to China's difficulties with domestic legalization. Following a counterfactual reasoning, one can argue that the Guomindang state-building practices, particularly the legal reforms of the 1930s, might have led to the abolition of extraterritoriality had Japan not invaded China and thus forced Western countries to delay their decisions to abolish extraterritoriality in China.[110]

Although the American decision to abolish extraterritoriality was structured within the context of a normative shift away from extraterritoriality and China's legal reforms, this decision also coincided with the growth of new forms of extraterritorial jurisdiction compatible with American hegemony. For example, while the extraterritoriality negotiations were in progress, the State Department became aware of a potential problem: American military personnel in China who were soon to be without the protections of extraterritoriality. While the Secretary of State believed that international law allowed American jurisdiction over its military personnel abroad, he suggested that this was not enough protection and that the status of American military personnel should be safeguarded by a treaty or a diplomatic exchange. Rather than raising the issue during the extraterritoriality

[110] FO (676/64) set forth British plans for the gradual abolition of extraterritoriality in the 1930s. These plans were not carried out because of the Japanese occupation. For a similar argument, see Fishel (1952).

negotiations with China, the State Department decided to negotiate protections for American military members after the abolition. On May 21, 1943, China and the United States exchanged diplomatic notes that granted "… the adjudication of criminal offenses committed by members of the armed forces of the United States within the territory of China to the service courts and authorities of the military and naval forces of the United States."[111] In a further move to eliminate the Chinese concerns about "unequal treaties," the United States agreed "to make like arrangements to ensure to such Chinese forces as may be stationed in territory under American jurisdiction a position corresponding to that of the American forces in China."[112] With this agreement, U.S. extraterritorial jurisdiction in China continued until all the American forces had been withdrawn; this occurred after the revolution in 1949.

In certain respects, the American attempt to protect military personnel and the ensuing extraterritorial jurisdiction agreement differ from the earlier forms of extraterritoriality in China. The geographical scope of extraterritoriality expanded and globalized from the great powers' claiming jurisdiction in non-Western states where communities of Western foreigners resided to locations throughout the world where the great powers, most importantly the United States, had an interest in stationing their military. This geographical expansion of jurisdiction came with a contraction of jurisdiction in terms of people (military personnel) and cases (criminal). The basis of jurisdiction shifted from the differences of culture and legal system to the requirements of military necessity and efficiency. This transformation of extraterritorial jurisdiction, however, indicates the emergence of another form of legal imperialism based on American power, interest, and jurisprudence. It is still a fundamental infringement of sovereign equality based on limiting and denial of a lesser power's law. Power imbalances are inherent to this jurisdiction, as great powers station most of the military personnel in the territories of weaker states. Paradoxically, more than the earlier form of extraterritoriality, the new regime of extraterritorial jurisdiction has strengthened the hand of the great powers by allowing them greater flexibility. Under

[111] FRUS (1943 [Volume China]: 699).

[112] FRUS (1943 [Volume China]: 695–696). Also see Chiu (1979–1980).

this new regime, great powers could use extraterritorial jurisdiction selectively on certain people, issues, territories, and activities but not on others. I will elaborate the new forms of extraterritorial jurisdiction and legal imperialism and their relevance to American power and jurisprudence in the next chapter.

CONCLUSION

During its 101-year history, extraterritoriality in China survived major Chinese efforts to abolish it. Despite vehement and sometimes violent Chinese opposition to extraterritoriality, Western states maintained extraterritoriality until 1943. Western states' tenacity turned into an unexpected concession during the Second World War. The United States and the United Kingdom initiated the abolition process during a period when the abolition of extraterritoriality was not a particularly significant concern for the Chinese government. While Western concerns of power politics and Chinese modernization are important in understanding extraterritoriality politics, two factors explain the trends in Western policies with regard to extraterritoriality in China: legal institutionalization and the American-led normative shift away from traditional extraterritoriality.

The debates over extraterritoriality in China underscore two aspects of legal imperialism. One is the role of lawyers and jurists. In the nineteenth century, Western lawyers and jurists were crucial for the construction of a narrow understanding of sovereignty and law by reducing these concepts to European thought and practices and by delegitimating non-Western forms of law and sovereignty. In the twentieth century, Western lawyers and jurists became judges of non-Western legal development, deciding if such efforts fit the idealized positivist criteria. The role of positivist legal discourse and jurisprudence guided the members of the Commission on Extraterritoriality in China when they examined the Chinese legal system. Using idealized positivist benchmarks, their report revealed flaws in China's legal system, justified the continuation of legal imperialism, and recommended additional legal reforms. The Chinese use of positivist discourse to convince the great powers to abolish extraterritoriality backfired: While China stressed how it had fulfilled the mandated legal institutions, accepting Western standards made China accountable for a commitment to positivist standards and thus vulnerable to Western judgment.

The other lesson of legal imperialism highlighted by China's struggle to end extraterritoriality concerns power. Legal imperialism is not only about legal episteme, it is also about imperial power. The final blow to extraterritoriality came with the change of hegemonic ideas regarding the form and content of legal imperialism. Traditional extraterritoriality was developed within nineteenth-century legal positivism and the European, particularly British, imperial agenda. During the interwar years, American attitudes toward extraterritoriality started to shift, as evidenced by Secretary of State Kellogg's changing views. This shift became more visible toward the end of the Second World War when American officials embraced a different vision for international order than did their nineteenth-century British counterparts. The American preeminence in the post–WWII international order and its dominant legal episteme, American legal realism, transformed some traditional forms of legal imperialism and added new ones.

Conclusion

American Legal Imperialism – Extraterritoriality Today

Mainly through legal institutionalization, non-Western states secured the abolition of extraterritoriality, achieved their sovereignty on Western foreigners and commercial interest, and integrated themselves into Westphalian international society as formal equals. The Meiji rulers' legal codification and the spread of the Japanese state court system led to the early abolition of extraterritoriality in Japan in 1899. While the legal reforms of the Ottoman elite failed during the reorganization period, the legal reforms of the Kemalist elite in the early 1920s emerged as a bargain between Turkey and Western states over the abolition of extraterritoriality in the Lausanne Treaty of 1923. The Chinese leaders' failures to codify rules and consolidate legal authority in the 1920s explain the Western states' retention of extraterritoriality in pre-Guomindang China. The Guomindang legal reforms in the 1930s and normative change in the United States against extraterritoriality created the conditions for the abolition of extraterritoriality in 1943.

The rise and demise of nineteenth-century extraterritoriality reveal how certain conceptions and practices of law and sovereignty sometimes served the Western imperial interests. The practices of extraterritoriality, however, had some beneficial consequences for non-Western societies, in particular for their reformist elites. These practices stimulated the transformations of indigenous legal systems, speeding their "modernization" and the "positivization" of these legal systems, which bolstered rulers' claim to legal centralization. By means of imposing extraterritoriality and conditions to end it, Western imperial states spurred non-Western states' adaptation of positivist legal ideas, categories, and practices. Western demands reflected both the legal positivist worldview prevalent in the West since the early nineteenth century and the belief that legal institutionalization of non-Western states could open new commercial and investment opportunities for Western merchants. Western great powers' support of non-Western legal development was not always consistent but it was conditional: When it was not clear that non-Western legal reforms could contribute to Western imperial interests or, worse, could undermine such interests, Western states did not support these reforms. Additionally, they undermined the reforms by not conceding on extraterritoriality and thereby kept Western foreigners and protégés, who controlled the important segments of local economies in places like the Ottoman Empire and China, out of Ottoman and Chinese law.

The rise and demise of extraterritoriality occurred within the debates about the meaning of sovereignty and the rights and responsibilities associated with it. These debates point out that two nineteenth-century developments – the dominance of legal positivism and Western colonial expansion – shaped "Westphalian" sovereignty. While legal positivist discourses and understandings about law changed, its core categories, like reducing law to sovereign commands backed by coercion, remained unchanged and became well established in legal, social, and political theory. Not only legal scholars, but also political and social thinkers, eventually accepted legal positivist categories to distinguish "law" from nonlaw, "sovereignty" from nonsovereignty, and "civilized" from noncivilized. Legal positivist formal and categorical approaches to law underlined arguments like "sovereignty means ultimate authority in a given territory" and "statehood requires the monopolization of legitimate means of violence within a territory" and established fundamental categories and ideas about state sovereignty in the nineteenth century.

In addition to Western thought and practice in the development of sovereignty, extraterritoriality reveals that Western colonial powers' encounters – particularly Britain's – with non-Western states in Asia and the Islamic world were integral to the development of a sovereignty doctrine. In these encounters, the practices of the British state and positive juridical categories and ideas reconstructed the sovereignty doctrine in part to legitimize Western powers' right to extend their authority into Asian and Islamic states that remained uncolonized but were deemed not fit for the category of "sovereign." While these states avoided colonization, they could not have the power to resist Western imperial expansion. Western powers imposed a system of extraterritoriality on these states and linked the recognition of non-Western law and sovereignty over Western citizens and commercial interest to non-Western legal institutionalization. In this process, legal institutionalization became a constitutive element of sovereign statehood for non-Western states and a building block for "Westphalian" sovereignty.

Although the constitutive role of domestic legalization in Westphalian sovereignty was due to the legal positivist worldview, debates about extraterritoriality undeniably show that a state's domestic law has significant international consequences. The structure and content of domestic law influence international politics including international trade, the rights of foreigners, as well as security, environmental, and financial regulations of other states. In European state formation, the revival of Roman law and the later dominance of positive law allocated states' rights and responsibilities in the clarification and enforcement of legal and property rights. The "law" required local rulers to standardize and systemize legal and property rights and enforce them through courts under the state's legal hierarchy. Each ruler of a sovereign state required other rulers to institutionalize state law. Once state law dominated the state's domains, state rulers held each other accountable in their respective domains. This reciprocal accountability established the foundation of the sovereign state system. In other words, modern sovereignty *requires* this reciprocal accountability in clarifying and enforcing standardized rules within one's own territorial domain. This is, in essence, modern sovereignty – establishing the foundations of a sovereign state system.

These international effects cause states to pay close attention to other states' legal systems, and powerful states often intervene in domestic legal systems of weaker states. Extraterritoriality was an example of such interventions. Both Western power and legal ideas were important in extraterritoriality. As realists have observed, power and interest matter when a state extends its authority into another state; when in conflict, powerful states often compromise the authority of weaker states. Non-Western powers were too weak to avoid extraterritoriality, and law and sovereignty became instrumental tools for the legitimization of the powerful state's legal expansion. Yet, power and interest tell only part of the story of extraterritoriality. From a realist perspective, it is not clear how legal systems contribute to a state's material capability and why powerful states intervene in and change domestic legal arrangements of weaker states. Moreover, legal ideas, such as what constitutes law, justice, property rights, and legal procedures, were important factors in Western powers' interventions into non-Western legal systems. These categories were defined, in part, by the dominant legal episteme – legal positivist understandings, discourses, categories, underlying values of law – not by dominant power.

By pointing to the role of domestic legal systems in international society and its expansion, English School scholarship moves in the right direction. However, it fails to realize the expansive role the legal differences between Western and non-Western societies play in international society and underestimates the constitutive role legal institutions play in its emergence and expansion by focusing on the cultural and civilization qualities of legal systems. The crucial debates in nineteenth-century Western interactions with non-Western states focused on legal institutions rather than issues like manners, diplomatic etiquette, or gender equality. Law seemed to be the defining character of the standard of "civilization." Furthermore, in many debates, the form of the legal system, rather than its content of law, appeared significant to distinguish "civilized" from "uncivilized." In other words, for a nineteenth-century "state of law," the form of the legal system, the codification of legal rules, the consolidation of legal authority through state courts, and the creation of a unified hierarchy of state courts – the qualities reflecting formal categorical thinking of legal positivism – mattered considerably. Admittedly, it is difficult to distinguish the influence of the form from the content as non-Western states I discussed adopted European codes rather than writing their own codes reflecting their respective legal traditions in terms of content. But the debates about the Ottoman Land Law and *Mecelle*, which were codes based on *Sharía*, and European acceptance of the Ottoman Land Law's application to Westerners confirm the importance of the formal structure of law rather than the cultural and civilizational qualities of its content.

The imposition of extraterritoriality and the conditions Western states set for its termination shaped legal reorganization of the states this book examined like Japan, the Ottoman Empire, and China, as well as others like Thailand, Korea, Iran, and Egypt. Throughout the nineteenth and early twentieth centuries, the rulers of these states constantly negotiated with European rulers prior to each major step in their state's legal reorganization. Because of the importance both parties placed on these negotiations, extraterritoriality became a centerpiece of international and domestic politics in non-Western states. Non-Western rulers faced three major pressures: 1) from Western powers for legal modernization in the form of legal positivization as a precondition to end extraterritoriality; 2) from increasingly vocal antiimperialist, nationalist, and xenophobic groups for immediate abolition of extraterritoriality; and 3) from conservative and religious groups as well as local notables against legal modernization, centralization, and positivization. Eventually, non-Western rulers secured legal modernization and centralization as Western states demanded, ended extraterritoriality as nationalist groups demanded, and eliminated traditional and religious elite as well as local notables. Japan completed its legal modernization under the Meijis in the 1890s, Turkey under the republican elite in the 1920s, and China under the Guomindang in the 1930s. These reforms were key for these states in ending extraterritoriality in Japan in 1899, Turkey in 1923, and China in 1943.

While the abolition of extraterritoriality in China heralded the end of an era of extraterritoriality, the United States' reinstating its jurisdiction over American military personnel in China signaled the emergence of a new form of extraterritorial jurisdiction. Postwar American governments have created new forms of extraterritorial jurisdiction and established new methods of legal expansion that were "more suited to the open liberal trading system America and its allies had created and, moreover, reflected the dramatic extent of postwar U.S. hegemony."[1] The instances are familiar: the increasing use of U.S. federal courts to enforce American foreign policy goals abroad, the removal of local courts' authority over American military personnel and contractors, the use of multilateral institutions for

[1] Raustiala (2009: 91).

global regulations, and American courts' regulatory reach abroad on issues like securities, antitrust, and environment.[2]

In the rest of this conclusion, I sketch the broad patterns of postwar American legal expansion that intervene and shape legal ideas, categories, and structures of other states. I compare this American legal imperialism with nineteenth-century British legal imperialism, relate American legal imperialism to American legal realism, and discuss the effects of globalization and the "war on terror" on American legal imperialism. These preliminary remarks have two goals. First, I suggest that legal imperialism is a powerful conceptual tool to examine the post–World War II international order, in particular to discern some of the forms of American foreign policy that often do not get much attention in international relations scholarship. Second, I propose that both the American legal episteme and its postwar hegemony are important to understand American extraterritorial jurisdiction.

Like its British predecessor, a major American goal in legal expansion has been to open foreign markets and investment opportunities to American companies and in this process to solve legal differences between the American legal system and others in a way reflecting American interest. Besides, the United States follows a policy of legal intervention; it uses its domestic courts to claim jurisdiction over certain activities abroad that may affect American prosperity and security. To expand commercial opportunities to American commercial interest, the American government mostly opted for multilateral arrangements.[3] Postwar multilateral arrangements commonly known as the Bretton Woods system allowed America to confront and change other states' legal systems reflecting America's trade interest and priorities. The multilateral nature of these arrangements moderates and conceals their imperialist quality, and some of these arrangements may reflect genuine collaboration in international society. However, there are also similarities with nineteenth-century extraterritoriality. For example, the membership conditions and conditionality requirements these arrangements impose on weaker states are reminiscent of nineteenth-century exclusionary standards. Besides, these multilateral arrangements construct and embody a global legal episteme through which other states reorganize their legal systems. For example, lesser

[2] See Putnam (2009).

[3] Ikenberry (2001: 29–49) calls this a hegemonic order.

powers are expected to reform their legal systems to implement modern legal ideas, categories, and practices, such as good governance, the rule of law, and intellectual property, defined and judged by American and other Western states, reminding us of Western states' exporting legal positivist ideas and practices to non-Western states in the late nineteenth and early twentieth centuries.

In addition to the use of multilateral arrangements and organizations to expand and export American legal ideas and practices, the American government uses a second form of legal expansion that takes a bilateral form, resembling the relationship between imperial centers and their "clients" in the periphery. Substantiated by unequal treaties, the asymmetric imperial relationships between America and its clients allow America to expand its legal reach in the client's territory. Unlike the British overseas military bases and leased territories, which "existed almost exclusively within the context of formal empire"[4] and under British sovereignty, the American overseas empire operated informally, with the client state continuing to hold de jure sovereignty and America holding de facto sovereignty on the leased territory. While the United States had leased territories such as the Panama Canal and military bases such as Guantánamo naval base in Cuba in the early part of the twentieth century, World War II transformed the American so-called leased empire and allowed America to project its military capacity worldwide. In 2007, the United States has 823 facilities of different sizes (14 large, 20 medium, 742 small, and 47 "other" sites) in 39 states.[5]

Military base agreements allow America to extend its legal authority beyond the territorial limits of military bases because America can also claim jurisdiction over cases that involve American military members, contractors, and accompanying civilians outside the military bases. Although the Allies granted immunity to American military personnel during wartime, they did so on an ad hoc basis. With a significant number of American military personnel stationed in Western Europe after 1945, the Allies and the United States agreed formally on

[4] Calder (2007: 8). For a discussion about the evolution of the American military base system and its differences from British imperial practices, see Calder (2007: chapter 1) and Sanders (2000: chapters 1 and 2).

[5] See the report of the Office of the Deputy Under Secretary of Defense (Installations and Environment) http://www.defenselink.mil/pubs/BSR_2007_Baseline.pdf.

the jurisdictional status of military personnel.[6] The agreement eventually turned into NATO's Status of Forces Agreement (SOFA) and became a prototype for the United States that has now more than 100 SOFAs with other states regulating the jurisdictional status of American forces. Through these SOFAs, the United States claims jurisdiction over its military personnel, contractors, and their families abroad and projects its military and political authority worldwide without a formal colonial relationship with client states.[7]

In addition to getting "consent" through multilateral or bilateral arrangements, there is a third and final form of American legal expansion that is a unilateral extension of American legal authority abroad. America and, following the American precedent, the European Union and some EU states individually like Britain and Germany, increasingly use their courts to exert unilateral extraterritorial jurisdiction. These powerful actors often use this type of jurisdiction to extend their regulatory reach, relying on a legal principle known as the effects doctrine. The effects doctrine refers to an actor's claim of jurisdiction abroad to prevent an activity that may influence its regulations on issues like environment, securities, and antitrust.[8]

The extraterritorial application of American antitrust laws illustrates the evolution of the effects doctrine and its change under postwar American hegemony.[9] Although the 1890 Sherman Act declared a universal jurisdictional claim by making "every contract, combination in the form of trust or otherwise, or conspiracy, in restraint of trade or commerce among the several states, or with the foreign nations"[10] illegal, American courts refrained its extraterritorial application before 1945. For example, in its *American Banana* decision (1909), the Supreme Court ruled against the application of the Sherman

[6] Baxter (1958), Erickson (1994), and Norman (1995–1996).

[7] Schmitt (2001–2002) and Jung and Hwang (2002–2003).

[8] Varghese (2001–2002). America also invokes the effect doctrine as a part of its foreign policy, applying the economic sanctions laws to other countries. For the extraterritorial applications of the Helms-Burton Act and other states' countermeasures against its extraterritorial applications, see Muse (1996–1997), Glossop (1998), and Clark (1999). For a recent comprehensive analysis of effects-based American extraterritorial jurisdiction, see Raustiala (2009: chapter 4).

[9] For the evolution of the extraterritorial application of American antitrust laws, see Lytle (1997), Beckler and Kirtland (2003), Chang (1992–1993), and Kim (2003).

[10] For the text of the Sherman Act, see http://www.usconstitution.com/ShermanAntiTrustAct.htm.

Act to punish the United Fruit Co. for noncompetitive activities in Panama and Costa Rica. Upholding the absolute territoriality principle, the court reasoned that the application of U.S. laws was limited to the physical boundaries of the United States. After 1945, however, U.S. courts began to enforce the Sherman Act abroad and defined the effects doctrine with the *Alcoa* decision (1945). The Second Circuit, sitting for the Supreme Court, claimed that the Aluminum Co. of America (Alcoa) set up a Canadian corporation to fix the prices of aluminum that were being imported to the United States and concluded that any business activity that is illegal in the United States would be illegal outside of its borders if the act both intended to and actually did effect the U.S. economy. Following the *Alcoa* decision and using the effects doctrine, the U.S. Department of Justice aggressively asserted American jurisdiction over foreign companies whose actions impacted the proper functioning of American markets despite fierce criticism that these practices were received from the American Allies, particularly from Western Europe.[11]

So far, I have described the multilateral, bilateral, and unilateral American foreign policy tools by which the United States expands its legal authority abroad directly or induces legal change in these countries that impact American interest. Many of these instruments of legal imperialism emerged under American hegemony after 1945, suggesting the key role of American power in their formation and application. In addition to the rise of American power and the change of American interest, a distinctively American legal thought accompanied the rise of American legal expansion. The early nineteenth-century legal positivism, with its formal and categorical approach, shaped British legal imperialism; the early twentieth-century American legal realism and its pragmatism shaped American legal imperialism. While legal formalism and its categorical approach, sometimes called "classical legal thought," was also influential in the United States in the nineteenth century, its strength in the United States started to decline by the start of the new century. By the 1930s, a new legal episteme, collective legal discourses, and understandings with distinctive emphasis on policy and interest became influential in American legal thought.[12]

[11] Raustiala (2009: 111–117).
[12] Raustiala (2009: 107–111).

Postwar American extraterritorial jurisdiction has been embedded in American legal thought that was shaped in American legal, political, and social circumstances of the 1920s and 1930s, such as the expansion of the federal regulatory system. An important element in this new legal thought was legal realism. Legal realism emerged in part as a reaction to the formalism of positivism: While positivism subsumes law into the legislative act of a sovereign and postulates a deductive method in applying the law, realism emphasizes law's ability to adjudicate conflicting interests and policy options. This interest and policy-oriented legal approach that blurred the boundaries of international law and foreign policy became very influential in American international legal scholarship in the 1940s and 1950s and found its clearest articulation in the New Haven "policy science" scholars such as Harold Lasswell and Myres McDougal. These scholars "repudiated the positivist notion of law as a body of rules and sought instead to systemize the different tasks of lawyers as decision specialists in a process of authoritative decision aimed at clarifying and implementing the community interest in world public order."[13] In this system, the role of jurists and the function of law were to balance economic, social, and political interests with an overall goal of demonstrating the global validity and applicability of liberal-democratic values.[14] Kal Raustiala points to the epistemic change in the evolution of American extraterritorial jurisdiction:

> It is nonetheless true that the rise of effects-based extraterritoriality coincides with the *decline of classical legal thought and the rise of balancing and "interests analysis."* It would be very surprising if these theoretical evolutions, in the air in the interwar years, had no effect on judges faced with hard questions about jurisdiction, or on regulators considering what sorts of claims might prevail before a judge. Certainly *Alcoa* and the extraterritorial decisions that followed exhibited a concern with interests, a focus on the functions that legislation is meant to perform, and a willingness to balance and to look past existing doctrine to the social result that flowed from judicial decision making. All of the principles reflected, or at least tracked, the *major shifts underway in American legal thought.*[15]

[13] Kingsbury (2003: 2).
[14] Duxbury (1995: 175).
[15] Raustiala (2009: 111, my italics).

I suggest neither that American legal thought can be reduced to a single approach nor that the rise of American legal imperialism can be reduced to changes in legal thought. As recent studies show, international factors like the end of the Cold War, globalization, and terrorism have been the primary reasons for the recent growth of America's extraterritorial jurisdiction.[15] The "Westphalian" sovereignty shaped within the legal positivist episteme of the nineteenth century remains central in the international system. Yet its claim of exclusive territorial jurisdiction does not seem to limit the reach of American authority bolstered by American power and interest and justified by American legal thought, which requires the analysis of competing interests, rather than the positivist deduction of legal judgments from legal concepts, categories, and codes. An American official acknowledges this need of balancing between "Westphalian" sovereignty and American security in justifying the Predator strikes against suspected Al Qaeda militants in the tribal areas of Pakistan: "There's a balance between respecting full Pakistani sovereignty, even in places where they're not capable of exercising that sovereignty, and the need for our force protection."[16] The official's analysis of competing interests of sovereignty and security reflects the uneasy compromise between legal positivism and American legal thought in the current international legal jurisprudence. As Benedict Kingsbury observes, the "dominant jurisprudential approach to the global practice of international law continues to be positivist" but contemporary positivist influence was often "attenuated by the pragmatic needs to ameliorate disputes, ensure international institutions can operate effectively, and respond to demands of global governance."[17]

Sometimes the expedient American denial of another state's laws coincides with the geographical limitations of American law, creating the absence of jurisdiction over a group of people, or a "vacuum of law,"[18] such as over the civilians accompanying armed forces and military contractors abroad.[19] In 2000, following the U.S. Court of Appeals dismissal of a case against a civilian who impregnated his

[15] For this literature, see Parrish (2009) and Raustiala (2009).
[16] *New York Times*, October 27, 2008.
[17] Kingsbury (2003: 9).
[18] Singer (2004).
[19] Raustiala (2009: 140–149).

teenage stepchild in American military housing in Germany because federal criminal law applied exclusively to the territorial United States, Congress enacted the Military Extraterritorial Jurisdiction Act (MEJA) of 2000. This act extended federal criminal jurisdiction to civilians accompanying the armed forces abroad if the civilians engage in any conduct that would be punishable by imprisonment for more than one year if that conduct were to occur in the United States.[20]

While MEJA extended U.S. military jurisdiction over military personnel and contractors, in June 2003, American authorities granted civil and criminal immunity to American contractors employed by civilian agencies like the State Department or the Central Intelligence Agency.[21] The contractors' immunity prevented the application of Afghan and Iraqi jurisdiction over a large number of people who are legally authorized by American authorities to use force. This immunity voided Iraq's jurisdiction, yet U.S. federal criminal law did not have jurisdiction. This legal void was illustrated by a case in the Abu Ghraib prison that occurred in November 2003 when a detainee died during an interrogation by a CIA officer and a CIA linguist contractor. This crime went unpunished. Similarly, in Baghdad's Green Zone, an employee of the contractor Blackwater killed one of the bodyguards of an Iraqi vice president in December 2006. As of this writing, this Blackwater employee has not been brought to trial because of the jurisdictional gap. While the contractor was immune from Iraqi laws, he was also out of reach of U.S. federal laws. A final example of this jurisdictional gap occurred in September 2007 when military contractors employed by Blackwater shot unarmed Iraqi civilians, leaving seventeen dead and twenty-four wounded. While a federal investigation of this massacre is underway, Blackwater's legal immunity may protect its employees from receiving any serious punishment for the crimes they committed.

In sum, legalization, legal intervention, and legal exclusion have become important issues in international relations and American foreign policy. In postwar international politics, American governments did not expand territoriality but opted instead for a policy of legal

[20] Fallon and Keene (2001).
[21] Liptak (2004).

expansion, employing tools of extraterritorial jurisdiction, and removing groups like private security contractors in Iraq and Afghanistan from the purview of law. To explain international politics and the role of American hegemony in postwar international relations, some international relations scholars turn to issues related to international law and legalization.[22] As the rise and demise of nineteenth-century extraterritoriality and contemporary American extraterritoriality show, law could serve the imperial interest. Law, however, served and could serve the creation of a more egalitarian and peaceful international society that can foster recognition of global diversity and cultivate dialogue and civilization. A better appreciation of the janus-like nature of law requires further research on the nexus of the legalization, legal episteme, and legal imperialism.

[22] Goldstein Kahler, Keohane, and Slaugher (2000) and Finnemore and Trope (2001).

Bibliography

A. Datasets

David Singer and Melvin Small. *National Material Capabilities Dataset.* http://www.umich.edu/~cowproj/capabilities.html.

David J. Singer and Michael Wallace. *Intergovernmental Organizations Dataset.* http://www.icpsr.umich.edu/cgi/archive.prl?study=5520.

B. Documentary and Archival Sources

1856. *Protocols of Conferences Held at Paris Relative to the General Treaty of Peace.* London: British Archives.

1882. *Foreign Relations of the United States.* Washington, DC: Government Printing Office.

1882–1896. *Tokei Nenkan [Japan's Statistical Year Book].* Tokyo: Tokeiin.

1884. *Further Correspondence Respecting the Revision of the Treaty between Great Britain and Japan.* London: National Archives.

1884. *Treaties and Conventions between the Empire of Japan and Other Powers.* Tokyo: The Foreign Office.

1899. *Treaties and Conventions between the Empire of Japan and Other Powers.* Tokyo: The Foreign Office.

1906. Meeting in Support of Belgian View. *London Times.* London: 3.

1907. Joris Released. *London Times.* London: 3.

1907. The Joris Case and the Turkish Capitulations. *The American Journal of International Law.* 1: 485.

1922. *China Year Book.* Shanghai: North China Daily News & Herald.

1922. *Conference on the Limitation of Armament (1921–1922),* Washington, DC: Government Printing Office.

1923. *China Year Book.* Shanghai: North China Daily News & Herald.

FRUS. *Foreign Relations of the United States*. Various years and volumes. Washington, DC: Government Printing Office.
1924. "Treaty of Lausanne." *American Journal of International Law* XVIII (Supplement): 1–116.
1924. *China Year Book*. Shanghai: North China Daily News & Herald.
1925. *China Year Book*. Shanghai: North China Daily News & Herald.
1926. *China Year Book*. Shanghai: North China Daily News & Herald.
1931. *The Civil Code of the Republic of China*. Nanking.
1937–1943. *China Handbook*. New York: The Macmillan Company.
DBFP. 1972. *Documents on British Foreign Policy 1919–1939*. London: Majesty's Stationary Office.
E 1528/1/44.1923. *British Secretary's Notes of Meeting Held in Lord Curzon's Room at the Beau Rivage Hotel*, Lausanne (February 4, 1923). London: National Archives.
Cmd. 1814. 1923. *Records of Proceedings and Draft Terms of Peace. Lausanne Conference on Near Eastern Affairs 1922–1923, Lausanne*. London: National Archives.
FO 371/10348. 1925. *Memo: Outstanding Questions with Siam; Further Correspondence Respecting the Affairs of Siam, 1908; and Further Correspondence Respecting the Affairs of Siam, 1909*. London: National Archives.
FO 371/11646. 1926. *China – Abolition of Extraterritoriality*. London: National Archives.
FO 371/11647. 1926. *China – Abolition of Extraterritoriality*. London: National Archives.
FO 371/31657. 1942. *Extraterritoriality – China 1942*. London: National Archives.
FO 371/31660. *Extraterritoriality Negotiations*. London: National Archives.
FO 371/35679. *Extraterritoriality Negotiations*. London: National Archives.
FO 676/64. *Extraterritoriality*. London: National Archives.
FO 881/4763. 1881–1882. *Further Correspondence Respecting the Revision of the Treaty between Great Britain and Japan 1881–1882*. London: National Archives.
FO 881/4778. 1883. *Memorandum of Views of Her Majesty's Government of the Question of the Revision of Treaties with Japan*. London: National Archives.
FO 881/4938. 1883. *Further Correspondence Respecting the Revision of the Treaty between Great Britain and Japan, 1883*. London: National Archives.
FO 881/5072. 1894. *Further Correspondence Respecting the Revision of the Treaty between Great Britain and Japan*. London: National Archives.
FO 881/6317.1926. *Extraterritoriality Commission*. London: National Archives.

FO 881/6488. 1893. *Further Correspondence Respecting the Revision of the Treaty between Great Britain and Japan, 1893*. London: National Archives.

FO 881/6582. 1894. *Further Correspondence Respecting the Revision of the Treaty between Great Britain and Japan, 1984*. London National Archives.

FO 881/659. 1856. *Persons Enjoying British Protection in the Levant*. London: National Archives.

FO 881/981. 1858. *Report from Hornby to Earl of Malmesbury*. London: National Archives.

FO 881/998. 1859–1861. *Papers Relating to Administrative and Financial Reforms in Turkey 1859–1861*. London: National Archives.

Prime Minister Office Files. National Archives. 1942. File Number 3740. Churchill to Roosevelt, August 9, 1942.

C. Books and Articles

Abernethy, David B. 2000. *The Dynamics of Global Dominance: European Overseas Empires, 1415–1980*. New Haven: Yale University Press.

Ahmad, Feroz. 2000. "Ottoman Perceptions of the Capitulations 1800–1914." *Journal of Islamic Studies* 11 (1): 1–20.

Akyıldız, Ali. 1993. *Tanzimat Dönemi Osmanlı Merkez Teşkilatında Reform, 1836–1856 [Reforms in the Ottoman Central Administration During the Reorganization Period, 1836–1856]*. Istanbul: Eren.

Alderson, Kai and Andrew Hurrell, Eds. 2000. *Hedley Bull on International Society*. New York: St. Martin's Press.

Alexandrowicz, C. H. 1962. "Doctrinal Aspects of the Universality of the Law of Nations." *British Yearbook of International Law* 37: 506–515.

1967. *An Introduction to the History of the Law of Nations in the East Indies (16th, 17th and 18th Centuries)*. Oxford: Clarendon Press.

1969. "New and Original States: The Issue of Reversion to Sovereignty." *International Affairs* 45 (3): 465–480.

Allain, Jean. 2004. "Orientalism and International Law: The Middle East as the Underclass of the International Legal Order." *Leiden Journal of International Law* 17 (2): 391–404.

Anderson, Perry. 1979. *Lineages of the Absolutist State*. New York: Verso.

Anghie, Antony. 1999. "Finding the Peripheries: Sovereignty and Colonialism in Nineteenth-Century International Law." *Harvard International Law Journal* 40 (1): 1–71.

2005. *Imperialism, Sovereignty and the Making of International Law*. Cambridge: Cambridge University Press.

Ashley, Richard K. 1984. "The Poverty of Neorealism." *International Organization* 38 (2): 225–286.

1989. "Untying the Sovereign State: Double Reading of the Anarchy Problematique." *Millennium: Journal of International Studies* 17: 227–262.

Austin, John. 1832. *The Province of Jurisprudence Determined.* [Reprint Amherst, NY: Prometheus Books, 2000.]

Badie, Bertrand. 2000. *The Imported State: The Westernization of the Political Order.* Stanford: Stanford University Press.

Baldwin, David A. 1979. "Power Analysis and World Politics: New Trends Versus Old Tendencies." *World Politics* 31 (2): 161–193.

Bardakçı, Murat. 1999. "1905' te idama mahkûm edip serbest bırakmıştık" [In 1905, We Sentenced Him to Death and then Released Him]. *Hurriyet Daily.* March 14, 1999. p. 9.

Bartelson, Jens. 1995. *A Genealogy of Sovereignty.* Cambridge: Cambridge University Press.

Barzel, Yoram. 2002. *A Theory of the State: Economic Rights, Legal Rights, and the Scope of the State.* Cambridge: Cambridge University Press.

Baumgart, Winfried. 1981. *The Peace of Paris, 1856: Studies in War, Diplomacy, and Peacemaking.* Santa Barbara, CA: Clio Press.

Baxter, R. R. 1958. "Criminal Jurisdiction in the NATO Status of Forces Agreement." *International and Comparative Law Quarterly* 7: 72–81.

Beasley, G. W. 1989. "Meiji Political Institutions" in Marius B. Jansen (Ed.), *The Cambridge History of Japan, Vol. 5: The Nineteenth Century.* 618–673.

Beaulac, Stéphane. 2003. "Emer de Vattel and the Externalization of Sovereignty." *Journal of the History of International Law* 5 (2): 237–292.

2004. "The Westphalian Model in Defining International Law: Challenging the Myth." *Australian Journal of Legal History* 8 (2): 181–213.

Beckler, Richard W. and Matthew H. Kirtland. 2003. "Extraterritorial Application of U.S. Antitrust Law." *Texas International Law Journal* 38: 12–25.

Bederman, David J. 2001. *International Law Frameworks.* New York: Foundation Press.

Bentham, Jeremy. 1970. *Of Laws in General.* London: The Athlone Press.

Benton, Lauren. 2002. *Law and Colonial Cultures: Legal Regimes in World History, 1400–1900.* Cambridge: Cambridge University Press.

Berkes, Niyazi. 1998. *Development of Secularism in Turkey.* New York: Routledge.

Bickers, Robert A. 1999. *Britain in China: Community Culture and Colonialism, 1900–1949.* Manchester: Manchester University Press.

Biersteker, Thomas J. 2002. "State, Sovereignty and Territory," in Walter Carlsnaes, Thomas Rise, and Beth A. Simmons (Eds.), *Handbook of International Relations:* Thousand Oaks, CA: Sage. 155–176.

Blaney, David L. and Naeem Inayatullah. 2002. "The Westphalian Deferral." *International Studies Review* 2 (2):1–28.

Bloch, Marc. 1961. *Feudal Society.* Chicago: University of Chicago Press.

Borg, Dorothy. 1947. *American Policy and the Chinese Revolution, 1925–1928*. New York: American Institute of Pacific Relations.

Bozkurt, Gülnihal. 1989. *Gayrimüslim Osmanlı Vatandaşlarının Hukuki Durumu [Legal Position of Non-Muslim Ottoman Citizens]*. Ankara: Türk Tarih Kurumu.

1998. *Azınlık İmtiyazları-Kapütülasyonlardan Tek Hukuk Sistemine Geçiş [from Minority Privileges and Capitulations to Uniform Legal System]*. Ankara: Atatürk Araştırma Merkezi.

Braude, Benjamin and Bernard Lewis, Eds. 1982. *Christians and Jews in the Ottoman Empire: The Functioning of a Plural Society*. New York: Holmes & Meier.

Bull, Hedley and Adam Watson. 1984. *The Expansion of International Society*. Oxford: Clarendon Press.

Bull, Hedley. 1977. *The Anarchical Society*. New York: Columbia University Press.

1979. "Natural Law and International Relations." *British Journal of International Studies* 5 (2): 171–181.

1996. "International Theory: The Case for a Classical Approach," in J. A. Vasquez (Ed.), *Classics of International Relations*. Upper Saddle River, NJ: Prentice Hall: 76–81.

Buzan, Barry. 1993. "From International System to International Society: Structural Realism and Regime Theory Meet the English School." *International Organization* 47: 327–352.

Buzan, Barry, Charles Jones, and Richard Little. 1993. *The Logic of Anarchy: Neorealism to Structural Realism*. New York: Columbia University Press.

Calder, Kent E. 2007. *Embattled Garrisons*. Princeton: Princeton University Press.

Callahan, William A. 2004. "Nationalising International Theory: Race, Class, and the English School." *Global Society* 18(4): 305–323.

Campbell, David. 1992. *Writing Security*. Minneapolis: University of Minnesota Press.

Chan, K. Chan. 1977. "The Abrogation of British Extraterritoriality in China, 1942–1943." *Modern Asian Studies* 11: 257–291.

Chang, Richard T. 1984. *The Justice of the Western Consular Courts in Nineteenth-Century Japan*. Westport, CT: Greenwood Press.

Chang, Seung Wha. 1992–1993. "Extraterritorial Application of U.S. Antitrust Laws to Other Pacific Countries." *Hastings International and Comparative Law Review* 16: 295–320.

Checkel, Jeffrey T. 1998. "The Constructivist Turn in International Relations Theory." *World Politics* 50 (2): 324–348.

Chen, Jianfu. 1999. *Chinese Law: Towards an Understanding of Chinese Law, Its Nature and Development*. Boston: Kluwer Law International.

Ch'ien, Tuan-shãeng. 1950. *The Government and Politics of China*. Cambridge: Harvard University Press.

Chiu, Hungdah. 1979–1980. "The United States Status of Forces Agreement with the Republic of China." *Boston College International and Comparative Law Review* 3: 67–88.

Churchill, Winston. 1929. *The World Crisis 1918–1928: The Aftermath*. New York: Charles Scribner Sons.

Cin, Halil and Ahmet Akgündüz. 1989. *Turk Hukuk Tarihi: Kamu Hukuku [Turkish Legal History: Public Law]*. Konya: Selçuk Üniversitesi Yayınları.

Clark, Harry L. 1999. "Dealing with U.S. Extraterritorial Sanctions and Foreign Countermeasures." *University of Pennsylvania Journal of International Economic Law* 20 (1): 61–96.

Clifford, Nicholas R. 1991. *Spoilt Children of Empire: Westerners in Shanghai and the Chinese Revolution of the 1920s*. Middlebury, VT: Middlebury College Press.

Commission on Extraterritoriality. 1926. *Report of the Commission on Extraterritoriality*. Washington, DC: Government Printing Office.

Copeland, Dale C. 2003. "A Realist Critique of the English School." *Review of International Studies* 29: 427–441.

Cotterrell, Roger. 1989. *The Politics of Jurisprudence: A Critical Introduction to Legal Philosophy*. Philadelphia: University of Pennsylvania Press.

Curley, Tyler. 2009. "Social Identity Theory and EU Expansion." *International Studies Quarterly* 53 (4): 647–666.

Dare, Philip Ned. 1975. *John Bingham and Treaty Revision with Japan: 1873–1885*. Lexington: University of Kentucky.

Deudney, Daniel. 1996. "Binding Sovereigns: Authorities, Structures, and Geopolitics in Philadelphian Systems," in T. J. Biersteker and C. Weber (Eds.), *State Sovereignty as Social Construct*. Cambridge: Cambridge University Press: 190–239.

Dewey, John. 1894. "Austin's Theory of Sovereignty." *Political Science Quarterly* 9 (1): 31–52.

Dixit, Avinash K. 2004. *Lawlessness and Economics: Alternative Modes of Governance*. Princeton: Princeton University Press.

Donnelly, Jack. 1986. "International Human Rights: A Regime Analysis." *International Organization* 40 (3): 599–642.

1998. "Human Rights: A New Standard of Civilization?" *International Affairs* 74 (1): 1–23.

2000. *Realism and International Relations*. Cambridge: Cambridge University Press.

Doyle, Michael. 1986. *Empires*. Ithaca, NY: Cornell University Press.

Dunne, Tim. 1998. *Inventing International Society: A History of the English School*. New York: St. Martin's Press.

Dunne, Timothy. 1995. "The Social Construction of International Society." *The European Journal of International Relations* 1 (3): 367–389.

Duxbury, Neil. 1995. *Patterns of American Jurisprudence*. Oxford: Clarendon Press.

Dyck, Edward Van. 1881. *Capitulations of the Ottoman Empire*. Washington, DC: Government Printing Office.

Eastwood, R. A. and G. W. Keaton. 1929. *The Austinian Theories of Law and Sovereignty*. London: Methuen.

Ellickson, Robert C. 1991. *Order Without Law*. Cambridge: Harvard University Press.

Erickson, Richard J. 1994. "Status of Forces Agreements: A Sharing of Sovereign Prerogative." *Air Force Law Review* 37: 137–154.

Epstein, Mortimer. 1908. *The Early History of the Levant Company*. London: G. Routledge & Sons.

Eroğlu, Hamza. 1967. *Türk Devrim Tarihi* [*History of Turkish Revolution*]. Ankara: Kardeş Matbaası.

Eryılmaz, Bilal. 1990. *Osmanlı Devletinda Gayrimüslim Tebaanın Yönetimi [Administration of Non-Muslim Subjects in the Ottoman State]*. İstanbul: Risale Basın-Yayın Ltd.

1992. *Osmanlı Devletinde Millet Sistemi [Millet System in the Ottoman Empire]*. İstanbul: Agaç Yayıncılık.

Fairbank, John King. 1964. *Trade and Diplomacy on the China Coast: The Opening of Treaty Ports 1842–1854*. Cambridge: Harvard University Press.

Fallon, Andrew D. and Theresa A. Keene. 2001. "Closing the Legal Loophole? Practical Implications of the Military Extraterritorial Jurisdiction Act of 2000." *Air Force Law Review* 51: 271–292.

Fenwick, Charles G. 1914. "The Authority of Vattel." *The American Political Science Review* 8 (3): 375–393.

Feuewerker, Albert. 1976. *The Foreign Establishment in China*. Ann Arbor: Center for Chinese Studies.

Finnemore, Martha and Stephen J. Toope. 2001. "Alternatives to 'Legalization': Richer Views of Law and Politics." *International Organization* 55 (3): 743–758.

Fishel, Wesley R. 1952. *The End of Extraterritoriality in China*. Berkeley: University of California Press.

Floor, Willem. 1983. "Change and Development in the Judicial System of Qajar Iran (1800–1925)," in E. Bosworth and C. Hillenbrand (Eds.), *Qajar Iran: Political, Social, and Cultural Change 1800–1925*. Edinburgh: Edinburgh University Press: 113–147.

Foster, John Watson. 1903. *American Diplomacy in the Orient*. Boston, New York: Houghton, Mifflin and Company.

Fox, Grace Estelle. 1969. *Britain and Japan, 1858–1883*. Oxford: Clarendon Press.

Fukuyama, Francis. 2004. *State-Building: Governance and World Order in the 21st Century*. Ithaca, NY: Cornell University Press.

Fung, Edmund S. K. 1987. "The Chinese Nationalists and the Unequal Treaties 1924–1931." *Modern Asian Studies* 21: 783–819.

Ganz, A. Harding. 1977. "German Navy in the Far East and Pacific: The Seizure of Kiatschou and After," in J. A. Moses and P. Kennedy (Eds.), *Germany in the Pacific and Far East 1870–1914*. St. Lucia, Queensland: Queensland University Press: 115–136.

Giddens, Anthony. 1987. *The Nation-State and Violence*. Berkeley: University of California Press.

Goldstein, Judith, Miles Kahler, Robert O. Keohane, and Anne-Marie Slaugher. 2000. "Legalization and World Politics." *International Organization* 54 (3): 385–399.

2001. "Response to Finnemore and Toope." *International Organization* 55 (3): 759–760.

Gönen, Yasemin Saner. 2000. "The Judicial Privileges of Foreigners in the Ottoman Empire," in K. Ciçek, E. Kuran, N. Göyünc, and İ. Ortaylı (Eds.), *The Great Ottoman-Turkish Civilization*. Ankara: Yeni Türkiye (III): 676–688.

Gong, Gerrit. 1984. *The Standard of "Civilization" in International Society*. Oxford: Clarendon Press.

Greif, Avner. 1993. "Contract Enforceability and Economic Institutions in Early Trade: The Maghribi Traders' Coalition." *American Economic Review* 83 (3):525–548.

Griswold, Whitney A. 1938. *Far Eastern Policy of the United States*. New York: Harcourt, Brace and Company.

Gross, Leo. 1948. "The Peace of Westphalia, 1648–1948." *American Journal of International Law* 42 (1): 20–41.

Grundman, Rock. 1980. "The New Imperialism: Extraterritorial Application of United States Law." *International Lawyer* 14: 257–266.

Hall, Stephan. 2001. "The Persistent Spectre: Natural Law, International Order and the Limits of Legal Positivism." *European Journal of International Law* 12 (2): 269–307.

Hall, William Edward. 1894. *Foreign Powers and Jurisdiction of the British Crown*. Oxford: Clarendon Press.

Hanioğlu, M. Şükrü. 2008. *A Brief History of the Late Ottamon Empire*. Princeton: Princeton University Press.

Hanioğlu, M. Şükrü. 2010. "Westphalian Eurocentrism in International Relations Theory." *International Studies Review*.

Hart, H. L. A. 1971. "Bentham's *Of Laws in General*." *Cambrian Law Review* 2: 24–34.

Henderson, Dan Fenno. 1968. "Law and Political Modernization in Japan," in R. E. Ward (Ed.), *Political Development in Modern Japan*. Princeton: Princeton University Press: 387–456.

Henkin, Louis, Richard Crawford Pugh, Oscar Schachter, and Hans Smit. 1993. *International Law: Cases and Materials*. St. Paul, MN: West Publishing.

Hertslet, Lewis. 1845. *Treaties and Conventions Between Great Britain and Foreign Powers*. Volume VI. London: Henry Butterworth.

Hinckey, Frank E. 1906. *American Consular Jurisdiction in the Orient*. Washington, DC: W. H. Lowdermilk.

Hoare, James. 1994. *Japan's Treaty Ports and Foreign Settlements: The Uninvited Guests, 1858–1899*. Folkestone, Kent: Japan Library.

Hobbes, Thomas. 1969. *The Elements of Law, Natural and Politic*, Ferdinand Tonnies (Ed.), 2nd ed. New York: Barnes & Noble.

Hobson, John M. 2000. *The State and International Relations*. Cambridge, Cambridge University Press.

Holland, Thomas Erskine. 1898. *Studies in International Law*. Oxford: Clarendon Press.

Hornby, Edmund. 1928. *An Autobiography*. Boston: Houghton Mifflin.

Horowitz, Richard S. 2005. "International Law and State Transformation in China, Siam, and the Ottoman Empire during the Nineteenth Century." *Journal of World History* 15 (4): 445–486.

Hsu, Immanuel C. Y. 1960. *China's Entrance into the Family of Nations: The Diplomatic Phase 1858–1880*. Cambridge: Harvard University Press.

Huang, Philip C. 2001. *Code, Custom, and Legal Practice in China: The Qing and the Republic Compared*. Stanford: Stanford University Press.

Hurewitz, J. C. 1961. "Ottoman Diplomacy and the European State System." *The Middle East Journal* XV (2): 141–152.

Hussain, Nasser. 2003. *The Jurisprudence of Emergency: Colonialism and the Rule of Law*. Ann Arbor: University of Michigan Press.

İnalcık, Halil. 1960. "Imtiyazat." *Encyclopaedia of Islam* [3]: 1178–1195.

Inkle, Frank W. 1967. "The Triple Intervention: Japan's Lesson in the Diplomacy of Imperialism." *Monumenta Nipponica* 22 (1/2): 122–130.

İnönü, İsmet. 1987. *Hatıralar [Memoirs]*. İstanbul: Bilgi Yayınevi.

Iriye, Akiye. 1986. "Japanese Aggression and China's International Position 1931–1949." *Cambridge History of China*. Cambridge: Cambridge University Press.

Jackson, Robert H. 1990. *Quasi-States: Sovereignty, International Relations and the Third World*. Cambridge: Cambridge University Press.

1993. "The Weight of Ideas in Decolonization: Normative Change in International Relations," in Judith Goldstein and Robert O. Keohane (Eds.), *Ideas & Foreign Policy*. Ithaca, NY: Cornell University Press: 111–138.

Janis, M. W. 1984. "Jeremy Bentham and the Fashioning of International Law." *American Journal of International Law* 78: 405–418.

Jensen, De Lamar. 1985. "The Ottoman Turks in Sixteenth Century French Diplomacy." *Sixteenth Century Journal* 16 (4): 451–470.

Jansen, Marius B. 1968. "Modernization and Foreign Policy in Meiji Japan," in R. E. Ward (Ed.), *Political Development in Modern Japan*. Princeton: Princeton University Press: 149–188.

1989. "Introduction," in M. B. Jansen (Ed.), *The Cambridge History of Japan*, vol. 5. Cambridge: Cambridge University Press: 1–49.

Jessop, Bob. 1990. *State Theory: Putting the Capitalist State in Its Place*. Cambridge: Polity Press.

John, Michael. 1989. *Politics and Law in Late Nineteenth-Century Germany: The Origins of Civil Code*. Oxford: Oxford University Press.

Johnston, W. Ross. 1973. *Sovereignty and Protection: A Study of British Jurisdictional Imperialism in the Late Nineteenth Century*. Durham, NC: Duke University Press.

Jones, Francis Clifford. 1931. *Extraterritoriality in Japan and the Diplomatic Relations Resulting in Its Abolition, 1853–1899*. New Haven, CT: Yale University Press.

Jung, Youngjin and Jun-Shik Hwang. 2002–2003. "Where Does Inequality Come From? An Analysis of the Korea–United States Status of Forces Agreement." *American University International Law Review* 18: 1103–1142.

Jupille, Joseph and James A. Caporaso. 2009. "Domesticating Discourses: European Law, English Judges, and Political Institutions." *European Political Science Review* 1 (2): 205–228.

Kahler, Miles. 1984. *Decolonization in Britain and France: The Domestic Consequences of International Relations*. Princeton: Princeton University Press.

2000. "Legalization as Strategy: The Asia-Pacific Case." *International Organization* 54 (3): 549–572.

Kajima, Morinosuke. 1967. *The Emergence of Japan as a World Power, 1895–1925*. Rutland, VT: C. E. Tuttle Co.

Kamikawa, Hikomatsu. 1958. *Japan-American Diplomatic Relations in the Meiji-Taisho Era*. Tokyo: Pan-Pacific Press.

Kasaba, Reșat. 1988. *The Ottoman Empire and World Economy: The Nineteenth Century*. Albany: SUNY Press.

Kayaoğlu, Turan. 2005. "Sovereignty, State-Building, and the Abolition of Extraterritoriality." Unpublished dissertation. University of Washington: Seattle.

2007. "The Extension of Westphalian Sovereignty: State-Building and the Abolition of Extraterritoriality." *International Studies Quarterly*. (51) 3: 649–676.

Keeton, G. W. 1969. *The Development of Extraterritoriality in China*. New York: Howard Fertig.

Kennedy, David. 1997. "International Law and the Nineteenth Century: History of an Illusion." *Quinnipiac Law Review* 99: 112–113.

Kennedy, Paul M. 1977. "Germany and the Samoan Tridominium, 1889–1898: A Study in Frustrated Imperialism," in J. A. Moses and P. M. Kennedy (Eds.), *Germany in the Pacific and Far East, 1870–1914*. St. Lucia, Queensland: Queensland University Press: 88–114.

1986. *The Rise and Fall of British Naval Mastery*. London: Ashfield Press.

1987. *The Rise and Fall of Great Powers*. New York: Random House.

Keohane, Robert O. 1986. *Neorealism and Its Critiques*. New York: Columbia University Press.
Kim, Marie S. H. 2009. "Customary Law and Colonial Jurisprudence in Korea." *American Journal of Comparative Law* 57 (1): 205–247.
Kim, Won-Ki. 2003. "The Extraterritorial Application of U.S. Antitrust Law and Its Adoption in Korea." *Singapore Journal of International and Comparative Law* 7: 386–411.
Kingsbury, Benedict. 2002. "Legal Positivism as Normative Politics: International Society, Balance of Power and Lassa Oppenheim's Positive International Law." *European Journal of International Law* 13 (2): 401–436.
Kocabaşoğlu, Uygur. 2004. *Majestelerinin Konsolosları [Majesty's Consuls]*. İstanbul: İletişim.
Koskenniemi, Martti. 1989. *From Apology to Utopia: The Structure of International Legal Argument*. Helsinki: Finnish Lawyers' Publishing.
2004. *The Gentle Civilizer of Nations: The Rise and Fall of International Law, 1870–1960*. Cambridge: Cambridge University Press.
Krasner, Stephan D. 1978. *Defending the National Interest: Raw Materials Investments and U.S. Foreign Policy*. Princeton: Princeton University Press.
1984. "Approaches to the State: Alternative Conceptions and Historical Dynamics." *Comparative Politics* 16 (2): 223–246.
1985. *Structural Conflict: The Third World against Global Liberalism*. Berkeley: University of California Press.
1989. "Sovereignty: An Institutional Perspective," in J. A. Caporaso (Ed.), *The Elusive State: International and Comparative Perspectives*. Newbury Park, CA: Sage: 69–96.
1993. "Westphalia and All That," in Judith Goldstein and Robert O. Keohane (Eds.), *Ideas and Foreign Policy: Beliefs, Institutions, and Political Change*. Ithaca, NY: Cornell University Press: 235–264.
1995. "Compromising Westphalia." *International Security* 20 (3):115–151.
1999. *Sovereignty: Organized Hypocrisy*. Princeton: Princeton University Press.
2001. "Organized Hypocrisy in Nineteenth-Century East Asia." *International Relations of the Asia-Pacific* 1: 173–197.
2004. "Sharing Sovereignty: New Institutions for Collapsed and Failing States." *International Security* 29 (2): 85–120.
Kratochwil, Friedrich. 1986. "Of Systems, Boundaries, and Territoriality: An Inquiry into the Formation of the State-System." *World Politics* 39: 27–52.
1995. "Sovereignty as 'Dominium': Is There a Right to Humanitarian Intervention?" in M. Mastanduno and G. Lyons (Eds.), *Beyond Westphalia: National Sovereignty and Humanitarian Intervention*. Baltimore: Johns Hopkins University Press: 21–42.

Lachs, Manfred. 1987. *The Teacher in International Law.* Dordrecht: Martinus Nijhoff.

Lane-Poole, Stanley and F. Victor Dickins. 1894. *The Life of Sir Harry Parkes, K.C.B., G.C.M.G., Sometime Her Majesty's Minister to China & Japan.* London, New York: Macmillan.

Langer, William L. 1951. *The Diplomacy of Imperialism 1890–1902.* New York: Alfred A. Knopf.

Leue, W. H.-J. 1992. "Legal Expansion in the Age of Companies," in W. J. Mommsen and J. A. De Moor (Eds.), *European Expansion and Law: The Encounter of European and Indigenous Law in 19th- and 20th-Century Africa and Asia.* Oxford: Berg: 129–158.

Lewis, Bernard. 1968. *The Emergence of Modern Turkey.* London: Oxford University Press.

Lieberson, Stanley. 1992. "Small N's and Big Conclusions: An Examination of the Reasoning in Comparative Studies Based on a Small Number of Cases." *Social Forces* 70 (2): 307–320.

1994. "More on the Uneasy Case for Using Mill-Type Methods in Small-N Comparative Studies." *Social Forces* 72: 1225–1237.

Liebesny, Herbert I. 1955. "The Development of Western Judicial Privileges," in M. Khadduri and H. J. Liebesny (Eds.), *Law in the Middle East,* Washington, DC: The Middle East Institute: 309–334.

Liptak, Adam. 2004. "Who Would Try Civilians from U.S.? No One in Iraq." *New York Times.* May 26, 2004: A11.

Little, Richard. 1995. "Neorealism and the English School: A Methodological, Ontological, and Theoretical Reassessment." *European Journal of International Relations* 1:1–21.

Liu, Shih Shun. 1925. *Extraterritoriality: Its Rise and Its Decline.* New York: Columbia University Press.

Louis, Roger. 1971. *British Strategy in the Far East, 1919–1939.* Oxford: Clarendon Press.

Lynn, Martin. 1999. "British Policy, Trade and Informal Empire in the Mid-Nineteenth Century," in A. Porter (Ed.), *The Oxford History of the British Empire: The Nineteenth Century* (III). Oxford: Oxford University Press: 101–121.

Lytle, Courtney G. 1997. "A Hegemonic Interpretation of Extraterritorial Jurisdiction in Antitrust: From American Banana to Hartford Fire." *Syracuse Journal of International Law and Commerce* 24 (4): 41–76.

Macfie, Alexander Lyon, Ed. 2000. *Orientalism: A Reader.* New York: New York University Press.

Mackinnon, Donald M. 1966. "Natural Law," in Herbert Butterfield and Martin Wight (Eds.), *Diplomatic Investigations.* London: George Allen & Unwin: 74–88.

Majeed, J. 1990. "James Mill's 'The History of British India' and Utilitarianism as a Rhetoric of Reform." *Modern Asian Studies* 24 (2): 209–224.

Marder, Arthur Jacob. 1940. *The Anatomy of British Sea Power: A History of British Naval Policy in the Pre-Dreadnought Era, 1880–1905*. New York: A. A. Knopf.

MacDonald, Paul. 2004. "Networks of Domination: Social Ties and Imperial Rule in International Politics," unpublished manuscript.

Mearsheimer, John J. 2001. *The Tragedy of Great Power Politics*. New York: W. W. Norton.

Memorandum. 1922. *The Capitulations: Memorandum Submitted on Behalf of the Non-Official British Community in Constantinople*. London: Page & Thomas Ltd.

Merryman, John Henry. 1969. *The Civil Law Tradition*. Stanford: Stanford University Press.

Midgley, E. B. F. 1975. *The Natural Law and the Theory of International Relations*. New York: Barnes & Noble.

Milton, Philip. 1982. "David Hume and the Eighteenth-Century Conception of Natural Law." *Legal Studies* 2 (1): 14–34.

Mitzen, Jennifer. 2005. "Reading Habermas in Anarchy." *American Political Science Review* 99 (3): 401–417.

Moravcsik, Andrew. 2000. "The Origins of Human Rights Regimes." *International Organization* 54 (2): 217–252.

Moulder, Frances. 1977. *Japan, China and the Modern World Economy*. Cambridge: Cambridge University Press.

Murphy, Alexander B. 1996. "The Sovereign State System as Political-Territorial Ideal," in T. J. Biersteker and C. Weber (Eds.), *State Sovereignty as Social Construct*. Cambridge: Cambridge University Press: 81–120.

Nicolson, Harold. 1974 [1934]. *Curzon: The Last Phase 1919–1925*. New York: Howard Fertig.

Nish, Ian. 1968. *The Story of Japan*. London: Faber.

1998. *The Iwakura Mission to America and Europe*. London: Routledge.

Norman, Adam B. 1995–1996. "The Rape Controversy: Is a Revision of the Status of Forces Agreement with Japan Necessary?" *Indiana International and Comparative Law Review* 6 (3): 717–740.

North, Douglass C. and Robert Thomas. 1973. *The Rise of the Western World: A New Economic History*. Cambridge: Cambridge University Press.

North, Douglass C. 1981. *Structure and Change in Economic History*. New York: W. W. Norton & Company.

North, Douglass Cecil. 1990. *Institutions, Institutional Change, and Economic Performance*. Cambridge: Cambridge University Press.

Nussbaum, Arthur. 1954. *A Concise History of the Law of Nations*. New York: Macmillan.

Onuf, Nicholas Greenwood. 1998. *The Republican Legacy in International Thought*. Cambridge: Cambridge University Press.

Oppenheim, Lassa. 1908. "The Science of International Law: Its Task and Method." *The American Journal of International Law* 2 (2): 313–356.

Ornsby, Robert. 1884. *Memoirs of James Robert Hope-Scott of Abbotsford*, 2nd edition. London: J. Murray.

Örücü, Esin. 1992. "The Impact of European Law on the Ottoman Empire and Turkey," in W. J. Mommsen and J. A. D. Moor (Eds.), *European Expansion and Law: The Encounter of European and Indigenous Law in 19th and 20th Century Africa and Asia*. New York: BERG.

Osiander, Andreas. 2001. "Sovereignty, International Relations, and the Westphalian Myth." *International Organization* 55 (2): 251–288.

Paine, S. C. M. 2003. *The Sino-Japanese War of 1894–1895: Perceptions, Power, and Primacy*. Cambridge: Cambridge University Press.

Parrish, Austen L. 2009. "Reclaiming International Law from Extraterritoriality." *Minnesota Law Review*. 93: 101–161.

Perez, Louis G. 1999. *Japan Comes of Age: Mutsu Munemitsu and the Revision of the Unequal Treaties*. Madison, NJ: Fairleigh Dickinson University Press.

Philpott, Daniel. 2001. *Revolutions in Sovereignty: How Ideas Shaped Modern International Relations*. Princeton: Princeton University Press.

Pitts, Jennifer. 2003. "Legislator of the World? A Reading of Bentham on Colonies." *Political Theory* 31 (2): 200–234.

Platt, Demond Christopher Martin. 1971. *The Cinderalla Service: British Consuls Since 1825*. London: Longman.

Poggi, Gianfranco. 1978. *The Development of the Modern State: A Sociological Introduction*. Stanford: Stanford University Press.

Poggi, Gianfranco. 1990. *The State: Its Nature, Development and Prospects*. Stanford: Stanford University Press.

Polat, Necati. 2000. "Three Contemporaries: The International, Bentham, and De Sade." *Social Text* 18 (4): 1–23.

Pollard, Robert Thomas. 1933. *China's Foreign Relations, 1917–1931*. New York: Macmillan.

Pound, Roscoe. 1954–1955. "The Chinese Civil Code in Action." *Tulane Law Review* 29: 227–422.

Putman, Tonya L. 2009. "Courts Without Borders: Domestic Sources of U.S. Extraterritoriality in Regulatory Sphere." *International Organization* 63(3): 459–490.

Quan, Lau-king. 1939. *China's Relations with the League of Nations*. Hong Kong: The Asiatic Litho Printing Press.

Ramseyer, J. Mark and Frances McCall Rosenbluth. 1995. *The Politics of Oligarchy: Institutional Choice in Imperial Japan*. Cambridge: Cambridge University Press.

Raustiala, Kal. 2009. *Does the Constitution Follow the Flag?* Oxford: Oxford University Press.

Reus-Smit, Christian. 1999. *Moral Purpose of the State*. Cambridge: Cambridge University Press.

2002. "Imagining Society: Constructivism and the English School." *British Journal of Politics and International Relations* 4 (3): 487–509.

Ruggie, John G. 1983. "Continuity and Transformation in the World Polity: Toward a Neorealist Synthesis." *World Politics* 35 (2): 261–285.
Ruggie, John Gerard. 1993. "Territoriality and Beyond: Problematizing Modernity in International Relations." *International Organizations* 47: 139–174.
Rumble, Wilfrid E. 2005. *Doing Austin Justice: The Reception of John Austin's Philosophy of Law in Nineteenth-Century England*. London: Continuum.
Ruskola, Teemu. 2002. "Legal Orientalism." *Michigan Law Review* 101 (1): 179–234.
2005. "Canton Is Not Boston: The Invention of American Imperial Sovereignty," *American Quarterly* 57: 859.
2008. "Colonialism Without Colonies: On the Extraterritorial Jurisprudence of the U.S. Court for China." *Law & Contemporary Problems* 71: 217–242.
Ryosuke, Ishii. 1958. *Japanese Legislation in the Meiji Era*. Tokyo: Pan-Pacific Press.
Said, Edward. 1979. *Orientalism*. New York: Vintage Books.
Sanders, C. T. 2000. *America's Overseas Garrisons*. Oxford: Oxford University Press.
Savolainen, Jukka. 1994. "The Rationality of Drawing Big Conclusions Based on Small Samples: In Defense of Mill's Methods." *Social Forces* 72: 1217–1224.
Schmidhauser, John R. 1997. "The European Origins of Legal Imperialism and Its Legacy in Legal Education in Former Colonial Regions." *International Political Science Review* 18 (3): 337–351.
Schmitt, Glenn R. 2001–2002. "Closing the Gap in Criminal Jurisdiction over Civilians Accompanying the Armed Forces Abroad." *Catholic University Law Review* 51: 55–134.
Scott, David. 2008. *China and the International System, 1840–1849*. Albany: SUNY Press.
Scully, Eileen. P. 2001. *Bargaining with the State from Afar: American Citizenship in Treaty Port China, 1844–1942*. New York: Columbia University Press.
Shapiro, Martin M. 1981. *Courts*. Chicago: University of Chicago Press.
Shaw, Malcolm N. 2002. *International Law*, 5th ed. Cambridge: Cambridge University Press.
Siebold, Baron Alexander von. 1901. *Japan's Accession to the Comity of Nations*. London: K. Paul, Trench, and Trubner & Co.
Silberman, Bernard S. 1993. *Cages of Reason: The Rise of the Rational State in France, Japan, the United States, and Great Britain*. Chicago: University of Chicago Press.
Simpson, Gerry. 2004. *Great Powers and Outlaw States: Unequal Sovereigns in the International Legal Order*. Cambridge: Cambridge University Press.

Singer, David. 1996. "The Incomplete Theorist: Insight without Evidence," in J. A. Vasquez (Ed.), *Classics of International Relations*, Upper Saddle River, NJ: Prentice Hall: 82–90.

Singer, Pater Warren. 2004. "War, Profits, and the Vacuum of Law: Privatized Military Firms and International Law." *Columbia Journal of Transnational Law* 42 (2): 520–550.

Snyder, Jack. 1991. *Myths of Empire: Domestic Politics and International Ambition*. Ithaca, NY: Cornell University Press.

Sonyel, Salahi R. 1975. *Turkish Diplomacy 1918–1923: Mustafa Kemal and the Turkish National Movement*. London: Sage Publications.

Soosa, Nasim M. 1931. "The Legal Interpretation of the Abrogation of the Turkish Capitulations." *Dakota Law Review* III (7): 335–364.

Sousa, Nasim. 1933. *The Capitulatory Regime of Turkey: Its History, Origin, and Nature*. Baltimore: Johns Hopkins Press.

Soyeshima, Taneomi. 1910. "Japan's Foreign Relations," in S. Okuma (Ed.) *Fifty Years of New Japan*. London: Smith, Elder & Co.: 93–121.

Spagnolo, John P. 1991. "Portents of Empire in Britain's Ottoman Jurisdiction." *Middle Eastern Studies* 27 (2): 256–282.

Spence, Jonathan. D. 1990. *The Search for Modern China*. New York: W. W. Norton.

Spruyt, Hendrik. 1994. *The Sovereign State and Its Competitors*. Princeton: Princeton University Press.

Stivachtis, Yannis A. 1998. *The Enlargement of International Society: Culture Versus Anarchy and Greece's Entry into International Society*. London: Macmillan Press.

Stokes, Eric. 1959. *The English Utilitarians and India*. Oxford: Clarendon Press.

Strang, David. 1996. "Contested Sovereignty: The Social Construction of Colonial Imperialism," in Thomas J. Biersteker and Cynthia Weber (Eds.), *State Sovereignty as Social Construct*. Cambridge: Cambridge University Press: 22–49.

Strayer, Joseph R. 1973. *On the Medieval Origins of the Modern State*. Princeton: Princeton University Press.

Suganami, Hidemi. 1984. "Japan's Entry into International Society," in H. Bull and A. Watson (Eds.), *The Expansion of International Society*. Oxford: Clarendon Press: 185–200.

Suzuki, Shogo. 2009. *Civilization and Empire: China and Japan's Encounter with European International Society*. New York: Routledge.

Taylor, Veronica. 1997. "Beyond Legal Orientalism," in Veronica Taylor (Ed.), *Asian Laws Through Australian Eyes*. Sydney: Law Book: 47–64.

Teschke, Benno. 2003. *The Myth of 1648: Class, Geopolitics, and the Making of Modern International Relations*. London: Verso.

Thomson, Janice E. 1995. "State Sovereignty in International Relations: Bridging the Gap between Theory and Empirical Research." *International Studies Quarterly* 39 (2): 213–233.

Thomson, Janice. 1994. *Mercenaries, Pirates & Sovereigns: State-Building and Extraterritorial Violence in Early Modern Europe.* Princeton: Princeton University Press.

Tilly, Charles. 1975. "Reflections on the History of European State-Making," in Charles Tilly (Ed.), *The Formation of National States in Western Europe.* Princeton: Princeton University Press: 3–83.

Tilly, Charles. 1992. *Coercion, Capital, and European States, AD 990–1992.* Cambridge: Blackwell.

Trotter, Ann (Ed.) 1996. *British Documents on Foreign Affairs: Reports and Papers from the Foreign Office Confidential Print. Series E. Asia, 1914–1939.* Volume 30, China, November 1925–June 1929. Bethesda: University Publications of America.

Tung, William L. 1970. *China and the Foreign Powers: The Impact of and Reaction to Unequal Treaties.* Dobbs Ferry, NY: Oceana Publications.

Varghese, Tracy P. 2001–2002. "The WTO's Shrimp-Turtle Decisions: The Extraterritorial Enforcement of U.S. Environmental Policy Via Unilateral Trade Embargoes." *The Environmental Lawyer* 5: 421–455.

Walker, R. B. J. 1993. *Inside/Outside: International Relations as Political Theory.* Cambridge: Cambridge University Press.

Walker, Thomas Alfred. 1893. *The Science of International Law.* London: C. J. Clay and Sons.

Wallace, Michael and J. David Singer. 1970. "Intergovernmental Organization in the Global System, 1815–1964: A Quantitative Description." *International Organization* 24: 239–287.

Wallerstein, Immanuel. 1979. *The Capitalist World-Economy.* Cambridge: Cambridge University Press.

Ward, Robert Edward and Dankwart A. Rustow. 1964. *Political Modernization in Japan and Turkey.* Princeton: Princeton University Press.

Warg, Paul A. 1958. *Missionaries, Chinese, and Diplomacy.* Princeton: Princeton University Press.

Watson, Adam. 1984. "European International Society and Its Expansion," in H. Bull and A. Watson (Eds.) *The Expansion of International Society.* Oxford: Clarendon Press: 13–32.

1987. "Hedley Bull, States Systems and International Society." *Review of International Studies,* 13: 147–155.

1992. *The Evolution of International Society.* New York: Routledge.

Weber, Cynthia. 1995. *Stimulating Sovereignty: Intervention, the State and Symbolic Exchange.* Cambridge: Cambridge University Press.

Weber, Max. 1978. *Economy and Society* [Volume 2]. Berkeley: University of California Press.

Wendt, Alexander and Daniel Friedheim. 1996. "Hierarchy under Anarchy: Informal Empires and the East German State," in T. J. Biersteker and C. Weber (Eds.), *State Sovereignty as Social Construct.* Cambridge: Cambridge University Press: 240–277.

Wendt, Alexander. 1999. *Social Theory of International Politics*. Cambridge: Cambridge University Press.

Westlake, John. 1894. *Chapters on the Principles of International Law*. Cambridge: Cambridge University Press.

Westney, D. Eleanor. 1987. *Imitation and Innovation: The Transfer of Western Organized Patterns to Meiji Japan*. Cambridge: Harvard University Press.

Wight, Martin. 1966. "Western Values in International Relations," in Herbert Butterfield and Martin Wight (Eds.), *Diplomatic Investigations*. London: George Allen & Unwin: 89–131.

1977. *Systems of States*. Leicester: Leicester University Press.

1991. *International Theory*. New York: Holmes & Meier.

Williams, William A. 1988. *The Tragedy of American Diplomacy*. New York: Norton.

Wong, Dong. 2005. *China's Unequal Treaties*. Lanham, MD: Lexington Books.

Wood, Alfred Cecil. 1935. *A History of the Levant Company*. London: Oxford University Press.

Wood, Hugh McKinnon. 1943. "The Treaty of Paris and Turkey's Status in International Law." *American Journal of International Law* 37 (2): 262–274.

Wright, Quincy. 1939. *The Existing Legal Situation as It Relates to the Conflict in the Far East*. New York: Institute of Pacific Relations.

Yamawaki, Haruki. 1904. *Japan in the Beginning of the 20th Century*. London: Murray.

Yıldız, Hakkı Dursun. 1992. *150 Yılında Tanzimat [The 150th Anniversary of the Reorganization]*. Ankara: Türk Tarih Kurumu Basımevi.

Yoshihara, Kunio. 1994. *Japanese Economic Development*. New York: Oxford University Press.

Yuichi, Inouye. 2000. "From Unequal Treaty to the Anglo-Japanese Alliance, 1867–1902," in I. N. Y. Kibata (Ed.), *The History of Anglo-Japanese Relations* (Vol. I). London: Macmillan.

Yurdusev, Ali Nuri. 2003. *Ottoman Diplomacy*. New York: Palgrave.

Zhang, Yongjin. 1991. "China's Entry into International Society: Beyond the Standard of 'Civilization.'" *Review of International Studies* 17: 3–16.

1991. *China in the International System, 1918–20: The Middle Kingdom at the Periphery*. New York: St. Martin's Press.

Zubaida, Sami. 2003. *Law and Power in the Islamic World*. New York: I. B. Tauris.

Zurcher, Erik J. 1993. *Turkey: A Modern History*. New York: I. B. Tauris.

Index

Abernethy, David, 5, 18n4
Abu Ghraib, 202
Adams, Walter A., 183
Alcoa decision. *See* extraterritorial jurisdiction
Ali Pasha, 121
Allies
  agreement on foreign legal advisers (Turkey), 145
  judicial demands from Turkey, 139
  occupying Turkey (1919–1922), 129
  position on extraterritoriality, 136
  preparation for Lausanne Conference, 132
  rejection of Ottoman unilateral abolition of extraterritoriality, 105
  united on extraterritoriality, 134
American Banana decision. *See* extraterritorial jurisdiction
American Chamber of Commerce in Shanghai, 166
American consular courts. *See* United States
American hegemony. *See* United States
American legal imperialism. *See* United States
American military personnel in China. *See* U.S. State Department
Anderson, Perry, 47
Anghie, Anthony, 17n3
antitrust laws. *See* extraterritorial jurisdiction
Aoki, Shuzo, 88
Aoki-Kimberley Treaty, 66, 88, 92, 97
Arinori, Mori, 79, 84
Associated American Chambers of Commerce of China, 167
Association for the Reform and Codification of the Law of Nations, 159
Atatürk (Mustafa Kemal), 80 , 129, 135
  nationalist resistance against occupation, 135
Austin, John, 4, 25, 33
  Austinian sovereignty, 26, 27
Australia, 130
Austria, 129
  abolition of extraterritoriality (China), 161

Austria *(cont.)*
abolition of extraterritoriality (Ottoman Empire), 104
Aydın, Cemil, 119

Bairoch, Paul, 74
Beaulac, Stéphane, 25n29
Belgian extraterritoriality (Ottoman Empire), 3
Bentham, Jeremy, 4, 25, 33
Benton, Lauren, 7n10, 63n64
Berlin Conference (1885), 34, 45n16
Bertie, Francis, 76
in extraterritoriality negotiations, 96
Bismark, 71
Blackwater killings in Iraq, 202
Bloch, Marc, 35
Borah, William E., 169
Bowring, John, 33n63, 33
Bretton Woods system. *See* United States
Britain
abolition of extraterritoriality (China). *See* China
abolition of extraterritoriality (Japan). *See* Aoki-Kimberley Treaty
abolition of extraterritoriality (Turkey). *See* Lausanne Conference, Lausanne Treaty
Bonar Law's policy on Turkey, 131
British business groups and missionaries in China, 166–171
British citizens criticize abolition of extraterritoriality (Japan), 100–102
British Consular Court at Hyogo, 2
British empire and legal episteme, 12
British extraterritorial empire, 3–6
British hegemony and the nineteenth-century international system, 20
British imperialism and legal orientalism, 33
British imperialism and Westphalian sovereignty, 20
British legal imperialism, 196
British Supreme Court at Istanbul, 6, 124
British Supreme Court at Shanghai, 6, 172
business groups and abolition of extraterritoriality, 100
and Chinese nationalism on extraterritoriality, 179–180
collapse of Lloyd George government over Turkish debacle, 130
concerned with legal reforms (Japan), 97
debates about Greco-Turkish war, 131
demanding legal reforms (China), 153
domestic politics and extraterritoriality in Japan, 99
dominions' response to mobilization for a Turkish war, 130
extraterritoriality and Foreign Jurisdiction Act, 30
extraterritoriality negotiations (China), 179–181
facing Chinese nationalism on extraterritoriality, 179–180
Foreign Office debating extraterritoriality in China during WWII, 182–185
foreign policy (China), 156

instruction on extraterritoriality to Sir Skinner Turner, 172
judicial demands from China, 165
linking extraterritoriality and legal reforms (China), 176, 179, 186–187
linking extraterritoriality and legal reforms (Turkey), 142
Naval Defense Act, 72
not participating in Triple Intervention, 72
Sino-Western alliance, 185
started bilateral negotiations with China, 180
its supremacy challanged in East Asia, 70–73
and Turkish nationalist movement (1919–1922), 128–131
British Chamber of Commerce of Turkey and Balkan States, 133
British Colonial Office, 6, 29
British Foreign Office, 8, 29, 122
assessing Japanese power, 76
discussions about extraterritoriality (Ottoman Empire), 123
divided on extraterritoriality in China, 182
justifying Tokyo Conference decision, 87
British Law Officers, 29
role in formulating British extraterritoriality, 43
British legal imperialism. *See* Britain
British Supreme Court at Shanghai. *See* Britain
Bull, Hedley, 59, 112
Bulwer, William (Sir), 123
Burton, James L., 168
business groups
and extraterritoriality in China, 166–171
Cadogan, Alexander, 182
Caliphate. *See* Ottoman Empire
Canada, 130
capitulations. *See* Ottoman Empire
Cevdet Pasha, 120
Chicago Bar Association, 172
Child, Richard W., 141
China
abolition of German and Austrian extraterritoriality, 161
adopted civil law system, 173
attempts to replace magistrate courts with modern courts, 164
bilateral negotiations with European powers, 177
challenging extraterritoriality, 152
change in American position on extraterritoriality, 184
Chinese codes and legal positivist codes compared, 162
Chinese reformists compared with Meiji and Tanzimat reformists, 153
codification, 178 , 178–179
Commission on Extraterritoriality, 171–176
demanding the abolition of extraterritoriality in Washington Conference, 161
demanding the abolition of extraterritoriality (1929), 179
demanding the abolition of extraterritoriality (Guomindang), 177
demanding the abolition of extraterritoriality in Paris Conference (1919), 161
early legal reforms, 166
establishment of diplomatic institutions, 158–159

China *(cont.)*
extraterritoriality negotiations (1930s), 179–181
failure of Qing and early republican legal reforms, 165
and great powers' spheres of influence policy, 155–156
Guomindang legal reforms, 177–181
Hull's reasons to abolish extraterritoriality in China, 184
inefficiency of Law Codification Commission, 171
internal weakness, 154
international organization membership, 159–160
Japanese occupation of Manchuria, 181
Law Codification Commission, 163
in League of Nations, 159–160
legal reforms and abolition of extraterritoriality, 186–189
legal reforms and extraterritoriality, 154
Legislative Yuan and codification, 177
modern legal reforms, 163
modernization of the court system, 178–179
motivation for reforms, 155
National People's Convention rejecting extraterritoriality, 181
New Government Reforms, 154
nobility's resistance to legal reforms, 154
participation in the Hague Peace Conferences, 159
place in international society, 157–161
political disintegration, 153–154
post–WWI internatioanal environment, 156
problems with early legal reforms, 163–165
Qing legal reforms, 154
rejecting American draft treaty on extraterritoriality, 181
replacing Greece in League of Nations' Council, 160
The Report of the Commission on Extraterritoriality in China, 173–175
Republican period, 154
rise and decline of extraterritoriality in China, 151–152
Sino-Western alliance, 185
split within the Guomindang, 180
treaty ports system, 155
U.S. agrees to gradual abolition of extraterritoriality in China, 180
unification under Guomindang, 177
warlords' resistance to legal reforms, 154, 164
China Association, 100, 101
Chinese Communist Party, 182
Ching-wei, Wang, 181
Churchill, Winston, 130
on extraterritoriality in China, 182
Clifford, Nicholas R., 149
codification in China. *See* China, Commission on Extraterritoriality, legalization
codification in Japan. *See* Japan, legalization
codification in Ottoman Empire and Turkey. *See* Ottoman Empire, Turkey, legalization
Comisión Mixta, 7n10

Commission on Extraterritoriality, 49–50, 157, 165, 167, 171–176, 187, 189
debates on Chinese codification, 174
debates on Chinese courts, 174
establishment, 171–172
influence on American decision on extraterritoriality, 175–176
influence on British policy, 176
influence on Chinese legal reforms, 177
influence on Western policy, 179
linking abolition of extraterritoriality to Chinese legal reforms, 174
The Report of the Commission on Extraterritoriality in China, 173–175
requiring legal positivist standards, 173
role of lawyers, 172
Commission on the Regime of Foreigners. *See* Lausanne Conference
Commodore Perry. *See* Japan
Concert of Europe, 111
Constructivism, 9, 19, 30
and English School, 58
Convention of the Red Cross Society, 89
Crimean War, 70 , 111
Curzon (Lord), 130
rejecting Turkish arguments at Lausanne Conference, 142

Declaration of the Maritime Law, 89
Department of Juridical Ordinances. *See* Ottoman Empire
Doyle, Michael, 18n4
Dyck, Edward Van, 126

Earl Granville, 79, 84
East India Company, 33, 41, 42n7
Eden, Anthony
favors abolition of extraterritoriality in China, 182
effects doctrine. *See* extraterritorial jurisdiction
Egypt, 123, 195
Enomoto. *See* Japan
English School, 9, 31, 58–61 , 63, 109, 119, 146, 194
on China in international society, 157–161
comparing Japan and the Ottoman Empire, 88
defining international society, 59
explaining extraterritoriality (Japan), 88–92
on extraterritoriality, 58–61
and legal imperialism, 194
legal reforms and extraterritoriality (Turkey), 146
and legalization, 61, 194
legalization and legal reforms, 158
and missionaries' pro-abolition stand on extraterritoriality (China), 170–171
on Ottoman Empire in international society, 113
on Western intervention in China, 157
Eurocentrism, 9, 17, 22
extraterritorial groups, 21
extraterritorial jurisdiction
Alcoa decision, 199
American Banana decision, 198
and American hegemony, 195
American influence, 196

extraterritorial jurisdiction *(cont.)*
American legal realism, 199–201
antitrust laws, 198
effects doctrine, 198
evolution, 200
Military Extraterritorial Jurisdiction Act (MEJA) of 2000, 201–202
postwar American extraterritorial jurisdiction, 196–203
role of U.S. Department of Justice, 199
Sherman Act (1890), 198
Status of Forces Agreement (SOFA), 198
unilateral application, 198
extraterritoriality
and English School, 58–61
explaining abolition of extraterritoriality, 11–12, 61
great powers competition, 56
and legalization, 51–54
non-Western legal reforms, 195
non-Western normative challenge, 48
non-Western reaction, 45–50
normative shift against extraterritoriality, 182–187
reaction of antiimperialist movements, 46
and realism, 54–58
rise of extraterritoriality, 41–45

Far Eastern Affairs Division. *See* U.S. State Department
Fishel, Wesley R., 150
Foreign Jurisdiction Act, 30. *Also see* Hope-Scott, James R.
enactment, 41–45
extraterritoriality, Britain
Foreign Jurisdiction Act (1843), 44n13, 44
Foreign Jurisdiction Act (1890), 44n15
the influence on American extraterritoriality, 20n16
and Order in Council decisions, 44
Foster, John W., 76
France, 70
extraterritoriality in China, 179
French Consular Court at Hanoi, 172
Franco-Russian naval alliance, 72
Fraser, Hugh, 95, 96
French Chamber of Commerce of Constantinople, 133
Fung, Edmund S. K., 150n4

Garroni, Marquis, 138, 140, 143
George, Lloyd, 130, 134, 135
Germany, 70, 129
abolition of extraterritoriality in Ottoman Empire, 105
in East Asia, 71
end of extraterritoriality (China), 161
German Civil Code (influence in China), 163
German colonial policy, 71
Giddens, Anthony, 36
Gong, Gerrit, 92, 150, 157
See English School
on Japan, 88
legal reforms and extraterritoriality, 146
Granville (Lord), 87
great powers
collaboration on extraterritoriality (Japan), 70
competition over Ottoman Empire, 110–111
open door policy toward China, 156
rivalry in East Asia, 70–73, 152

and Scramble of Africa, 64
spheres of influence policy (China), 155–156
Triple Intervention, 72
Greco-Turkish war, 129, 135
Greece, 129
Grotius, Hugo, 23
Grotian sovereignty, 23
Gülhane Fermanı. *See* Imperial Edict (1839)
Guomindang. *See* China
Guomindang legal reforms, 177–181, 187, 191
codification, 178

Hague Peace Conferences, 159
Hall, William E., 26
Hamilton, Maxwell M., 185
developing a normative argument against extraterritoriality, 183
Hayashi (Baron)
comments on Turkish legal reforms, 143
Helms-Burton Act, 198n7
Hikomatsu, Kamikawa, 80
Hinckley, Frank E., 92
Hobbes, Thomas, 25
Holland, Thomas E., 27
on Foreign Jurisdiction Act and extraterritoriality, 45
Hope-Scott, James R., 43
role in formulating extraterritoriality, 43–44
Hornby, Edmund, 124–126
role in establishment of British Supreme Court at Istanbul, 124
Hsu, Immanuel C. Y., 158
Huang, Philip, 163
Hull, Cordell, 184
reasons to abolish extraterritoriality in China, 184
Hume, David, 25

Imperial Edict (1839), 114
imperialism. *See* legal imperialism
Inoue, Kaoru, 85
International Conventions for the Protection of Property and Copyright, 97
international society. *See* English School
International Telegraphic Convention, 89
Iran, 3, 12, 46, 63 , 81, 123, 195
Iriye, Akira, 150
İslahat Fermanı. *See* Reform Edict (1856)
Islamic law, 119
İsmet Pasha, 130, 138, 142
arguing for extraterritoriality violates Turkish sovereignty, 141
on Ottoman legal reforms, 138
rejecting Allies' demands, 141
rejecting foreign legal advisers, 144
Istanbul Conference (proposed), 122
Iwakura Mission, 66, 78 , 88, 92

Japan
arrival of Commodore Perry (1853), 89
codification, 92
comparison with Ottoman Empire, 105
diplomatic note to Britain for further legalization, 97
Enomoto pleads Diet for legal reforms, 94
extraterritoriality in China, 179
Great Japan Society and foreigners, 95
influence of Japanese Civil Code in China, 163

Japan *(cont.)*
international organization membership, 89
Japanese power and extraterritoriality, 78
joining International Conventions for the Protection of Property and Copyright, 97
legal institutionalization and the abolition of extraterritoriality, 92–98
legal system and extraterritoriality, 80
Meiji Revolution, 74
occupation of Manchuria, 181
response to Triple Intervention, 77
rise and decline of extraterritoriality in Japan, 67
split among Western foreigners on extraterritoriality, 99
Tokugawa legal system, 81
Western business groups and abolition of extraterritoriality, 100
Western foreigners and extraterritoriality, 98–102
xenophobia, 89, 95
Japan arrival of Commodore Perry (1853), 73
Jones, F. C., 80
Joris, Charles Edouard, 2

Kaishek, Chiang, 177 , 180, 183
Kellogg, Frank B., 169, 172, 173
favoring the abolition of extraterritoriality (China), 170
influenced by Commission on Extraterritoriality, 175–176
Kennedy, Paul, 74
Kingsbury, Benedict, 201
Korea, 71, 195
Koskenniemi, Martti, 19n7, 24n29
Krasner, Stephen, 19, 24n29, 54
organized hypocrisy and extraterritoriality, 54–58
Kratochwil, Friedrich, 36

Land Law (Ottoman). *See* Ottoman Empire
Lasswell, Harold, 200
Latin America, 7, 63n64
Lausanne Conference, 61 , 106, 134–147, 143, 177
Allies' judicial demands from Turkey, 139
Allies' preparation for, 132
Commission on the Regime of Foreigners, 138, 140, 143
debates about foreign legal advisers, 144
debates about Judicial Declaration, 143–147
debates on sovereign territoriality and equality, 138
ending of the first phase, 145
failure of the first phase, 140
first phase, 136–145
protection of foreigners, 138
second phase, 145–146
Subcommission on the Judicial Rights of Foreigners, 139
Turkey rejecting Allies' judicial demands, 140
Lausanne Treaty, 105, 136, 145
Law, Bonar, 131
Law Codification Commission. *See* China
Lawrence, T. J., 27
League of Nations, 159
legal advisers. *See* Lausanne Conference
legal episteme, 4, 17

American imperial legal episteme, 196
British imperial legal episteme, 18, 19
Dutch imperial legal episteme, 23
imperial legal episteme, 20, 22, 23
Spanish imperial legal episteme, 22
legal imperialism, 13, 189
and colonization of Africa, 34
definition, 6
English School, 194
extraterritoriality as, 34
imperialism and sovereignty, 18
influence on non-Western legal reforms, 191–192
and international law, 13
and power politics, 54
the role of lawyers, 172
the role of lawyers in American legal imperialism, 200
and Westphalian sovereignty, 192
legal institutionalization. *See* legalization, Japan, Ottoman Empire, Turkey, China
legal naturalism, 22, 23
and sovereignty, 23, 28
legal orientalism, 30–35, 162
definition, 32
legal positivism, 4, 12, 23, 25, 27, 162, 192
in Commission on Extraterritoriality, 173
compared to legal realism, 200
development, 24–26
and extraterritoriality, 176
extraterritoriality in China, 174, 189
and international law, 26–30
and legal orientalism, 33
and power politics, 194
in *The Report of the Commission on Extraterritoriality in China*, 175
role in Westphalian sovereignty, 192, 201
legal realism, 12, 199–201
American extraterritorial jurisdiction, 199
American legal imperialism, 199
compared to legal positivism, 200
role in American legal imperialism, 199–201
legalization, 13, 21, 35, 38–39
abolition of extraterritoriality, 191
abolition of extraterritoriality (Japan), 98
abolition of extraterritoriality in China, 174, 186–189
abolition of extraterritoriality in China and legal reforms, 186–187
and the abolition of extraterritoriality (Japan), 96
and abolition of extraterritoriality (Turkey), 143
adopting civil law tradition (Japan), 97
as a condition for the abolition of extraterritoriality (China), 153
codification in China, 178
codification in Japan, 93
codification in Turkey, 136 ,
defined, 38–39
in China, 178–179
and English School, 60 , 158
and extraterritoriality, 51–54
and extraterritoriality (China), 152, 176, 179
international consequences of domestic legalization, 37

legalization *(cont.)*
its influence on non-Western domestic politics, 47–48
in Japan, 92–95
Judicial Declaration (Turkey), 143–147
Law Codification Commission (China), 163
and legal imperialism, 191–192
legal reforms (China), 166
modernization of court system in China, 178–179
Ottoman reforms and Meiji reforms compared, 146
problems with early Chinese legal reforms, 165
and protection of foreigners, 138
role in European state building, 35n70, 193
sovereignty and extraterritoriality (Turkey), 140
state building and legalization, 35–39
in Turkey, 135–136
and Westphalian sovereignty, 35–39
the influence of legal fragmentation on trade, 12
The Report of the Commission on Extraterritoriality in China, 173–175
the role in European state building, 35n70, 193
Legislative Yuan. *See* China
Levant Company, 41
its abolition, 41–43
Liaodong Peninsula, 72, 77
Lorimer, James, 110

MacDonald, Paul, 34
Mackay Treaty (1902), 153
MacMurray, John V. A., 168
criticizing missionaries on extraterritoriality, 169
Mao, 149
McDougal, Myres, 200
Mearsheimer, John, 74, 75
Mecelle. *See* Ottoman Empire
Meiji reforms, 153, 191
codification, 92
compared to Guomindang reforms, 178
compared to other non-Western legal reforms, 81
compared to Ottoman reforms, 119
completion of legal reforms, 92–95
Criminal Code of 1880, 86
early legal reforms, 80–84
affect on extraterritoriality, 84
failure of early reforms, 82
growth of Japanese power, 73–78
international context, 69–70
Law of the Organization of Courts, 93
legalization required to end extraterritoriality, 96
reform of the court system, 84
mercantile companies. *See* Levant Company, East India Company
Meter Convention, 89
Military Extraterritorial Jurisdiction Act (MEJA) of 2000. *See* extraterritorial jurisdiction
millet system. *See* Ottoman Empire
missionaries, 68
American Board of Commissioners for Foreign Missions, 168
American missionaries lobby to end extraterritoriality (China), 168–170

in China, 167
demanding the abolition of extraterritoriality (China), 169
demands rejected by U.S. State Department, 168
and English School argument on extraterritoriality, 170–171
and extraterritoriality, 56
on extraterritoriality (China), 167
and extraterritoriality in China, 166–171
Federal Council of Churches of Christ, 169
Foreign Missions Conference, 168
mixed courts, 123
Mutsu Munemitsu, 96

Naff, Thomas, 107, 112
National People's Convention. *See* China
Nizamiye Mahkemeleri. *See* Ottoman Empire
Normanton, 2
North, Douglas, 36
Nur, Rıza
defending Turkish draft of Judicial Declaration, 144

Opium War, 73, 149
Oppenheim, F. L., 27
Order in Council. *See* Foreign Jurisdiction Act
Organized Hypocrisy. *See* Krasner, Stephen
orientalism, 31. *Also see* legal orientalism
Ottoman Empire. *Also see* Turkey, Laussane Conference
1876 Constitution, 115n24
admission to international society, 109
British Foreign Office discussions about extraterritoriality, 123
capitulations and extraterritoriality, 104n1
claims to Caliphate, 8
in Concert of Europe, 111
dissolution, 128
establishment of Ministry of Foreign Affairs, 108
establishment of Ministry of Justice, 114
establishment of permanent diplomatic institutions in Europe, 108
Edmund Hornby's reports on legal reforms, 124
in First World War, 129
great powers' competition, 110–111
international organization membership, 108
Land Law, 194
Land Law and extraterritoriality, 127–128
legal fragmentation, 116–119
legal reforms and legal reorganization, 114–121
major attempts to end extraterritoriality, 104n1
Mecelle, 115n24, 120, 194
millet system and legal fragmentation, 41, 117, 119
Nizamiye Mahkemeleri, 118
place in European diplomacy, 108
place in international society, 113
reorganization of religious courts, 118
state control over religious courts, 118
Tanzimat reforms, 114–121
Tanzimat reforms compared to Meiji reforms, 119

Ottoman Empire *(cont.)*
U.S. State Department report on legal reforms, 127
ulema and Tanzimat legal reforms, 120
ulema's reaction to legal reforms, 119, 147
unilateral abolition of extraterritoriality (1914), 104
Western business groups and extraterritoriality, 134

Paris Conference (1856), 48, 61 , 104, 106, 111n15, 116, 127
compared to Washington Conference, 155
extraterritoriality discussions, 122
Paris Conference (1919), 48, 161
Paris Treaty (1856), 112, 128, 139
admission of Ottoman Empire into international society (Article 7), 109
Parkes, Harry (Sir), 80, 86
objections to end extraterritoriality (Japan), 85
Permanent Court of International Justice, 143
Petersen, Maurice, 182
Poggi, Gianfranco, 36
postcolonial perspective, 31
Privy Council, 6
protégés, 45, 102, 192
China, 152
in Ottoman Empire and Japan, 102

Raustiala, Kal, 198n7, 200
realism. *Also see* Stephen Krasner
and extraterritoriality, 54–58
extraterritoriality and power politics, 193
Reform Edict (1856), 114, 116, 121
Report of the Commission on Extraterritoriality. *See* Commission on Extraterritoriality
Roman law, 11, 36, 47, 193
Rosebery (Lord), 95, 99
Ruggie, John, 36
Rumbold, Horace (Sir), 140
criticizing Turkish draft of Judicial Declaration, 144
Russell, J. (Lord), 123
Russia. *Also see* Soviet Union
and Orthodox population of the Ottoman Empire, 111n15
role in East Asia, 69
Russian extraterritoriality, 64
Russian Revolution, 131
Trans-Siberian Railway, 71
Vladivostok Harbor, 71

Said, Edward, 31
Scramble of Africa. *See* great powers
Scully, Eileen, 49
Sèvres Treaty, 130, 135
Shapiro, Martin, 162
Sherman Act. *See* extraterritorial jurisdiction
Shikai, Yuan, 174
Siebold, Alexander von, 79
Sino-Japanese War (1895), 69, 72
Sino-Japanese War (1937–1945), 182
Sousa, Nasim, 131
South Africa, 130
sovereign equality
debates at Lausanne Conference, 138
sovereignty and extraterritoriality
Allies' argument for the compatability of, 143

debates at Lausanne Conference, 143
in extraterritoriality negotiations (China), 179–181
international norm against extraterritoriality, 183
normative shift against extraterritoriality, 187
and power politics, 193
Soviet Union
abolition of extraterritoriality, 65
abolition of extraterritoriality (Turkey), 131
Congress of the Peoples of the East in 1920, 131
support for Turkish nationalists, 131
Soyeshima, Taneomi (Count), 76
Spruyt, Hendrik, 37
standard of "civilization." *See* English School
Status of Forces Agreement (SOFA). *See* extraterritorial jurisdiction
Strawn, Silas H., 172
on Chinese legal system, 173
Kellogg's instruction on extraterritoriality, 172
links extraterritoriality to Chinese legal reforms, 173
Subcommission on the Judicial Rights of Foreigners. *See* Lausanne Conference
Suganami, Hidemi, 88

Tang Code, 162, 163
Tanzimat, 153
compared to Chinese reforms, 154, 178
legal reforms, 114–121
territorial sovereignty
and territorial jurisdiction, 11
debates at Lausanne Conference, 138
Thailand, 3, 12, 33, 46, 63 , 123, 171, 195
Thomson, Janice, 51n30, 57
Tilly, Charles, 35n70
Tokugawa. *See* Japan
Tokyo Conference (1882), 61 , 66, 69, 79, 84–87, 96, 172
Toussaint, G. Ch., 172
Treaty Concerning the Formation of General Postal Union, 89
Treaty of Shimonoseki, 77
Triple Intervention, 72, 72 , 77
Turkey, 136 . *Also see* Ottoman Empire, Lausanne Conference, Lausanne Treaty
abolition of communal courts, 136
abolition of religious courts, 136
agreement for Judicial Declaration at Lausanne Conference, 145
codification, 136
the influence of Young Turks nationalism, 137
legal reforms, 135–136, 191
Ministry of Justice, 144
Ottoman legal reforms and Turkish legal reforms compared, 136
position on extraterritoriality at Lausanne, 137
rejecting Allies' judicial demands, 140
Turner, Skinner (Sir), 172

U.S. Department of Justice, 199
U.S. District Court for China, 2, 6n7
establishment, 50, 152

U.S. State Department, 126, 137, 166
concerned with lack of reforms in China, 171
debates about extraterritoriality in China during WWII, 182–185
Far Eastern Affairs Division and extraterritoriality, 168, 183
negotiates extraterritoriality for military personnel in China, 188
and norms against extraterritoriality, 184
policy on extraterritoriality (Turkey), 132
rejects the missionaries' demands, 168
report on Ottoman legal reforms, 127
ulema. *See* Ottoman Empire
unequal treaties, 46, 181, 188
United States
agrees to the gradual abolition of extraterritoriality in China, 180
American business groups and missionaries in China, 166–171
American consular courts, 18
American hegemony, 12
American legal imperialism, 13, 196
draft treaty on extraterritoriality, 180
extraterritorial jurisdiction and military bases, 197
extraterritorial jurisdiction using effects doctrine, 198
extraterritoriality negotiations with China (1930s), 179–181
foreign policy (China), 156
Foreign Relations Committee and extraterritoriality (China), 169
halts extraterritoriality negotiations (China), 181
hegemony and Bretton Woods system, 196
Hull's reasons to abolish extraterritoriality in China, 185
initiating extraterritoriality negotiations, 182
Iraq War and extraterritorial jurisdiction, 203
judicial demands from China, 165
linking abolition of extraterritoriality to Chinese legal reforms, 186–187
linking extraterritoriality to legalization (China), 175–176
Military Extraterritorial Jurisdiction Act (MEJA) of 2000, 201–202
new forms of extraterritorial jurisdiction, 195
new forms of extraterritorial jurisdiction in China, 188
policy change on extraterritoriality, 184
position on extraterritoriality (Turkey), 137
postwar extraterritorial jurisdiction, 196–203
Sino-Western alliance, 185
started bilateral negotiations with China, 180
Universal Postal Union Convention, 89
Uruguay, 7
US v. Demenil, 2

Vattel, Emer de, 24, 25n29
Vattelian sovereignty, 24

Vitoria, Francisco de, 22
  Vitorian sovereignty, 22

Walker, Thomas A., 27
Wang, Ch'ung-hui, 161
warlords. *See* China
Washington Conference, 48, 61 , 155, 165, 171, 177
Watson, Adam, 157
Weber, Max, 36, 47
Westphalia, Peace of (1648), 14, 27
Westphalian sovereignty, 9, 18, 19, 23, 24n29, 24, 30, 201
  and British legal imperialism, 17–22
  invention, 27
  and legal imperialism, 193
  and legal positivism, 192
  and legalization, 35–39
  and transnational legal structures, 7
Wilhelm, Kaiser, 71

xenophobia. *See* Japan

Zhang, Yongjin, 159

Lightning Source UK Ltd.
Milton Keynes UK
UKOW04f0613191213

223340UK00001B/119/P

9 781107 617889